Matters of Life and Death

Matters of Life and Death

PERSPECTIVES ON PUBLIC HEALTH,
MOLECULAR BIOLOGY, CANCER,
AND THE PROSPECTS FOR
THE HUMAN RACE

John Cairns

PRINCETON UNIVERSITY PRESS

PRINCETON, NEW JERSEY

Library of Congress Cataloging-in-Publication Data
Cairns, John, 1922–.
Matters of life and death : perspectives on public health,
molecular biology, cancer, and the prospects for the
human race / John Cairns.
p.   cm.
Includes bibliographical references and index.
ISBN 0-691-02872-9 (cloth : alk. paper)
1. Life (biology).   2. Molecular biology.
3. Cancer.   I. Title.
QH501.C33   1997   574.8′8—dc20   96-18026   CIP

Contents

Foreword

THE ALFRED P. SLOAN FOUNDATION has had a continuing interest in encouraging public understanding of science. Science in this century has become a complex endeavor. Scientific statements may reflect many centuries of experimentation and theory, and are likely to be expressed in the language of advanced mathematics or in highly technical vocabulary. As scientific knowledge expands, the goal of general public understanding of science becomes increasingly important and difficult to achieve.

Only a small number of scientists can contribute to this goal. A special few combine scientific ingenuity and writing virtuosity. John Cairns is one of those special few.

For many years, the Sloan Foundation has tried to recruit Dr. Cairns to write for our book series aimed at the general reader. During the 1980s he was preoccupied with his teaching and research at Harvard and was unable to accept our invitation. But when he moved back to his native England in the early 1990s and we renewed our invitation, he accepted.

The book he has written is a sparkling gem of lucid, absorbing, and instructive exposition on a range of topics. The Sloan Foundation is proud to have initiated this volume and to be associated with its publication.

Arthur L. Singer, Jr.
Vice-President (retired)
ALFRED P. SLOAN FOUNDATION
April 26, 1996

Preface

ONE EVENING in October 1957, I was standing among a group of people on the roof of one of the buildings at the California Institute of Technology, waiting for our first chance to see Sputnik I. In the gathering darkness the tiny pinpoint of light suddenly appeared exactly at the calculated time, rushing across the sky with unimagineable speed. We watched in silence until it lost the sun and was gone. There was a pause. And then, from the other nearby roofs, across the evening air, we could hear the sound of clapping.

Xenophon captured for posterity one of the most romantic moments in history with his description of the sound of distant shouting when the Greeks retreating from Persia caught sight of the sea from the top of a hill. The soldiers were shouting because they now knew that they were safe, and home in their element. The clapping I heard on that October night was not for any personal triumph but for the triumph of all humankind. Here was *Homo sapiens* at his best, one group acknowledging a common cause by applauding their rivals. This, I thought, is the essence of the arts and sciences.

The fashion these days is to present science as a cut-throat competition between a bunch of near-delinquents hotly in pursuit of wealth and fame. It makes a better story. (Also, it sells better, because most people do not understand much science and are happy to believe that the whole enterprise is somewhat despicable.) But I do not think that the sciences, or the arts, operate that way. Certainly, not many of the scientists I know are at all predatory. Most are happy to help one another and most would agree that their lives have been greatly enriched by the sense of being part of a communal effort.

At the end of 1991, after spending almost fifty years in one branch of biology or another, I retired from the Harvard School of Public Health. This should be a time of calm reflection, but I find myself dogged by a sense of indebtedness—partly, of course, to the many people who have helped and inspired me in my career but also to the enterprise of science itself. Looking back, I realize how exciting my life has been. That is the thing about science. It grips and it fascinates. During your lifetime, your horizons are being continually extended, mostly thanks to the work of others but also, slightly, through your own endeavors. You wrestle with some problem for months or years and, as you do experiments and read about other people's experiments, you find that the pieces of the puzzle are magically re-arranging themselves, as though you were watching a private display of some abstract form of evolution.

This continual evolution in understanding seems to me to be a form of human activity peculiar to the arts and sciences. In the arts it is almost impossible to explain. To take a famous example, we would like to know what exactly was happening as Beethoven worked his way through the eighty or so versions of the opening bars of his song cycle, *An die ferne Geliebte*, but his struggle defies analysis because it is too remote. We feel we recognize the rightness of the end result, presumably because Beethoven discovered something about the human mind, and we are overwhelmed because we know that we ourselves could not have made that journey, but it is not something that is open to analysis, even by other professionals. I remember hearing David Hockney giving a lecture on Van Gogh's "Night Café" and his being reduced to saying "fantastic!" over and over again because he found himself unable to explain what was so marvelous about the painting.

Science seems almost the opposite of that. Although many of the great discoveries of science are just as much the product of genius as the opening of Beethoven's song cycle or Van Gogh's painting, the steps leading to each discovery are easily understood if you are a scientist. Once they have been laid out in front of you, you have the joy of feeling that you could have done it yourself.

Most people are not scientists. They benefit from the end results—hybrid corn, penicillin, transistors, and so on—but the joy escapes them. That, I think, is why I have this vague feeling of indebtedness and guilt. For years I have been enjoying myself, doing something most people cannot understand. In fact, I have been especially lucky for I have worked in so many different fields. I started in medicine, drifted into bacteriology and virology, went from there into molecular biology, and then moved temporarily into cancer research. This was followed by ten years in a school of public health. Finally, I returned to the molecular biology of bacteria. The sequence was not planned, but each move introduced me to a new problem and delighted me with a new literature.

When the Sloan Foundation asked me to write my autobiography, I refused because I felt I do not have the proper temperament for a good book about myself. A couple of years later they suggested that I should write a popular account of some scientific topic rather than an autobiography. This seemed more manageable, so I said I would write a history of mortality. In trying to write that book I discovered that I am by nature an essayist and have neither the knowledge nor the skill to write a whole book on one subject. So I settled for a set of essays on the various subjects that have interested me, at one time or another during my scientific career. It so happens that the subjects are connected and can be arranged in a fairly logical sequence, although I was not lucky enough to meet them in the right order. But that is to be expected; as Kierkegaard said, life has to be lived forward, but it can only be understood backward. When the subjects are correctly arranged, they trace a path that touches upon many of the major divisions of biology.

Much of the pleasure of being a scientist comes from being part of a communal effort and being able to observe at close quarters the continual evolution in our understanding of the world around us. I have met a lot of very clever people and I have had a lot of fun, and I feel I am lucky to have been a scientist. When I look back on my career it is this sense of being a privileged witness to a communal effort that is my source of greatest pleasure, and it is this feeling that I want to pass on to my readers.

But there is more to it than that. The last 150 years have seen a sequence of discoveries in biology that will in time be judged to have been as important as the Copernican revolution. Yet they are not nearly so accessible. The implication of Galileo's discovery of Jupiter's moons was all too obvious, whereas few of the great discoveries in biology were instantly understandable even by biologists. The main purpose of these essays is to give a simple description of some of the great developments in the biological sciences, including the science that underlies the preservation of human health. My hope is that the book will give each reader a better understanding of living systems and of certain factors that affect the human condition. To make it easier, I have tried to show how each discovery came about, starting right at the beginning. In other words, the essays are specifically designed to be read by people who know nothing about science.

Acknowledgments

I AM GRATEFUL to the Sloan Foundation for support during the writing of this book. The diagrams were drawn by Vicki Martin. An early version of the first chapter was published in Mannheimer Forum in 1985, and a later version in *Diet, Nutrition and Health*, edited by K. K. Carroll (McGill-Queens University Press) in 1989. Many friends and relatives have been forced to read parts of the text, and I would like to thank David Attlee, Victoria Cairns, David Dressler, David Freedman, Roy Gould, David Hunter, Kirk Jensen, Jonothan Logan, Christopher Longuet-Higgins, Cedric Mims, Julie Overbaugh, Richard Peto, Rainer Riester, Miranda Robertson, Leona Samson, my cousin Anthony Smith, my sister Elizabeth Nussbaum, and my wife Elfie, and various anonymous reviewers, for picking up numerous errors of style and for correcting countless factual errors. I am particularly indebted to my wife, who has had to put up with the stress without having any of the fun.

Matters of Life and Death

CHAPTER 1

A History of Mortality

> Happy the man who could understand the causes of things.
> —Virgil, *Georgics*

There are few pleasures in life so steadily exciting as the voyages of discovery that are made in libraries. It is the book next to the one you first reach for that makes the day and leads you to the unknown land. After a morning spent tunneling through the stacks, breathing in the subtle aroma of forgotten knowledge, I find that I emerge rejuvenated. A Persian proverb says that time spent fishing is not deducted from your life-span. Somehow I feel that time spent in a library may actually be added on.

Yet there are rules. As an experimentalist, I have spent much of my life counting things. This is what I am trained to do. And so when I took a job in 1980 at the Harvard School of Public Health, I looked around for something to count that would give me an understanding of public health. It had to be something that could be measured accurately; therefore it could not be "Health." So it had to be Death. If I wanted to find out what determines when we die, then I should first study the history of mortality. As I was to discover, this is not something you learn in medical school; in fact, as far as I could determine, you are not even taught it in schools of public health.

꧁꧂

HUMANS HAVE existed on this earth for some 3 million years. But only in the last 200 years has there been much change in the pattern of mortality. If you were born at any time before the middle of the eighteenth century, you had less than a 50 percent chance of surviving long enough to produce any children. Today, the world as a whole has an average life expectancy that is greater even than that achieved in Sweden by the end of the nineteenth century. Now, any inhabitant of the developed nations has a good chance of living long enough to overlap with some of his or her great-grandchildren.

Unfortunately, the nations of the world have not yet worked out how to cope with the consequences of this change in longevity, and the problems posed by the huge increase in population seem set to dominate human affairs for at least the next century.

As I have said, throughout the history of *Homo sapiens*, the balance of life and death hardly changed at all until about 1750. Populations were able to survive because each woman of reproductive age produced an average of five or six children; two or three of them were female, and one of these survived to be her mother's successor. That is the way it was, and it is still that way in many parts of the world—in the highlands of New Guinea, the forests of the Amazon, and the Kalahari Desert.

In most European nations, the drop in death rate began several generations before a drop in the birthrate, and that was why populations suddenly increased in the nineteenth and early twentieth centuries. In much of Africa and Asia, mortality is now dropping very quickly, but the birthrate has not changed and the population explosion in these nations has yet to run its course.

Medicine deals with individuals, and public health deals with populations. People's ideas about health have changed from one age to the next, but the distinction between the quick and the dead never changes; mortality is something you can measure. And I felt that until I knew exactly when death rates started to come down, I could not start to understand what kinds of things affect the health of populations.

Measurement of Life Expectancy: Life Tables

Collection of vital statistics has been a preoccupation of rulers and governments since the beginning of recorded history, because the size of a population determines how large an army can be mobilized and how much money can be raised in taxes.[1] The number of adult males in the tribes of Israel were counted by Moses and by King David as a prelude to their attacking the neighboring tribes; the Romans needed regular censuses so that they could tax their colonies; in 1086 the Normans recorded in the Domesday Book the size and taxable value of each village in conquered England. Interestingly, none of these early surveys were concerned with the longevity or mortality of the population being surveyed. In 1790, the first U.S. census was carried out for the democratic purpose of ensuring that each state would have the right number of representatives in Congress, but it went no further than to divide the population into slaves and free, whites and nonwhites, males and females, and specifically white males who were over age sixteen.

Although there had been no measurements of life expectancy, governments found themselves having to enact laws about life insurance and annuities.[2] Roman law, for example, accepted the simple rule that anyone under the age of twenty could expect to live for another thirty years, and anyone over twenty could expect to live to the age of sixty. In seventeenth-century England, the official table for calculating annuities (certified by Newton himself) assumed that each person, irrespective of age, would survive on average for an additional ten years. At the end of the seventeenth century, the English government embarked on the business of selling annuities, partly as a primitive form of national insurance but mainly as yet another way of borrowing money. Unfortunately, the formula it used for calculating life expectancy was so unrealistic that annuities became a very good investment for foreign capital. This led to a desperate search for some way of finding out what was the exact relationship between age and death rate. An English businessman, John Graunt, had published an estimate for London in the middle of the seventeenth century[3] which he had worked out as a way of determining London's total population, but his method involved a lot of guesswork.

The answer was eventually found by the English astronomer Edmund Halley,[4] who learned that the town of Breslau had, for some years, been keeping a record of age at time of death for every death within the city. He obtained a copy of the register covering a period of five years, and with this and a record of the number of births in the city he was able to construct the first *life table*. Because such life tables are the foundation for all discussions of population, Halley's analysis is worth discussing in some detail.

In the 1690s, the Breslau registry of births reported that, on average, 1,238 children were born each year. The register of deaths showed that each year, on average, 348 children died before their first birthday; if we assume that there had been no net immigration or emigration of infants during this period, it follows by subtraction that each year, on average, 890 children (the 1,238 who were born, less the 348 who had died) survived at least to celebrate their first birthday. Each year, sixty-nine children died who were between one and two years old; this implies that each year only 821 of those 890 children would survive to their second birthday. The same calculation can then be made for every subsequent year of life using the average number of deaths observed in each one-year age group, up to the age of eighty-three, beyond which point there were no recorded deaths during the five years of records presumably because there were so few people still alive in their eighties. The final result shows us how many of the 1,238 children born in any one year would on average live to celebrate any particular birthday.

Halley realized that this procedure would be valid only if there had been no movement of people in or out of the city and no change in annual birthrate or in the force of mortality for the previous eighty years.

TABLE 1.1
A Life Table from the Seventeenth Century

The first complete Life Table, prepared for the city of Breslau at the end of the seventeenth century by the astronomer Edmund Halley. On average, 1,238 children were born in the city each year, and the table shows how many of this annual crop of children would still be alive at each subsequent birthday up to the age of 83. The numbers published by Halley were slightly different from those shown here because his objective was to calculate the number of people alive at any one moment, rather than the number reaching each successive birthday. For example, the number of children who were in their first year of life on any arbitrarily chosen day would be somewhere between 1,238 (the annual birthrate) and 890 (the number surviving a whole year). Thus the first entry in his table was 1,000; subsequent entries were roughly halfway between the adjacent numbers shown here (855 in the second year of life, 798 in the third, and so on).

Age	Number	%	Age	Number	%	Age	Number	%	Age	Number	%
0	1238	100	21	586	47	42	422	34	63	207	17
1	890	72	22	581	47	43	412	33	64	197	16
2	821	66	23	576	47	44	402	32	65	187	15
3	776	63	24	570	46	45	392	32	66	177	14
4	744	60	25	564	46	46	382	31	67	167	13
5	716	58	26	558	45	47	372	30	68	157	13
6	692	56	27	551	45	48	362	29	69	147	12
7	665	54	28	542	44	49	352	28	70	137	11
8	654	53	29	534	43	50	342	28	71	126	10
9	643	52	30	527	43	51	331	27	72	115	9
10	637	51	31	519	42	52	320	26	73	104	8
11	630	51	32	511	41	53	309	25	74	93	8
12	624	50	33	503	41	54	298	24	75	83	7
13	619	50	34	494	40	55	287	23	76	73	6
14	615	50	35	485	39	56	277	22	77	63	5
15	613	50	36	476	38	57	267	22	78	53	4
16	610	49	37	467	38	58	257	21	79	44	4
17	607	49	38	458	37	59	247	20	80	36	3
18	603	49	39	449	36	60	237	19	81	29	2
19	598	48	40	440	36	61	227	18	82	23	2
20	592	48	41	431	35	62	217	18	83	18	1

Source: E. Halley, "An Estimate of the Degrees of the Mortality of Mankind. Drawn from Curious Tables of the Births and Funerals of the City of Breslau; with an Attempt to Ascertain the Price of Annuities upon Lives." Phil. Trans. Roy. Soc. Lond. 17: 596–610, 1693.

Also, the table's forecast of the likely fate of the children born in the 1690s would be accurate only if the force of mortality remained unchanged for the next eighty years; for example, the calculation assumes that in 1740, when the children born in 1690 would reach fifty years of age, they would be subject to the precise annual mortality that was being

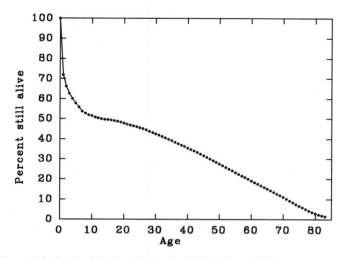

Figure 1.1. Survival in Breslau in the 1690s (from Halley; see note 4).

suffered by those who had reached age fifty in 1690 (i.e., were born in 1640). Because he only had records for five years, he could not exclude errors due to migration or to changes in birthrate or mortality, although he pointed out that during this period the annual birthrate roughly equaled the annual death rate, as it should under steady-state conditions; (actually, he observed that there were on average sixty-four fewer deaths than births each year, but he attributed this to some deaths having occurred in foreign wars and therefore not being counted, so he surreptitiously made up the difference by adding a few extra deaths to the older age groups). Halley realized that he could have checked some of his assumptions if a census of the population had been taken, because the table can also be read as an estimate of the age distribution of the population at any given moment, and therefore the total of about 34,000 for all the numbers in the table should equal the total population of Breslau. Halley's statistics are shown in table 1.1. Most of us, however, are happier with graphs than tables, so I will henceforth show life tables as figures, starting with a graphical version of Halley's life table in figure 1.1.

For many purposes it is convenient to summarize such a table by calculating the average number of years lived by the members of the population. In this case, you would take the total number of years lived by a typical cohort of 1,238 Breslau infants whose fate is described in the table and divide it by 1,238. The calculation proceeds as follows. You might choose to assume that the 348 who died in their first year died halfway through the year and so contributed 174 person-years to the total; the sixty-nine who died in their second year contributed 1.5 years each, or 103.5 person-years; and so on. From the total of all those person-years divided by 1,238, we get an estimate of *average life expectancy* at age zero. For Breslau in 1690 it was 26.4 years; in modern Breslau (Wroclaw), a newborn infant has a life expectancy of over 70.

Halley's method for estimating the force of mortality can be used whenever we have records of age at time of death, provided there are reasons to think that the total size of the population is not changing. For example, we can determine the approximate life expectancy of prehistoric man, because we can determine the age of the skeletons in Palaeolithic and Neolithic burial sites. Similarly, the Roman obsession with astrology made them record on each tombstone the exact date of birth and death, and this gives us the age at death for at least those people who were important enough to deserve a gravestone. And of course the births and deaths in the ruling families of Europe are part of recorded history. From such records we can therefore estimate the life expectancy for certain groups of people in the distant or not-so-distant past, and this will be the subject of the next two sections of this chapter.

For the more recent past, however, Halley's procedure is not adequate. When the size of a population is rapidly increasing (as it was in the industrial nations from about 1750 onward), the number of births each year exceeds the number of deaths. Since the deaths are occurring among cohorts that were born many years earlier when the annual birthrate was lower by some unknown amount, we have no way of deducing the original size of each birth cohort or how many of them are still alive; therefore, in these cases it is not possible to translate total numbers of deaths into age-specific death rates. If we want to measure life expectancy in an unstable population, we have to know the number of people in each age group (i.e., we have to have carried out a census).

Fortunately, early in the nineteenth century it became the custom in many nations to conduct regular censuses that recorded, among other things, each person's age. Indeed, many of the reforms in public health that came later in the century were stimulated by these surveys, because they showed for the first time just how appalling were the conditions in cities like Paris and London. Before dealing with these more modern statistics we should, however, go back to the beginnings of humankind.

Mortality Up to A.D. 1700

One of the most extensive and best documented Palaeolithic burial grounds was found in a cave at Taforalt in Morocco. Forty thousand years ago this was apparently the site of a small community. They have left us 186 skeletons, and these give us a distribution of age at time of death which can then be translated into a life table. (Halley's calculations were based on the observed birthrate and the number of deaths in each age group in Breslau; we know nothing about the birthrate in Taforalt, so we have to assume that the number of births in any given period of time—in this instance, the functioning life of the cemetery— roughly equaled the number of deaths.) Figure 1.2 shows the life table for Palaeolithic man compared with a similarly constructed life table for a Neolithic settlement of early agriculturalists living in Hungary around 3000 B.C.[5] and with the life table for a contemporary tribe of hunter-gatherers living in the Kalahari Desert of Africa.[6] (Because there were few very young skeletons in the burial grounds, it seems likely that these people seldom extended the ceremony of burial to dead infants; so rather arbitrarily I have assumed that, in each population, 60 percent of newborns survived to the age of five.)

Compared to the changes that are to come later, these three curves are remarkably similar; indeed, their similarity suggests that they are fairly accurate. The present day !Kung seem to be doing slightly better than our distant ancestors, but overall the pattern of birth, life, and death seems to be much the same for the three groups. The !Kung have been carefully studied over many years and the dynamics of their population are well documented. On average, each breeding woman produces 4.5 children. Of these, 2.25 are girls, and of them one survives to be the replacement for her mother. In this way, births balance deaths, and the population tends to maintain itself at a constant level from one generation to the next. For the ancient communities shown in figure 1.2, mortality was somewhat higher, so each breeding woman must have had to produce about six children to maintain the population.

This was the pattern of life and death over the countless generations that came before recorded history, and we should expect to find that natural selection has achieved this pattern by an appropriate balance between the rates of human development and aging and the natural rate of reproduction. Several factors come into the equation.[7] The mother in a nomadic family has to carry some of the baggage plus the youngest child, but she cannot easily carry more than one child and if there happen to be two small children in the family, the younger one is likely to be left behind; so births ideally should be spaced more than two or three years apart. But the death rate for children makes it necessary for each breeding woman to be able to produce six children, so it follows that she has to be fertile for about twenty years. This is very different from the modern woman, who is fertile for about thirty years and can readily produce a dozen children or more. But, at low levels of nutrition, a woman does not become fertile until she is almost twenty. Furthermore, the diet

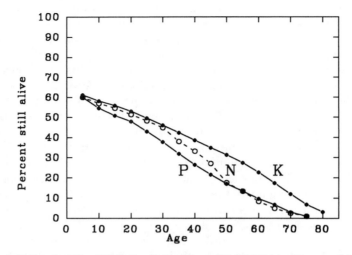

Figure 1.2. Survival for (P) Palaeolithic Man, (N) Neolithic Man, and (K) the contemporary !Kung tribe (from Acsadi and Nemeskeri; see note 5, and Howell; see note 6). Because there were few very young skeletons in the burial grounds, it seems likely that these ancient people seldom extended the ceremony of burial to dead infants; so rather arbitrarily I have assumed that, in each population, 60 percent of newborn infants survived to the age of five.

of nomads is difficult to eat if you have no teeth, so children have to be breast fed for about three years; because lactation tends to inhibit ovulation, especially at low levels of nutrition, the existence of one child therefore tends to inhibit the arrival of the next. However, each tribe must have some unexploited capacity for increase. Consequently, it is usual to find that in primitive societies part of the interval between successive children is being achieved by restrictive rules governing matrimony and by a certain amount of abortion and infanticide.

Homo sapiens has spent several hundred times longer being a hunter-gatherer than an agriculturalist, and the city dweller is a still more recent invention. So we should expect to find that much of our biochemistry and reproductive physiology was selected to be suitable for what we would now think of as an alien lifestyle. Certainly, many of our present diseases can be traced to our departure from the habits and lifestyle to which we were adapted. Cardiovascular disease is almost unknown in primitive rural communities. Similarly, although breast and colon cancer are now two of the commonest cancers in Europe and the United States, there are good reasons to think that they would be quite rare if we were to go back to the diet and breeding habits of our hunter-gatherer ancestors.

The invention of agriculture, around 10,000 years ago, vastly increased the capacity of land to support human populations. Palaeolithic communities seldom achieved densities higher than 0.1 person per square kilometer. Early Neolithic agriculturalists reached 1 per km², and by the time of the Roman Empire several countries had reached 15 per km²; (these numbers should be compared with the present value of about 30 for the United States and 100–200 for most countries in western Europe).[8] Presumably the increased productivity of the countryside, brought about by agriculture, improved the nutrition of its inhabitants and this then led both to an increase in their fertility and to a decrease in their mortality.

Agriculture brought other changes, however, that were initially much more important than the mere increase in population. It has regularly been observed that the inhabitants of agricultural communities have to work much harder than hunter-gatherers.[9] In this sense, agriculture can be seen as the invention that allows people to generate more food by working harder—in particular, more food than they themselves can consume. So it brings into existence societies where some people not only produce food for themselves but are forced to produce food for others—a development that has been called "macroparasitism."[10] Such societies are the essence of civilization. But with their arrival the human race acquired rulers and armies, and these had to be supported by yet more work, which in turn created the demand for more births to add to the working population—an idea that is explicit in the Roman choice of the word *proletarius* to describe the segment of the population who were not landowners and whose prime function was to produce offspring (*proles*).

It is difficult to disentangle the many interactions between the inventions of agriculture and the birthrate and death rate of these early populations, and the same problem will return when we consider the demographic changes that occurred at the time of the Industrial Revolution. However, one consequence of the invention of agriculture was of enormous importance for the evolution of human diseases, and that was the development of cities.

Once large numbers of people are in close contact with each other, infectious agents can survive from one year to the next even if they produce lifelong immunity in their host, because there will now always be a high enough concentration of fresh, susceptible children to keep the disease going.[11] So we see new human diseases arising that had probably never existed before, such as measles and smallpox. Even diseases that must have existed since the beginning achieved a prevalence they did not have among scattered, isolated communities.

We see this clearly from the records of Roman cemeteries (figure 1.3).[12] The life table for the inhabitants of the Roman colonies in

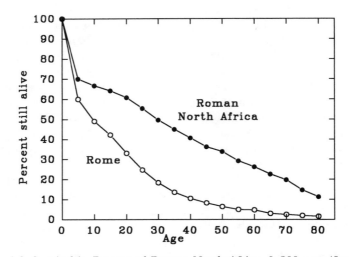

Figure 1.3. Survival in Rome and Roman North Africa, 0–200 A.D. (from Mac-Donell; see note 12). The Romans tended not to put up gravestones for small children, and we therefore have little information about infant mortality at that time. So the five-year survivals in this figure have been arbitrarily set at 60 percent for Rome (which is the value for seventeenth-century Breslau) and 70 percent for Roman North Africa. Even so the figure probably overestimates children's chances of surviving in Rome, because so many of its inhabitants came to Rome as young adults.

North Africa in A.D. 0–400 shows life expectancy to have been very like that of the !Kung. In contrast, Rome itself, even for those rich enough to deserve gravestones, was an extraordinarily hostile environment. There, the force of mortality was so overwhelming that senescence ceased to be very important: in any year, you had roughly a one in twenty chance of dying irrespective of your age. A physicist from outer space would describe the adult inhabitants of ancient Rome as having a half-life of about 14 years. If you sit down and try to work it out, you will see that the population of Rome could not possibly have sustained itself without transfusion from outside. The surrounding countryside had continually to provide Rome not only with the tribute of food and taxes but also with young recruits for its work force.

Ancient Rome may have been an extreme case, but it was not until the twentieth century that any city became able to sustain itself without some influx of people from outside. Rural life was what we would now call marginal subsistence; city life must have been a round of unimaginable squalor. And to think that just 200 years ago the historian Edward Gibbon declared, "If a man were called to fix the period of the world during which the condition of the human race was most happy and prosperous, he would, without hesitation, name that which elapsed from the death of Domitian [A.D. 96] to the accession of Commodus [A.D. 180]."[13] Plainly our idea of happiness is far removed from Gibbon's.

As we come up to the seventeenth and eighteenth centuries, any history of mortality cannot avoid some mention of the changes that were occurring in the intellectual, economic, and political scene: the English Revolution in the seventeenth century, followed by the Enlightenment and the American and French Revolutions in the eighteenth century—the beginnings of modern chemistry and physics—and the start of the Industrial Revolution. It was no chance coincidence that the eighteenth and nineteenth centuries ushered in the great change in the pattern of mortality. It is a change that the nations of the world have not yet learned how to accommodate. And it is the timing of this change that is the main topic of the chapter.

The Seventeenth and Eighteenth Centuries

Until the end of the eighteenth century, people's attitude toward disease seems to have been a matter of occasional activism against a background of passivity. Everyone knew that plague was a contagious disease which could be escaped by avoiding any contact with victims. That was why Boccaccio's talkative ladies and gentlemen were sequestered in the country in 1348. The very word "quarantine" comes from the practice, in fourteenth-century French and Italian ports, of holding ships at anchor off-shore for forty days if they had come from countries suffering plague. In contrast, the general force of mortality, as it weighed upon the populace from one year to the next, was treated as if it were immutable and not to be meddled with.

In England, a regular record of mortality was kept from the sixteenth century onward as a way of watching for outbreaks of plague. In 1662, John Graunt produced a study of the published Bills of Mortality for London, in which he showed that the city regularly recorded more deaths than births and was being maintained by immigrants from the country. He ascribed London's unhealthiness rather vaguely to pressures of population and to the ever-increasing smoke as the nation turned to coal for its source of heat. Even though he discussed the rise and fall of various diseases, he seems to have been uninterested in their causes. Indeed, he ends his book with the words ". . . whether the knowledge [of births and deaths, migration and disease] be necessary for many, or fit for others than our sovereign and his chief ministers, I leave to consideration."[14] Subsequently, in the eighteenth century, various schemes were proposed in England to improve the health of the public.

For example, in 1714 a Quaker called Bellers suggested that there should be a national health service, with special hospitals for the treatment of certain diseases.[15] But these ideas attracted little attention.

Indifference to the fate of humankind was not confined to England. In Germany, Johann Süssmilch published a treatise on population in 1741, entitled "Die göttliche Ordnung in den Veränderungen des menschlichen Geschlechts, aus der Geburt, dem Tode, und der Fortpflanzung desselben erwiesen," which can be roughly translated as "Proof for a God-given order to the changes in male and female births and deaths and the reproduction of human populations."

Times were changing, however. Within one generation, Johann Peter Frank produced the first of a series of books describing how the cities of Germany could be kept clean and free of disease, and how the authorities should encourage the population to produce children who then should be properly looked after, educated, and protected from accident. His system for the control of medical hygiene ("System einer vollständigen medicinischen Polizey") appeared in six volumes between 1779 and 1817, and may perhaps be counted as the first statement of the concept of public health. Unfortunately, it had little impact. About the same time, a similar scheme was proposed to the revolutionary Constituent Assembly of France by Dr. Guillotin, but it too was not acted upon, and his lasting fame rests on a much simpler idea.

What were needed were facts and figures, and it was the emergence of the statistics of life and death, at the end of the eighteenth century, that ushered in the revolution in health. For some years, records had been kept of the death rates in several European cities, and in the 1770s Richard Price, the English theologian and revolutionary, used these statistics to calculate what would have to be the rate of payment for any scheme that provided pensions in old age. (Price was one of the founders of the first life assurance company, and a pamphlet he wrote in England in 1776 supporting American independence had great influence on both sides of the Atlantic.) In a supplement to the second edition of his book of statistics, he commented on the great difference between urban and rural death rates.

> From this comparison it appears with how much truth great cities have been called the graves of mankind. [The comparison] must also convince all who consider it that . . . it is by no means strictly proper to consider our diseases as the original intention of nature. They are, without doubt, in general, our own creation. Were there a country where the inhabitants led lives entirely natural and virtuous, few of them would die without measuring out the whole period of present existence allotted them; pain and distempers would be unknown among them; and the dismission of death would come upon them like a sleep,

in consequence of no other cause than gradual and unavoidable decay. Let us then, instead of charging our Maker with our miseries, learn more to accuse and reproach ourselves.[16]

The end of the eighteenth century was above all a time of high ideals and the start of a chain of revolutions. That was when people began to collect statistics on mortality, and it seems to have been about then that some governments started to adjust to the idea that one of the responsibilities of the state was to provide a happy longevity for all its citizens rather than just for the rich and the powerful. It had seemed perfectly acceptable that Frederick the Great, in the pursuit of his family squabbles, should urge his troops on with the cry "You dogs, do you want to live forever?" Yet, less than twenty years later, Thomas Jefferson was writing a draft of the U.S. Declaration of Independence and asserting that we all have a right to "the preservation of life, liberty, and the pursuit of happiness."

It was about then, at the end of the eighteenth century or early in the nineteenth century, that life expectancy started to climb upward. For those lucky enough not to be in large cities, life expectancy had been roughly forty for hundreds or even thousands of years (except, of course, in times of famine and pestilence). Over the next 150 years, however, the industrial nations of the world were to see average life expectancy move up to seventy-five and beyond.

We would obviously like to know what actually were the technical, social, and political changes that produced such a sudden improvement in the human condition. How many of the changes were meant to improve public health and how many were fortuitous? How often did the reforms confer such conspicuous benefits that they were instantly accepted by everyone, and how often did they have to be forced on the population by some paternalistic authority? It is also worth considering what, at the time, were believed to be the causes of premature mortality; as we shall see, the arguments that raged over the causes of what we now call the infectious diseases were extraordinarily like some of the present arguments about the causes of cancer. By looking at this period, we may therefore hope to learn some important lessons about the way public health and preventive medicine tend to operate in practice.

The Origins of the Demographic Transition

When comparisons are being made between many different populations (e.g., each year's crop of children, born between 1540 and 1890) rather than just one or two at a time (as in the previous three figures), it is much simpler to describe each population in terms of its life expectancy (average number of years from birth to death) rather than try to carry in our minds the whole life table for each group. The calculation can be made in one of two ways. If you have a life table, you can work out the actual average number of years lived, for example, by those born on some particular date. But obviously you cannot work this out until every member of the cohort has died. It is therefore more usual to calculate a kind of hypothetical life expectancy; when, for example, someone says that the present life expectancy in Japan is eighty, what they mean is that a group of people would live for an average of eighty years if they had, in each year of their life, the exact mortality now shown by Japanese of that age; I shall call that "calculated life expectancy." In a world where death rates are going steadily downward, actual life expectancy will turn out to be better than the calculated value. Occasionally, as we shall see near the end of this chapter, disaster strikes and the opposite is true.

We can now start with the crude facts. The exact historical records of life and death in the ruling families of Europe show that, for the rich, life expectancy began to go up somewhere between 1650 and 1750.[17] The common people had to wait another 100 years before their lot improved[18] (figure 1.4). The developing nations of the world had to wait still longer, but for them the rise was still more dramatic (figure 1.5).

Even to this day, the rich tend to live longer than the poor. In most Western nations, life expectancy is still about ten years greater for the highest social classes than for the lowest;[19] in the United States, for example, the richest ethnic group are the Japanese, and the poorest are the Africans; the life expectancies for Japanese, Caucasian, and African women in 1960 were eighty, seventy-five, and sixty-seven, respectively.[20]

Surprisingly, the prime causes of the increase in life expectancy are still somewhat obscure. If the only information at our disposal were the statistics for the total population of a nation such as England, we would be forced to conclude that nothing happened to life expectancy until the middle of the nineteenth century, especially since we know that this was the time of great sanitary reform. But mortality had started to change much earlier for the rich, so before we give all the credit to the reformers of the nineteenth century, we should look at what was happening 100 years earlier.

The eighteenth century saw one conspicuous innovation in public health—the introduction of immunization against smallpox—and this may have had a significant effect on overall mortality. In Sweden, for example, smallpox was responsible for more than 10 percent of all deaths in the middle of the century, but the figure had dropped to about 1 percent 100 years later.[21] Indeed, in 1793, three years before Jenner's invention of vaccination, a plan was proposed to exterminate smallpox

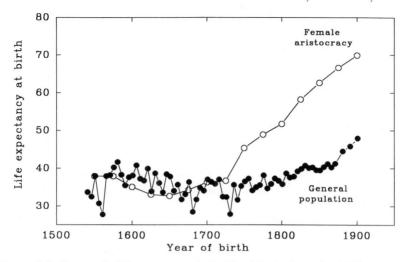

Figure 1.4. Changes in life expectancy in England. I give here the life expectancy for aristocratic females (from T. H. Hollingsworth; see note 17) because the men had warfare as an extra hazard. The life expectancy for the general population comes from Wrigley and Schofield; see note 18. Such accurate statistics for the general population were not available to the humanitarians of the eighteenth and nineteenth centuries.

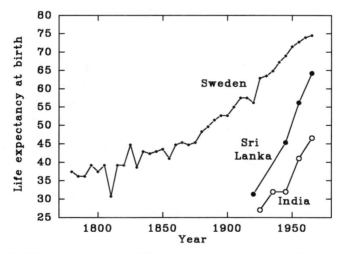

Figure 1.5. Changes in calculated life expectancy in Sweden (which was the first country to enter the demographic transition), Sri Lanka, and India.

from Great Britain by inoculating the entire population subcutaneously with virulent smallpox virus.[22] [In England the effect of inoculation and vaccination would have been masked (save perhaps among the rich) because industrialization was drawing people into cities; in the eighteenth century, London's share of England's population went from 5 percent to 12 percent, and this would have tended to raise mortality.]

Other important changes were taking place.[23] Increasing trade with the new world was bringing in new crops, plus the great wealth engendered by such trade. Agriculture was becoming vastly more sophisticated and efficient, so that many people probably had access to at least a more varied diet.[24] Bubonic plague vanished from Europe partly as the result of improvements in the design of buildings, which eliminated the black rat. Wool (which shrinks when washed) began to be replaced by cotton, so that it became practicable to wash your clothes repeatedly and therefore worthwhile to wash yourself at the same time, and people at last started to be fairly clean, which must have diminished the spread of many contagious diseases.[25]

Lastly, there seems to have been a great change in attitude of mind. Books on health became best sellers. In France, a book entitled *Avis au Peuple sur sa Santé* (Advice to People on their Health) (Tissot 1762) went through ten editions in six years, and a German equivalent, *Gesundheitkatechismus* (A Catechism for Health) (Faust 1794), sold 150,000 copies.

The emphasis of the times, at least among the reading public, seems to have been on cleanliness. Unfortunately, this could be extended to the general public only in those situations where there was some centralized authority—as in certain hospitals, army camps, and ships of the navy. For the poor, whether they lived in the city or the country, the struggle for survival allowed little time for inventiveness, and so they were not involved in these changes nor initially did they benefit from them. Nevertheless, we should date the beginnings of public health to at least as far back as the eighteenth century. (It is interesting that this tendency for advances in health to come first to the rich applies to this day; for example, the recent massive decline in cardiovascular mortality in the United States began on the West Coast and the Northeast and only later spread slowly into the center of the country.)[26]

Johann Peter Frank, who was mentioned earlier in connection with his treatise on public health published between 1779 and 1817, went to Pavia as professor of Clinical Medicine and Public Health and studied the state of medicine in northern Italy. As a result he reached the conclusion that most disease could be traced to the abject poverty imposed on the population by the nobility and clergy, who owned all the land. "After all the land has been divided among the powerful and rich, there is hardly any difference left between the common people and the very beasts of burden except that the beasts precede and pull the plow, while men guide and follow."[27] But his attempts at reform were fruitless even though he had the backing of the Emperor Joseph II. In his professorial graduation day address at the University of Pavia in 1790, "*De populorum miseria: morborum genitrice*" (Concerning the misery of the populace and the genesis of diseases) he asked, "Why is it that a vast amount of illness originates in the very society that men of old inaugurated in order to enjoy a safer life?" This is a question that could still be put to many of today's governments.

Although most of the conventional heroes of public health are nineteenth-century figures, I think the idea of public health can be traced back to the philosophers of the Age of Enlightenment. They were the ones who persuaded the world that the human condition is not the subject of Divine Will but is essentially a matter of choice.

The Nineteenth Century

The population of Europe has suffered at least two periods of great decline—during the Dark Ages which followed the fall of the Roman Empire, and during the fourteenth century when there was a succession of epidemics of plague, the worst of which killed one out of every three people.[28] But apart from these major setbacks, the number of people living in Europe had been growing fairly steadily at the rate of up to 7 percent per generation (i.e., had doubled every 300 years or so). In the eighteenth century, this was suddenly to change. Europe's population doubled in 100 years and would almost double again before reaching its present relatively stationary state; indeed, England went further, doubling between 1800 and 1850, and again between 1850 and 1900, which amounts to a 50 percent increase in each generation.

The exact process underlying this period of growth is still the subject of debate. Obviously, for a population to increase, births must exceed deaths. If the change is to be more than temporary, it must lead to an increase in the breeding population, either by an increase in birthrate or by a decrease in childhood mortality. Since the force of mortality did not change in England for the nation as a whole until after 1850 (figure 1.4), the explosion in population that occurred in the nineteenth century must initially have been the result of an increase in birthrate.

As mentioned earlier, the circumstances of a !Kung tribeswoman determine that she has rather little unexploited capacity for producing children. In contrast, the nineteenth-century European woman was plainly able to produce enough children to increase the population by more than 50 percent per generation, and nineteenth-century England was so organized (in terms of marriage and reproduction) that she did exactly that. Demographers have therefore had to decide whether there was a sudden change in marriage customs (proportion of women who married, how young they were, etc.) or in the fertility of married women, and how much the change was a physiological one (due perhaps to improvements in nutrition) and how much was the result of a conscious effort to have more children (i.e., an increase in fecundity). Incidentally, any explanation has to accommodate the awkward fact that a similar acceleration was occurring at the same time in India, China, and Japan; so perhaps one of the causes may have been a worldwide change in climate.[29] These changes are discussed in the final chapter.

Whatever the underlying cause, the increase in Europe's population was accompanied by a migration into the cities in pursuit of the wealth that was being generated by the Industrial Revolution. Over the course of 100 years, the populations of London and Paris increased about five-fold, and Berlin increased ten-fold. By 1900, London contained over 6 million people and the other two cities each contained 2–3 million. Because this growth occurred at a time when there were few if any restrictions on the design of buildings or minimum standards to be met by landlords, the major cities of the Western world maintained a squalor and level of mortality almost matching that achieved by ancient Rome.

The conventional view of the Industrial Revolution is that it worsened the lot of the masses, ruining the lives of those who went into the cities and impoverishing the countryside. Yet the statistics on mortality do not support this idea. Before I knew any better, I would have guessed that life in seventeenth-century Breslau was much like Wagner's idyllic portrait of life in sixteenth-century Nürnberg. In fact, Halley's life table shows that the conditions in Breslau were quite as bad as those of the worst of English cities (Liverpool) in 1860, which was about the worst time in the Industrial Revolution[30] (figure 1.6). As for life in the country, the semi-rural districts of England in the 1860s had a not much lower mortality than Roman North Africa more than 1,500 years earlier.

Perhaps the most important changes, however, were in people's thoughts about disease and death. The world was now ready for reform. The earliest numerical studies of mortality among the poor were carried out in France.[31] In 1829, in the first issue of *Annales d'hygiène publique et de médecine légale*, Villermé reported that in most paupers' prisons in France the average annual mortality was about 25 percent. The cause had to be the indifference of the authorities to the fate of the poor, rather than any calculated severity, because mortality was much lower in maximum security prisons where there was forced labor and the prisoners were watched over more closely. From prisoners, Villermé then turned his attention to the citizens of Paris. Figures were available for mortality, and the affluence of various districts could be assessed in-

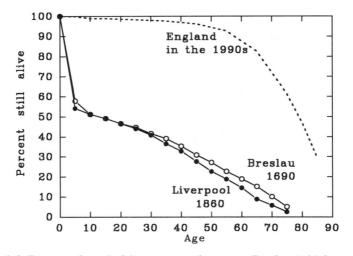

Figure 1.6. Pattern of survival in seventeenth-century Breslau (which may have been typical for the times), nineteenth-century Liverpool which had the lowest survival for any city in nineteenth-century England (from Farr; see note 30), compared to that in modern England (or any other modern Western nation).

directly by determining the proportion of people who paid rents that were high enough to be taxed. Using these statistics, he showed that mortality was about 50 percent higher in the poorest districts than in the richest. He went on to look at the great differences in mortality for different occupational groups and produced a table giving life expectancy at several ages for sixteen occupations. For example, at age ten the children of manufacturers and merchants could expect to live for another forty-two years, whereas for factory workers the figure was only twenty-eight years.

Villermé's second report, *Tableau de l'état physique et moral des ouvriers* (A tabulation showing the physical and moral condition of workers), came out in 1840 and was followed, two years later, by Chadwick's "Report on the sanitary conditions of the labouring population of Great Britain"[32] and then in 1845 by Engels' book *The Condition of the Working Class in England.*[33] The conclusion was all too clear. The businessman who built a factory and created jobs was bringing wealth to some but he was certainly not bringing health to the workers in the factory. For example, one of England's major sources of wealth was the manufacture of cotton fabrics (by the 1830s about 1 percent of the entire population was engaged in the cotton industry). The southern states of the United States were becoming the main suppliers of raw cotton, so we had a triangle of trade—slaves from West Africa to the United States, cotton from the United States to England, and cotton (and other) goods from England to Africa (and elsewhere). For people who were rich, cotton fabrics made it much easier to be comfortable and clean, and as mentioned earlier this cleanliness may have contributed to their increasing life expectancy; for both the West African slaves[34] and the English cotton spinners[35] life expectancy at birth seems to have been about twenty years.

The Industrial Revolution brought another, very unwelcome result. In 1831, trade with India introduced cholera to Europe for the first time,[36] and by the following year it had spread to the United States. Like plague, cholera is a readily identifiable disease and typically produces sudden violent outbreaks with a high mortality. For example, the 1892 outbreak in Hamburg (which at the time had a population of about five hundred thousand) produced a thousand new cases *each day* of whom half were to die; and one nineteenth-century epidemic in Cairo killed 13 percent of the inhabitants. Europe had been free of such cataclysmic epidemics for several generations. The last outbreak of plague had been in Marseilles in 1720, and smallpox could by now be fairly well contained thanks to vaccination. So the sudden appearance of a new epidemic disease precipitated a prolonged and historically very important controversy about the causes of mortality. It also stimulated the collection and use of proper statistics. Just as the plague of 1592 had been the stimulus for the collection and publication of the weekly London Bills of Mortality, so it was the arrival of cholera in the 1830s that made the British Parliament create, in 1848, a central Board of Health with the power to enforce the sanitary reforms that were being advocated by those who knew the statistics. The first half of the nineteenth century was therefore a time for assembling statistics, arguing about causes, and preparing for a reform in public health.

The main causes of death were certain infectious diseases that the industrialized nations have now almost completely eradicated (table 1.2).[37] Indeed, the most important of these (tuberculosis, diphtheria, cholera, dysentery, typhoid, and typhus) are caused by microorganisms that most people in the Western world should now never meet unless they travel. Some of these diseases are airborne, spreading directly from person to person; others are carried in food or water.

None of this, however, was known at the start of the nineteenth century. Smallpox had been shown to be contagious; the success of inoculation proved that. Plague and leprosy had for centuries been regarded as infectious. But the other diseases listed in table 1.2 were often not well distinguished one from another. For the most part, their incidence did not vary greatly from one year to the next, so there was ample excuse for not realizing that they were infectious. Furthermore, with the French and American Revolutions fresh in people's minds, it was very much part

TABLE 1.2
Death Rates (per million) in England and Wales

Deaths due to Infectious Diseases	1848–54	1971
Tuberculosis	2,901	13
Bronchitis, pneumonia, influenza	2,239	603[a]
Scarlet fever and diphtheria	1,016	0.
Other airborne diseases	1,103	3
Cholera and dysentery	1,819	33[b]
Other food and water borne diseases	1,743	2
Other infectious diseases	2,144	60
Total for all infectious diseases	12,965	714
Total for all noninfectious diseases	8,891	4,670

Source: T. McKeown. "The Role of Medicine: Dream, Mirage, or Nemesis." (London: The Nuffield Provincial Hospital Trust, 1976.
Notes:
[a] Predominantly pneumonia in the very old.
[b] Predominantly infantile diarrhoea.

of the mood of the times to look for political rather than technological solutions for the ills of humankind.

Villermé and Chadwick had shown that the greatest cities had the greatest mortality and that the poor lived less long than the rich. Since mortality went hand in hand with density of population and the general filth of cities, it was natural to propose that diseases were caused simply by the miasma (smell) of people and the filth and squalor that accompanies extreme poverty. So there arose, early in the century, a strong anticontagionist school which believed that diseases were, with a few exceptions, not due to infective agents transmitted from one person to another, but could arise spontaneously wherever the miasma of poverty existed. (The issue has fascinating similarities to the controversy, in the 1940s, about the origin of mutations; interestingly the arguments were resolved in opposite directions, but each controversy lies at the heart of a scientific discipline—respectively, clinical microbiology and classical genetics.)

The anticontagionists included some strange bedfellows.[38] Many scientists felt that the arguments of the contagionists were very weak and this rather negative reason made them, illogically, into anticontagionists; they did, however, remain experimentalists at heart and would fearlessly use themselves to prove that one or another disease was not contagious, the most famous instance occurring in 1892 when the German pathologist, von Pettenkofer, swallowed a culture of the newly isolated bacterium, *Vibrio cholera*, in the hope of proving that it was not a cause of disease (he escaped unscathed). The social reformers tended to be anti-contagionists because they believed that social reform was all that was needed to resolve the problem of disease. For example, another German pathologist, Rudolf Virchow, was a staunch believer in the social causes of diseases (e.g., that social conditions decided whether your disease appeared as typhus or typhoid). It was thanks largely to his efforts that Berlin was transformed into one of the healthiest cities in Europe, and von Pettenkofer was to do the same for Munich. (Actually, Virchow was not a committed anticontagionist; for example, early in his career he carried out a beautiful study of the epidemiology of measles in isolated communities which showed that it was an infectious disease with a fairly constant incubation period.)

Many priests were laissez faire anticontagionists because they wanted to believe that disease was a sign of sinfulness. Big business was anti-contagionist because it did not want any form of quarantine to interrupt international trade and it also did not want any social reform; its position was therefore at least internally consistent (unlike, for example, the present-day American tobacco industry which asks that the growers receive government subsidies and that the marketers be left free from any government interference with their right to advertise their lethal product). Last, even the medical establishment was occasionally driven by self-interest to take an anticontagionist stance; for example, in 1897 the New York Academy of Medicine opposed legislation that would make tuberculosis a notifiable disease, because the diagnosis would so often end up in the hands of the bacteriologists rather than the clinicians and this would diminish the power and prestige of the doctors.[39]

Certain unfortunate experiments greatly strengthened the anticontagionist cause.[40] Most of the people like von Pettenkofer, who deliberately used themselves as experimental animals, came to no harm; (many human pathogens are of rather limited virulence and tend to become attenuated on culture). In the 1820s, the French conducted a series of very careful studies of several outbreaks of yellow fever, in both the New World and the Old, and showed beyond doubt that the disease could arise in people who had not come into direct contact with other cases.[41] (Yellow fever was an unfortunate example to choose, because it is transmitted by mosquitoes and consecutive cases can therefore arise far apart from each other.) As a result of these studies, the French Academy of Medicine produced a strongly anticontagionist report in 1828, and this led to their taking a similar position on many other diseases, including cholera, and to the widespread abolition of quarantine. We should not blame them too much for this; the contagiousness of diseases such as plague and smallpox had been a more obvious and acceptable idea in earlier centuries when most people lived in small towns or villages, travel was slow and difficult, and a belief in contagion did not incur any cost.

It is easy to list the sequence of discoveries that should have been the decisive events in establishing, once and for all, that most mortality at that time was due to pathogenic microorganisms; hindsight makes wise men of us all. What actually happened seems to have been much less tidy. In 1840, a young German pathologist, Jacob Henle, produced a masterly review of the literature, "Von den Miasmen und Kontagien" (On miasmas and contagions), in which he outlined all the reasons for thinking that many of the common epidemic diseases were caused by microorganisms.[42] His argument was partly by analogy; fermentation and putrefaction had been shown in the 1760s by the Italian scientist, Spallanzani, to be the result of contamination with living creatures, such as yeasts and fungi, that do not arise spontaneously. Like the process of fermentation, the development of diseases such as measles, scarlet fever, or smallpox takes time (i.e., each disease has a characteristic incubation period); during this time the causative agent must be increasing in quantity because we know, from direct observation, that in a disease such as smallpox a single pustule contains enough of the agent to infect many people each of whom will, in due course, bear many pustules. It is this ability of the causative agents of smallpox and the other epidemic diseases to multiply which shows that they must be alive, since living creatures are the only things that can multiply in number. Unfortunately, Henle's reasoning seems to have had little influence on his contemporaries, and anticontagionism remained the dogma of the day. Indeed, it was not until the great argument between Pasteur and Liebig in the 1860s that the existence of microorganisms became widely accepted.

We should not be tempted into feeling that modern science has risen above all irrational prejudices. The same controversy surfaced again in the 1930s over the nature of the viruses of bacteria (bacteriophages) and once again the wrong side was temporarily victorious; Burnet, in Australia, believed that the bacteriophages were viruses and should be classified as living because they exhibited, as he put it, *genetic continuity* from one generation to the next. Unfortunately, Northrop and other American biochemists, who being biochemists were somewhat unreliable on matters of biology, argued that the bacteriophages were inanimate toxic enzymes which could induce a bacterium to make more such enzyme molecules but were not alive and could not multiply; and their view prevailed for several years—perhaps because Northrop had won a Nobel Prize and Burnet, at that time, had not.

In 1854, a third epidemic of cholera hit Europe, and it gave rise to two investigations that, at least in retrospect, should have settled once and for all what was the immediate cause of the disease and how it was spread. John Snow's report published in 1855 ("On the mode of communication of cholera") showed, beyond all doubt, that cholera was spread by contamination of water supplies.[43] Some 600 cases could be traced to one particular water pump in London. Furthermore, this local epidemic provided him with several significant "controls," for he noted that the people occupying a nearby brewery and workhouse (each of which had its own independent water supply) were spared, whereas someone who collected her water at the pump died of cholera even though she happened to live far away on Hampstead Hill. Snow's book, which describes the outbreak around the Broad Street pump in the district of Soho and a similar episode south of the river Thames in the suburb of Lambeth, is a *tour de force*. Indeed, it is now considered the beginning of investigative epidemiology. As it happened, another report was published at about the same time by Filippo Pacini describing and naming the unusual bacterium that is present in almost pure culture in the intestines of people dying of cholera.[44]

Neither of these reports seems to have made any lasting impression on the governments of the time. In England, the compiler of the Registrar General's Annual Reports, William Farr, came to believe as the result of further epidemiological studies that Snow was right, and it seems that many doctors were equally convinced and, by their efforts, cut short many outbreaks of cholera. But central authorities were not persuaded; indeed, shortly after this, Parliament abolished Chadwick's Board of Health, which until then had been responsible for sanitary reforms in the cities of England. The issue seems to have been the familiar one of power politics, the lobbying of certain vested interests and the gullibility of those who read newspapers. The *London Times* rejoiced in the decision, saying that "we prefer to take our chance of cholera and the rest than be bullied into health." Chadwick retired. Snow died at the age of forty-five. And although Pacini survived until 1883, he too died a disappointed man, unaware that his discovery was just about to be confirmed.

From the vantage point of the twentieth century, we can see that the central, scientific issue was the question of spontaneous generation. If some disease is caused by a miasma and can appear in a totally isolated community whenever the right physical conditions are present, then the causative agent must be capable of arising by spontaneous generation (i.e., is not like the living creatures we see around us, that can only increase by producing replicas of themselves). Conversely, if the disease spreads solely by direct contact (contagion), that must be because the causative agent is a living creature and cannot arise de novo. Although experiments had already been performed that seemed to exclude the possibility of spontaneous generation of the invisible causes of disease,

the issue remained in doubt until the 1860s, when Pasteur showed con-
clusively that any material or culture medium that had been properly
sterilized by heat would remain sterile indefinitely, provided it was
protected against microbial contamination from outside. His proof required the concept that substances can be sterilized by heat (Spallanzani's discovery, almost 100 years earlier). This may seem a trivial notion
but it is the foundation of the sophisticated technology that he and
others were developing for the study of bacteria. Once developed, these
techniques made it possible to identify all the major pathogenic bacteria
(i.e., the immediate causes of most of the diseases listed in table 1.2).

Appropriately, the dominant figure at this time was a pupil of Henle's,
Robert Koch. In 1882, Koch isolated the bacterium that is the cause of
tuberculosis, and in the following year he went to Cairo to investigate an
outbreak of cholera and quickly identified the bacterium that was responsible. On his return to Germany he was accorded a hero's recep-
tion, perhaps in part because the Egyptian exercise had been a joint (but
competitive) venture by Germany and France, and so Koch's success
could be given nationalistic overtones. It is an interesting piece of medical history that Koch never referred to Snow's work and it was not until
the 1930s that Snow came to be recognized as one of the founders of
modern epidemiology.[45]

Some doubters remained, however, even among the scientific community. Doctors could not have liked seeing so many of their cherished
beliefs cast aside. The bacteriologists must have seemed to them like
arrogant intruders, for this was really the first time that laboratory science had invaded the practice of medicine. As the president of the New
York Academy of Medicine said in 1885, "Have we not had enough yet of
the monthly installments of new bacilli which are the invariably correct
and positive sources of disease . . . ?"

Any residual doubts about the cause of cholera were settled by Koch's
study of the 1892 epidemic in Hamburg, in which he showed that the
hardest hit parts of the city were those that had the oldest water supply.
Interestingly, his epidemiological evidence was not so neat and clearcut
as John Snow's, a generation earlier. But now the world was ready for the
discovery and, more to the point, ready for all its implications. Over the
previous thirty or forty years there had been a revolution in people's
attitude to public health, and it was now widely accepted that health
and disease were proper subjects for legislation. Boards of Health had
been created in many European cities and the process of cleaning up
the environment was already well underway. As Virchow had put it,
"Medicine is a social science. . . . Politics is nothing but medicine on a
large scale." (Cicero had said rather the same thing almost 2000 years
earlier, although he probably meant that the prime consideration of the

law should be the welfare of the populace, rather than health and a freedom from disease, which he would not have thought of as controllable variables.)

With the knowledge that cholera is due to a bacterium, it became much easier to police the laws about water supply and sewage disposal and to enforce rules of quarantine during epidemics; for example, in the great outbreak of 1892, six infected ships visited the port of New York, but the local Board of Health was able to stop the disease from entering the city. Henceforth, any population could in principle be shown how to halt an epidemic of cholera by instituting a few simple precautions. It is important to note here that although the discovery of the bacterium *Vibrio cholerae* required some fairly high technology (good microscopes and all the other paraphernalia of bacteriologists), the end result was a solution to the problem that was within the reach of even the humblest peasant. Incidentally, this seems to have been true for many of the important discoveries in public health; in biology, as in other fields of human endeavor, knowledge itself is power.

The conquest of cholera is a particularly useful example because it illustrates so clearly the interplay between epidemiology and laboratory science—the kind of interplay, incidentally, that is becoming characteristic of much of present-day cancer research. But the final years of the nineteenth century were filled with other similar discoveries of enormous importance for the health of the human race. The transmission of malaria and yellow fever by mosquitoes, the role of symptomless carriers in the spread of diseases such as typhoid and diphtheria, the discovery of the immune system—the list seems endless. It was obviously one of those moments when a fresh cast of mind is sufficient to achieve a scientific revolution. To appreciate the full impact of these discoveries upon the health of the world, we must look at the twentieth century.

The Twentieth Century

Once they had identified the most important bacterial causes of human disease, the early bacteriologists moved on to study the mechanisms underlying acquired immunity to those diseases. The history of this period can be illustrated by considering the example of diphtheria. This is a disease, usually of the upper respiratory tract, that is dangerous because the bacterium *Corynebacterium diphtheriae* secretes a very potent toxin. In 1890, workers in Koch's laboratory showed that the blood of guinea pigs that had survived infection contained antibodies that would inactivate the toxin. Their discovery quickly led to two important developments—the mass production of antibodies (in horses) for the treatment of human cases of diphtheria, and the mass production of the bacterial toxin (suitably modified to diminish its toxicity) for the preventive immunization of human populations. This was the first time science offered not only a specific treatment (the use of secondhand antibodies against the bacterial toxin) but also a way of preventing an infectious disease (active immunization). These procedures (plus the antibiotics that came in the 1940s) are still, to this day, the weapons used to control diphtheria. So the history of the battle against diphtheria records what amounted to a competition between those who treat and those who seek to prevent. For example, since the 1890s the state of Massachusetts has kept a record of the number of cases of diphtheria occurring each year, what proportion of the cases were fatal, how much diphtheria antitoxin was distributed, and later (when immunization became practicable) how much modified toxin was distributed. The first thing we see (figure 1.7) is that the fatality of the disease had dropped steeply in the 1890s (before antitoxin became available) and has remained between 5 percent and 10 percent from then on. To judge from these overall numbers, therefore, treatment with antitoxin seems to have been of rather little avail; even with today's antibiotics, the fatality of cases is still about 10 percent.

There does, however, seem to have been some control over the incidence of diphtheria, because no major epidemics occurred after about 1907 (figure 1.8). This was the year the state installed health inspectors whose job it was to see that every case of a dangerous infectious disease was reported. Although these inspectors had very limited powers, they would advise about quarantine and could arrange for bacteriological tests to determine who were chronic carriers of diphtheria, and it seems not unreasonable to assume that the drop in incidence of diphtheria was at least partly because of their efforts. Finally, with the introduction of active immunization in the 1920s, diphtheria ceased to be an important cause of death. If therefore we look back over the history of this one disease, we would have to say that it was largely conquered by prevention—first as part of the general reduction in mortality from many diseases that came at the end of the nineteenth century (perhaps because of improvements in nutrition), somewhat later as the result of direct efforts to restrict the spread of the disease, and finally as the result of a specific program of immunization. Advances in the treatment of diphtheria (as opposed to its prevention), in particular the discovery of antibiotics, have had only a minor effect on mortality.

Most of us feel more confident with solutions that depend on high technology, perhaps because we feel more comfortable when we can point to some particular discovery as having been a turning point in human affairs. For this reason, the obvious impact of active immunization upon the incidence of infections like diphtheria tends to blind us to the effects of other less specific ways of controlling the spread of

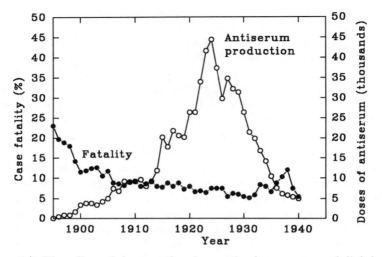

Figure 1.7. The effect of the use of antiserum in the treatment of diphtheria upon the fatality of diphtheria, in the state of Massachusetts.

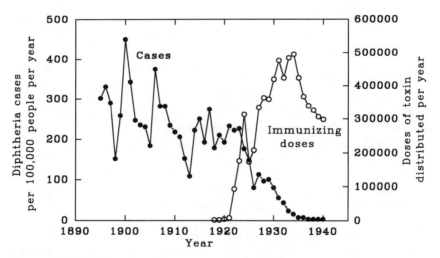

Figure 1.8. The effect of immunization with modified diphtheria toxin upon the annual incidence of new cases, in the state of Massachusetts.

infectious diseases. But we should remember that half of the reduction in mortality from diphtheria had already been achieved before the technological solution was available. Therefore we should now look specifically at the history of some infectious disease for which no technological solution was available.

The preeminent example is tuberculosis. As a cause of death this was far more important than diphtheria. In Massachusetts, early in the nineteenth century, one in 1,000 people died of diphtheria each year, but four times as many died of tuberculosis. No really effective treatment for tuberculosis became available until the 1950s, and immunization was never adopted on a large scale either in the United States or England. Yet the mortality went steadily downward. It is not clear exactly when this started; rates of 500 per 100,000 were not uncommon at the beginning of the nineteenth century, so the decline was probably well underway before the period covered by figure 1.9. The change could hardly have been caused by any deliberate attempt at prevention, because the disease was thought to be hereditary. Although Villemin showed, in France in 1865, that tuberculosis was transmissible to rabbits, his experiments seem not to have been believed and it was only when Koch isolated the bacterium, in 1882, that the contagiousness of tuberculosis became widely accepted. By then the death rate had already dropped by one-third or more.

Tuberculosis is a relentless indicator of social conditions. We can see this in the way the privations caused by World Wars I and II temporarily raised the mortality of the civilian population; in each war about 15,000 more people died from tuberculosis in Britain than would have been expected from the rates in the years either side of the two wars; and Vienna and Budapest, during World War I, achieved annual death rates of about 600 per 100,000. So we should be looking for possible social explanations for the drop in mortality in the nineteenth century. Various ideas have been proposed: for example, an increase in resistance of the population as the gradual epidemic of tuberculosis, brought about by urbanization, gained momentum, weeded out the most susceptible and then receded; or an improvement in nutrition thanks to new crops and advances in agriculture; or the increase in real wages resulting from the Industrial Revolution; or the improvement in people's living conditions brought about by publication of the very statistics we are discussing; or the isolation of cases in the workhouse which was the policy in England (but not in Ireland, where tuberculosis did not decline).[46] Apart from the first strictly biological explanation (which is largely supposition), these various underlying changes are known to have taken place and each of them was in some sense, directly or indirectly, a product of

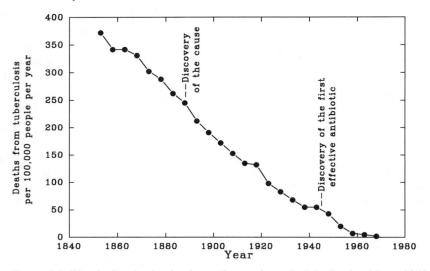

Figure 1.9. The decline in the death rate from tuberculosis in England from 1850 onward (from McKeown; see note 37).

the philosophical and technological revolutions of the eighteenth and nineteenth centuries. In short, if statistics on mortality are a fair index of the human condition, it seems that the fortunes of the masses were steadily improving in the second half of the nineteenth century, rather than going continuously downhill in the way Karl Marx predicted.

Looking at the smooth decline in mortality from tuberculosis shown in figure 1.9, it is tempting to say (as others have done) that the discoveries of the 1880s and 1890s had absolutely no impact on events. Yet when we read the annual reports of local authorities such as the Boards of Health of Massachusetts and New York, it is hard to believe that science was not making a contribution. Within one year of Koch's discovery of *Mycobacterium tuberculosis,* the Massachusetts Board had started on its campaign to eradicate bovine tuberculosis, and New York had made respiratory tuberculosis a notifiable disease (though it was not compulsorily notifiable until three years later). Interestingly, in some cities the medical profession resisted the idea that tuberculosis was contagious, because they felt that the principle of notifiability was an infringement of the delicately lucrative relationship between physicians and their patients; thus they complained that the New York Board was "not only, by means of alarming bacteriological edicts, directly interfering with the physician in the diagnosis of the patient, but in the end, by the creation of a public suspicion of his ignorance, possibly depriving him of one of the means of legitimate livelihood."[47]

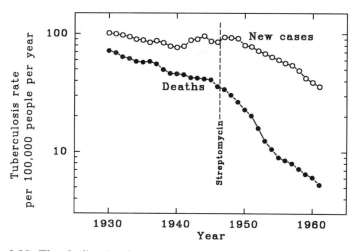

Figure 1.10. The decline in the death rate from tuberculosis and the rate of appearance of new cases, in the United States (from Lowell; see note 48).

The modern period in the campaign against tuberculosis in the United States started in 1930, when annual deaths were running at 70 percent of the rate of diagnosis of new cases (i.e., probably about half of the patients were eventually dying of their disease; figure 1.10).[48] This was the time when mass screening by chest x-ray came increasingly into play, and that was presumably why the incidence of new cases soon started to go up, rather than continue steadily downward. These extra cases were apparently not contributing to mortality, because the death rate went on declining until some time in the late 1940s, at which point it dropped away more steeply as antibiotics became available for the treatment of tuberculosis. By this time, the annual mortality had dropped from 400 to 30 per 100,000. Thus the invention of an effective treatment for tuberculosis did not arrive until more than 90 percent of the mortality had already been prevented by other means.

So we come to the end of this look at the revolution in the force of mortality. Over a period of about 100 years, the industrialized nations adopted a life-style that allowed them to avoid the major lethal infectious diseases and, with the notable exception of AIDS, now know how to treat many of the infections that slip through the protective shield of public health. The main spectacle of the second half of the twentieth century has been the spread of this revolution in mortality to the developing nations of the world who, as a consequence, will soon make up more than 80 percent of the human population. As mentioned earlier in the chapter, the population of the world as a whole now has an average life

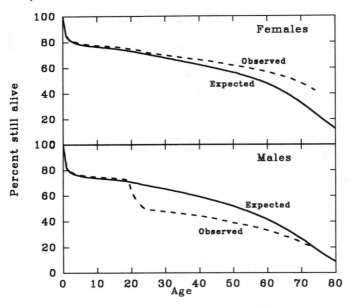

Figure 1.11. The observed survival of the males and females who were born in France in 1895, compared to the survival that would have been expected on the basis of the 1895 table of age-specific mortality rates (from Vallin; see note 49).

expectancy that is higher than the highest achieved for any nation by the end of the nineteenth century.

In this discussion of mortality I have left out one of the most important causes of premature death, namely war. But, in a sense, war is just another problem in public health. Sometimes the scale defies imagination. For example, all the advances of the twentieth century in public health and medicine were not enough to undo what happened to the cohorts who fought in World War I. Figure 1.11 compares (a) the expected survival of the children born in France in 1895, assuming that no further improvements in life expectancy would occur during their lifetime; and (b) the actual survival of these children.[49] As you might imagine, the female children lived longer than might have been expected, thanks to the steady drop in the force of mortality throughout the twentieth century. The males, however, have survived much less well than expected, because one-third of them were killed. For this group of males, all the advances in medicine and public health during their lifetime were not sufficient to compensate them for the losses they suffered in four years of war. They would have done better to have stayed away from the twentieth century.

Early in the history of public health, in the 1860s, the newly formed New York Board of Health wrote the following words in its second annual report: "The health department of a great commercial district which encounters no obstacles and meets with no opposition, may safely be declared unworthy of public confidence; for no sanitary measures, however simple, can be enforced without compelling individuals to yield something to the general welfare."[50] These words were written about the politics of health, but surely they apply just as well to the politics of peace.

Mortality and Medicine

Most people, doctors especially, find it hard to believe that the main advances of medicine did not arrive until long after most of the causes of untimely death had come under control. Many of us have had severe illnesses that responded dramatically to one or other of the weapons in the armory of modern medicine, and we like to imagine that we might have died but for this technology.

This picture of medicine as a triumphant technology is quite a new view. For example, in 1937 a committee in Washington was given the job of forecasting the advances in technology likely to take place in the next fifteen years.[51] Their report is discussed in some detail in the final chapter. For me, one of its most interesting features is that it omitted any mention of possible advances in medical care (other than the likely increase in cost). In 1937, medicine was apparently not considered a technology. Or perhaps no one thought that medicine might be subject to major advances.

All that changed after World War II, with the widespread use of antibiotics and the invention of some spectacular surgical procedures. But we should not forget that the first antibiotics, the sulfonamides in the early 1930s and penicillin in the 1940s, were discovered at about the time that life expectancy in Western nations had reached the biblical limit of three score years and ten. Perhaps one of the main consequences of the discovery of antibiotics has been the idea that every disease should be treatable, if we could but find its Achilles heal. In nineteenth-century London there were riots about the failure of the government to prevent the spread of cholera but no complaints about the way the disease was being treated; 150 years later there are riots about the lack of any treatment for AIDS, but great reluctance of many governments to become involved with preventive measures.

The misapprehension about the relative achievements of prevention and treatment stems largely from the medical profession. Doctors spend their lives treating patients, who come to them in a never-ending stream, and inevitably they see the answer to any disease in terms of treatment. That, after all, is their job. But the power of the medical lobby, particularly in the United States, has had several unfortunate consequences. For example, the predominately medical committee, assembled to advise Congress on President Nixon's War against Cancer early in the 1970s, included a few laboratory scientists but not a single cancer epidemiologist.[52] In consequence, over the next few years there was little or no effort to explore the possibilities for preventing cancer. Indeed, as late as 1989 Dr. Armand Hammer, the medical philanthropist, was proposing a massive increase in funds for the search for a cure for cancer (in particular, new forms of chemotherapy) in the mistaken belief that it was by the discovery of cures that diseases such as poliomyelitis, smallpox, typhoid fever, diphtheria, and tuberculosis were conquered.

Now, it might be argued that I am being unfair: although methods for prevention happened to come before any successful methods for treating the major diseases of mankind, one could imagine an alternative history where events occurred in a different order. In that case the credit would have gone to the professionals of medicine rather than of public health. But I do not believe it could have been the other way round. Consider the diseases listed by Armand Hammer. Poliomyelitis and smallpox can be prevented but they cannot be treated; diphtheria and typhoid, even today, are not easy to treat and have a case fatality rate that is not much less than that in the nineteenth century; and tuberculosis is not easy to control by treatment, as witness the increase in death rate seen whenever the poor become poorer, as they have in recent years especially in Russia and Eastern Europe.

Even today it is difficult to determine how much effect modern methods of treatment have on overall mortality. General mortality in the developed nations of the world dropped steadily between the 1950s and the 1970s, but only one-third of this drop was in causes of death that are considered to be treatable.[53] Most of the decline has been caused by a drop in the incidence of certain diseases. Mortality from stomach cancer, for example, has declined about tenfold in the last generation despite the absence of any effective treatment. So even now, prevention due to changes in life-style seems to be making the main contribution to the rise in life-span.

We can approach the problem in a different way. If we ask what factors are associated with high life expectancy in the different nations of the world, it turns out not to be the number of doctors or hospital beds for every 10,000 in the population, but things like the provision of a clean water supply and the level of literacy (figure 1.12).[54] So even at the end of the twentieth century, when there are cures for many diseases, it still seems that the health of nations depends more on the services

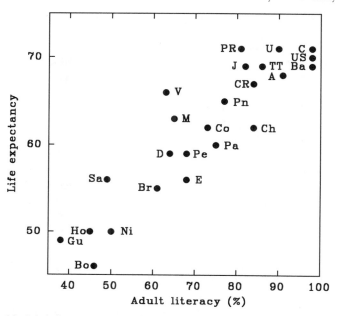

Figure 1.12. Adult literacy rates and average life expectancy in the nations of the Western Hemisphere in 1968. Argentina (A), Barbados (Ba), Bolivia (Bo), Brazil (Br), Canada (C), Chile (Ch), Colombia (Co), Costa Rica (CR), Dominican Republic (DR), Ecuador (E), El Salvador (S), Guatemala (Gu), Honduras (Ho), Jamaica (J), Mexico (M), Nicaragua (Ni), Panama (Pn), Paraguay (Pa), Peru (Pe), Puerto Rico (PR), Trinidad & Tobago (TT), United States (US), Uruguay (U), and Venezuela (V). (Missing are Cuba, Guyana, and Haiti, through lack of available statistics) (from Stewart; see note 54).

provided by their governments than on the services provided by their doctors.

There has, however, been a revolution in the practice of medicine. The first important change was the realization that many common medical procedures do more harm than good. We tend to imagine that the treatment of diseases is based on the results of some rational system of trial and error. Certainly, there have been notable instances where an established treatment was abandoned when it was found to do more harm than good; in a sixteenth-century battle the French surgeon Ambroise Paré ran out of hot oil to pour on the wounds of soldiers hit by gunfire and, as a result, discovered (and later reported) that simple bandaging produced better results. But such open-mindedness was exceptional. For example, an early nineteenth-century comparison of the fate of a group of patients with pneumonia, who were bled at various stages of their disease, showed that blood-letting did not affect either the average duration or the fatality of their disease;[55] most were ill for two or three weeks, and about 25 percent of them died. The author of this study did not go so far as to suggest that these patients might actually have done better if they had been left alone, but still he was attacked for daring to think that patients could be compared with one another. And it was not until well into the twentieth century that blood-letting fell out of favor. Proper clinical trials, which compared a treated group with untreated controls, did not come until after World War II, when the antibiotics had started to have an impact on the course of many infectious diseases. But even then the use of trials met with some opposition from clinicians who tended to dislike being guided by statisticians. Now, however, trials are being widely employed to find out which treatments and preventive measures are effective, and the influence of this upon medical practice is likely to be far-reaching.

This section should not, however, end on a negative note. In the past 150 years the practice of medicine has obviously undergone a complete revolution. Today, societies can prevent what were once the main causes of death among children and young adults, and the medical sciences have discovered the means for treating many diseases. In the case of accidents and violence, there has been spectacular success. All this has led to a great change in our expectations. We are no longer content to endure illness and disease: the maimed and the halt expect to be healed, and healed quickly.

At the same time, life seems to have become in many ways much more complicated, and there are still many people, especially among the rich, who look back nostalgically to the easy simplicities of the nineteenth century. Few of us, however, would happily make the journey back in time if we knew we would then have to consult a nineteenth-century doctor for a serious illness.

Future Developments

This chapter has surveyed the history of mortality in the developed nations. They were the first countries to undergo what is called the "demographic transition"—from a balance of high birthrate and high mortality to the new balance of low birthrate and low mortality. For the rich nations of the world it seems unlikely that there can be much more change in the pattern of mortality, because they have already attained a life expectancy that takes most of the population to the brink of senility. What these countries now have to do is learn how to run a nation where 25 percent of the population are receiving pensions and expensive health care and are too old to work, 20 percent of the population are too young to work, and there is less and less work for most of the remaining 55 percent.

From now on the important demographic changes are going to be in the less-developed nations. They represent the majority of humankind. It seems most unlikely that these nations will simply recapitulate what happened in the developed nations. For one thing, the scale is unimaginably greater and the pace of events is now much faster. Of all industrial nations, England had the fastest growth rate; in the middle forty years of the nineteenth century its population doubled. But several countries in Africa are now doubling every twenty-five years.

Because of the distortions of most maps of the earth, the inhabitants of the temperate zones tend to underestimate the size (and future importance) of countries near the equator. For example, the Sahara Desert is about the same size as the United States, and Africa as a whole could just about contain all of China, India, Canada, and the United States. The population of countries such as China, India, and Indonesia has been growing throughout the twentieth century, particularly in the last fifty years, but Africa's has only just started. Within 200 years, the Far East and Africa may each contain more people than are now present in the entire world.

Another difference between the temperate and equatorial nations is in their diseases. The tropics tend to have a greater abundance of native fauna and of potential vectors for disease, and in consequence tropical countries suffer particularly from diseases such as malaria, schistosomiasis, and yellow fever which pass through an intermediate host rather than directly from one person to another. These are the great killers. It was yellow fever that ended the French occupation of Haiti and was partly responsible for the Louisiana Purchase, which in 1803 roughly doubled the size of the United States. Even today, malaria remains the single most common cause of death in the world as a whole.

The developing nations have to face one additional problem that the nations of temperate climes were spared. In the nineteenth century there were no highly advanced nations lurking in the background and offering advice based on their own past experience but, in practice, more likely to use the developing nations as a market for things like cigarettes and surplus expensive weapons of war. Before we give any advice, we should first ask which parts of public health and medical practice give good value for money in our own country and which do not. This question of costs and benefits has not come into the chapter up to now even though it has recently become a big issue in most Western nations.

As a general rule, wealth and health go hand in hand. This is true for nations and for the different ethnic groups and social classes within a

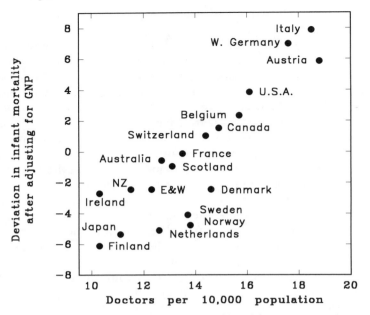

Figure 1.13. The relationship between the number of doctors in a nation and the extent to which that nation's infant mortality (deaths per 1,000 live births) deviates from a simple linear relationship between infant mortality and the value of the per capita Gross National Product (from Hart; see note 56).

given nation. As mentioned earlier, the life expectancy of the richest ethnic group in the United States (the Japanese Americans) is almost ten years more than that of the poorest (the African Americans), and roughly the same difference is seen between the professional classes and the unskilled manual workers at the bottom. These differences are seen in each Western nation, even in countries that provide free treatment for everyone.

So when we compare different nations and different systems of health care, some correction must be made for the nonspecific effects of wealth. In effect, we have to look at the simple relationship between GNP and some measure of health (such as infant mortality) and then ask whether the way the different nations deviate from this simple relationship can be attributed to some other variable (such as coal or cigarette consumption or the presence of too few doctors).

You might guess, for example, that the more doctors you have, the lower will be infant mortality. But in fact many studies have shown that the reverse is true (figure 1.13).[56] This does not, of course, mean that doctors are a cause of death in babies. Rather it suggests, to me at least, that countries can either manage infant and maternal care at the national level (which is mainly a matter of prenatal care and does not require advanced technology) or they can choose to wash their hands of the whole thing and let market forces determine what happens. And market forces will lead to an overabundance of doctors, because there is almost no limit to the opportunities for lucrative medical practice in countries with a rich aging population. (Incidentally, there does not seem to be much benefit in going above about ten doctors per 10,000 population, because an extension of the analysis to other age groups showed that no one, except possibly the very old, benefits from the presence of a large number of doctors.)[57] Judging, therefore, from the past and present experience of the industrialized nations, we should advise developing countries to go for the inexpensive forms of public health. And for their medical systems, they should try to imitate Japan and Finland rather than Italy and West Germany. That will give them better value for their money.

❧❧❧

The most important message of this chapter is simply that whenever statistics are available, it is folly not to use them. The countries of the world can be thought of as a huge ongoing experiment, using hundreds of millions of experimental animals. Admittedly, the experiment is poorly controlled, but it is very carefully monitored and, unlike most experiments, it does not cost you anything. If you want to study the impact of antibiotics on mortality, the first step is to ask what happened to life expectancy during the years when antibiotics first came into use. If you want to find out whether most cancers in the United States could be blamed on the petrochemical industry, why not start off by comparing the cancer rates in the United States with those in affluent but nonindustrialized countries like Iceland and New Zealand? If you want to check the efficacy of the war against cancer, surely the first step is to ask what changes, if any, have occurred in the national death rates from the various kinds of cancer.

Perhaps I am over-enthusiastic for all the columns and columns of figures that are published each year by the nations of the world. But my voyages among those numbers, during my time at the Harvard School of Public Health, changed the limited vision of health and medical care that I had acquired in medical school in the 1940s.

To have such an awakening in one's sixties must be counted an unexpected blessing.

Earlier in my life I had enjoyed another awakening which took place more gradually. In the last fifty years, *Homo sapiens* has come to understand roughly how living systems work and how such systems could have originated from inanimate matter. By chance, I was lucky enough to spend much of my working life on the fringes of this scientific revolution, watching it going on around me.

To an observer from outer space, writing a history of humankind, our sudden grasp of the principles of biology might well be considered more important than our recent increase in life expectancy. Yet most people today have little or no understanding of modern biology, and I have not seen any simple account of the origins of the revolution. So the next three chapters describe what I believe were the main discoveries. Two chapters cover the molecular biology of unicellular animals, and the third deals with the organization of multicellular systems. This last subject has come to be dominated by cancer research, and it therefore leads naturally into a chapter on the epidemiology of cancer. This, in turn, takes us back to the human condition, and a discussion of the population explosion and our prospects for the future.

CHAPTER 2

A History of Molecular Biology:
The Storage of Biological Information

The previous chapter showed that the conquest of premature mortality was largely the result of the general improvement in wealth, nutrition, and living conditions that accompanied the Industrial Revolution. This happened before the discoveries of science had had an impact on the treatment of any major disease. For that reason, the early history of public health is easily understood. Just about the only science in the story is the discovery of the microscopic causes of the infectious diseases. Although most people have never seen a bacterium under a microscope, we have all seen pictures of them in newspapers. So we have grown accustomed to the idea that we are surrounded by an invisible world of little creatures which are as much alive as we are.

The difficulty comes further down the scale when we have to consider the world of molecules and their component atoms. We are happy to accept that a human being is a billion times the size of a grain of sand, and even that this in turn is a billion times the size of a small bacterium; these things are visible objects. But many people have a problem with the next billionfold step, which takes us down to the smaller atoms such as carbon, nitrogen, and oxygen. It is an ancient idea that matter is not infinitely divisible and comes in units; that is the derivation of the word atom. But it is hard to be confident about the existence of these units, if they are not visible; (in fact, microscopes have recently been invented that can see down to the level of individual atoms, and one such picture is shown at the end of this chapter).

The giant step forward in our knowledge of this invisible world was surely the main achievement of the last 200 years of human history. The rules governing the behavior of atoms are now roughly understood, and we now think we understand how living systems work and also how they come into existence in an otherwise inanimate universe. This is exciting stuff and deserves to be more widely known.

From my own experience I know how hard it is for adults to make the transition into science. It is supposed to be an advantage to have had a classical education, but in my case the disadvantages seemed to outweigh the advantages. On leaving high school in 1939, I found myself having to absorb, as quickly as possible, the rudiments of botany, zoology, biochemistry, and physiology without having first acquired the slightest understanding of chemistry and physics. For someone with very limited powers of recall, forgetting Latin and Greek was easy. Replacing them with a general understanding of biology seemed a hopeless task for which I was ill-prepared and obviously unsuited, as was pointed out to me on several occasions by my various teachers at Oxford.

Most medical students find the courses in human anatomy the most burdensome part of their training, and I was no exception. But anatomy and physiology did not worry me in the way I was worried by biochemistry. It seemed reasonable that human anatomy should be complicated and that we should have to study the subject; the physical relationship of things in space is often very intricate, and if you intend to practice your trade within a certain defined space you ought to know something about the arrangements of the objects in that space. Also, I was not annoyed by physiology, that is to say the crude workings of the body, because it could be made to seem exciting, what with all those electrical charges zipping along nerve fibers and hormones rushing hither and thither, calling for more this and less that. But I was not happy with biochemistry. Either there was something wrong with it or (what appeared more likely) something wrong with me. There were, of course, many facts to assimilate about the chemistry of living creatures, but these facts did not give me any understanding of what was really going on.

I remember, as an undergraduate, spending hours in the Oxford Science Library, struggling to read a German monograph on metabolism. I had been given this task with the idea that the exercise would kill two birds with one stone; I would come to learn some biochemistry and would acquire a smattering of German. In fact, I achieved neither objective. The main protagonist of the book, as far as I can remember, was something called *Escherichia coli*. As I had yet to learn about bacteria, the name meant nothing to me. Much of the book was concerned with the way this little creature breaks down glucose into lactic acid and water or (when oxygen is available) into carbon dioxide and water. It was, of course, all very complicated and the story included accounts of many ingenious experiments. But as far as I can remember the author did not explain why the subject was interesting or, more important, what benefit *Escherichia coli* gained from all those chemical reactions.

To a demoralized eighteen-year-old, fresh from a school that put sport above everything else, a book like this presented an unresolvable dilemma. If you accepted the idea that a study of what is called intermediary metabolism would lead to a deep understanding of the meaning of life, you had to be prepared to familiarize yourself with something apparently as intricate as the railway systems of the world. But, as far as I could see, this maze of chemical reactions had no obvious connection with the characteristic manifestations of life, such as growth, movement, and the ability to reproduce; a map of the railways of the world does not tell you why people go on journeys. And to learn all this stuff seemed to require that I sacrifice some principle of which, at that time, I was only dimly aware. It was, I suppose, that the acquisition of facts can sometimes be a barrier to understanding, but I did not have sufficient courage to draw that conclusion. Luckily, I did in the end learn enough biochemistry to pass the exam and move on to clinical medicine.

Looking back, half a century later, I find there are many things I regret about my undergraduate years. Who doesn't? But I certainly do not totally regret the misery of having to pass exams in the various biological sciences before the advent of what is called molecular biology. If I had been born twenty years later and had been educated after rather than before the revolution in the biological sciences, I would have found it hard to comprehend the magnitude of the gulf between the 1930s and the 1950s and to appreciate fully the brilliance and vision of those who made the great discoveries that brought about the revolution. It really is an extraordinary story, and the nice thing about it is that you can understand it without having to learn much science. Also, although the dramatis personae—DNA, RNA, enzymes, and so on—are very, very small, they are real objects, not abstractions, and they behave in ways that seem eminently reasonable (something that could not be said for the protagonists of particle physics).

The subject of molecular biology has brought me much happiness in my life. Although I had no part in its origins I have, like many people, luxuriated in its unfolding. In this chapter and the next, I will try to show the reader the source of my pleasure. As I hope you will see, it is the sheer ingenuity of living systems that is so dazzling. Contemplating the political events in the world over the past fifty years, I often feel ashamed to belong to the human race. But I can at least feel proud of being alive—of being an example of a highly miniaturized system for handling information and for passing it on from one generation to the next, that is so miniaturized that it can generate something as complex as the human mind starting with a fertilized egg far, far smaller than the head of a pin.

One of the difficulties of understanding a great scientific discovery is that we find it hard to see how the discovery was made. What was the crucial experiment? Why was it done and what was it meant to show? In this history of molecular biology, I shall confine myself to a very limited set of experiments. Many things are left out, but I feel it better suits my purpose to give too little information than too much. It is best, however, if I start at the very beginning—that is to say, with the beginnings of chemistry—even though this may irritate some readers.

~~~

Chemistry in the Nineteenth Century

Modern chemistry really began in France at the end of the eighteenth century when Lavoisier showed that chemical reactions, contrary to popular opinion, do not involve any change in the total mass (weight) of the ingredients. When water is formed from the combination of two gases (to which he gave the names *oxygène* and *hydrogène*), the weight of the resulting water exactly equals the weight of the two gases. Similarly, when something is burned (is oxidized under the influence of heat), the weight of the products equals the weight of the starting material plus the weight of the oxygen; heat itself (*matière de feu*), he realized, has no weight. Last, he showed that the weights of the separate components (*molécules*) in these various reactions have fixed ratios, one to another; for example, water contains a certain fixed ratio of hydrogen to oxygen. Given a little more time, he would surely have deduced that the different *elements* (e.g., hydrogen, oxygen, carbon, phosphorus) exist in indivisible units (*atoms*), each with a characteristic weight. But Lavoisier was beheaded, and this final step in the Atomic Theory was left to an Englishman and a Swede, Dalton and Berzelius, ten to fifteen years later. (As one of Lavoisier's contemporaries said, "It only took them a moment to make that head fall, but a hundred years may not be sufficient to produce its equal.")

During the nineteenth century, the main types of atom (the elements) were identified and the rules governing their interactions were worked out. A molecule of water contains two hydrogen atoms and one oxygen; a carbon atom can combine with either one or two oxygen atoms, producing either carbon monoxide or carbon dioxide; a molecule of glucose has six carbons, twelve hydrogens, and six oxygens; and so on. The structure of certain simple molecules started to be understood; for example, glucose was shown to have five of its carbon atoms and one of its oxygens arranged in the form of a ring. The different elements were given the symbols by Berzelius that are used to this day—Na (natrium) for sodium, C for carbon, Cl for chlorine, and so on—and, toward the end of the century, the seventy or so known elements were seen to form an ordered series ranging from the lightest (hydrogen) to the heaviest (at that time uranium, which is about 238 times heavier than hydrogen, though heavier elements are now known).

Initially, the terminology must have seemed dangerously abstract. (A hundred years later a similar kind of abstraction arose in the science of genetics with the idea of the gene as the fundamental unit of inheritance, and in this case the abstraction gave rise to many useless arguments and much confusion.) Certainly, the atomic theory made several spectacularly successful predictions, but these only required knowledge of the relative masses of the different kinds of atom rather than their actual weights and so they did not constitute proof that atoms really exist.

Several methods for estimating the size of atoms were devised during the nineteenth century, and they all gave more or less the same answer.[1] The simplest method came from the measurement of the thickness of films of oil spread on water; as these films are, at their thinnest, only two molecules thick, it is possible to work out the space occupied by each molecule of oil and from this the space occupied by the atoms that made up these molecules. And once you know the space occupied by, say, an atom of carbon, you can work out how many atoms will be present in a gram of carbon. From this you can then work out the mass of all the other elements—that is to say, the relationship between the weight of any given substance and the number of atoms or molecules that it contains. A gram of hydrogen (the lightest element) was shown to contain slightly more than 6×10^{23} hydrogen atoms (this is called Avogadro's number); the carbon atom is twelve times heavier than hydrogen, and so a gram of carbon contains only one-twelfth as many atoms; the glucose molecule (made up of six carbon atoms, twelve hydrogens, and six oxygens) is 180 times heavier, and so when you buy a gram of glucose you are buying only about 3×10^{21} molecules; and so on.

In the last 180 years, nothing has come up to disturb the terminology originally invented by Berzelius. Of course, like most great truths, the system has undergone some minor modification and has needed some qualification. Eventually, atoms were seen not to be the ultimate units of matter but to be composed of an assortment of fundamental particles (which exhibit some singularly mysterious properties when studied in isolation). With the discovery of radium (which decays into lead plus helium), it became clear that some atoms are unstable. Last, the weight of ingredients in a reaction need not be conserved; during atomic fission and fusion a small fraction of the total mass of the participants is converted into energy. However, none of these qualifications play an important part in the history of molecular biology.

While the rules of chemistry were being worked out, the biological sciences were also moving into their modern phase. Three more or less independent developments in biology had their origins around the middle of the nineteenth century. These were (1) the cell theory, (2) the discovery of enzymes, and (3) the theory of evolution and the science of genetics.

Microscopy and the Discovery of Cells

Even the simplest magnifying lens is enough to show that the tissues of certain plants are made up of close-packed arrays of cells (a special use of the word "cell" that dates back to the seventeenth century). In animal tissues, this is not easy to see because the cells do not have such thick walls, so the generalization that all living tissues are made up of cells could not be made until the nineteenth century and the invention of better microscopes and the development of dyes that specifically color the different parts of the cell.

During development of animal embryos, some cells were observed to fuse together (for example, during the creation of muscle tissue), and this unfortunately led to the idea that just as cells could lose their individuality by fusion with each other they could arise out of some formless material by a process like crystallization. By the 1850s, however, it had become clear that every cell is descended from some other cell by a process of division in which one cell gives rise to two daughter cells. This was the first great simplification in the history of biology. Even the most complex of animals starts off as a single cell which, by a succession of cell divisions, gives rise to the multicellular system that is the whole, finished animal. During this process, the cells in the different organs of the body somehow acquire distinct forms appropriate for their function. The proper functioning of an animal is therefore the result of cooperation between an enormous number of what seem to be relatively independent units (cells) each of which somehow knows what it ought to be doing. We would now say that the cells are programmed to behave in different ways, but that is a modern way of describing it; in the nineteenth century, "program" had not yet become a verb and biologists did not have the computer as a handy metaphor.

Looking more closely it could be seen that each cell contains a distinct central region, the nucleus; this is more refractile and binds certain dyes much more strongly than the rest of the cell. By the 1880s, the microscopic anatomy of the different tissues of the body was being studied in ever greater detail. Methods had been invented for staining the different parts of the cell with various natural dyes (and later with synthetic dyes), and this led to the science of microscopic anatomy. Each of the organs of the body was found to contain different kinds of cells, which meant that the fertilized egg cell was able to produce many different kinds of descendants. If that were not complicated enough, the improved microscopes of the 1880s showed that intricate organization extends to much smaller levels than the whole cell. For example, cell nuclei were seen to undergo some very complicated changes in form just before cell division. The study of these changes played an important part in the history of molecular biology, but it is better that I discuss them a little later, in the section on the origins of genetics.

The idea of the cell as the unit of life became more firmly established as the result of a famous argument about the nature of fermentation.

Fermentation and the Discovery of Enzymes

One of the reactions studied by Lavoisier was the conversion of grape sugar into alcohol and carbon dioxide. Here too he found that the total weight of the ingredients did not change during the reaction. A hundred years earlier, the Dutch microscopist Anthony van Leeuwenhoeck had seen that fermentation is associated with tiny spherical particles, but he could not decide whether these were the cause or the product of the process. By the 1850s, however, it had become clear that fermentation is due to the presence of yeast particles and that these are minute living organisms that can be seen, under the microscope, to grow by cell division just like the much larger cells of plants and animals.

There followed a fascinating argument which has periodically recurred in various guises right up to the present. Justus von Liebig, the great German chemist, had embarked on a study of the multitude of carbon-containing compounds found in living creatures (the subject that is now called organic chemistry and extends to all the other, nonbiological compounds containing carbon) and he, initially at least, did not believe that yeast was alive and considered fermentation to be simply a matter of chemistry. But in the 1860s, Louis Pasteur showed that fermentation (and putrefaction) would occur only if yeasts or other microorganisms were present; furthermore, the nature of the chemical reaction in fermentation depended on what species of microorganism was present, one species converting sugar into alcohol and another converting it into vinegar and so on. Like the combatants in many arguments, Liebig and Pasteur pushed each other into taking extreme positions, for they were both rather cantankerous people. Pasteur, to his dying day, maintained that the chemical reactions achieved by living creatures could never be fully explained by chemists because they occurred inside cells and involved a mysterious vital force that he believed was the essence of all living things. (Many people find attractive the hypothesis that living systems contain something that is inexplicable; for example, the idea has recently resurfaced in the form of the Gaia Hypothesis, which postulates that all living creatures are part of some coordinately acting mysterious whole.)

Other instances were found where organic compounds were broken down into smaller compounds by nonliving substances (soluble ferments) released by living cells. Like yeast, these soluble ferments could cause the reaction of many times their own weight of sugar or whatever was the starting material in the reaction, and like each species of microorganism each kind of soluble ferment would carry out one particular kind of reaction. It was therefore conceivable that every one of the chemical reactions occurring within living cells is carried out by intracellular soluble ferments. Pasteur and his supporters chose not to believe this, and a special word *enzyme* (derived from the Greek *en zumé*, meaning "in yeast") was coined for the imagined vital intracellular equivalents to the inanimate soluble ferments that are able to work in the absence of any cells. By the end of the century, however, it had become clear that there is nothing distinct about the ferments that work inside cells. Pasteur's vitalism fell out of favor, and all "ferments" were simply called enzymes.

All enzymes appeared to be members of the class of biological molecules named "proteins" (so called because they were thought to be the primary, prototypal molecules associated with life). But vitalism did not disappear altogether and several people, including some notable chemists, were not happy with the thought that something as clever as an enzyme could reside in something as inanimate as a protein molecule. And it was not until the late 1920s that an enzyme was finally obtained in pure form and shown unquestionably to be a protein.

With the discovery of enzymes there arose a new branch of biology called biochemistry that was concerned with the chemical nature of the various substances present in living cells, with the various chemical reactions occurring inside cells, and with the enzymes that make these substances and bring about these reactions. We now all know that cells contain several classes of chemicals (proteins, fats, carbohydrates, and nucleic acids). However, rather than give an intimidating list, it is easier if I let the various components of living systems drift into my narrative as I go along. But before ending this section on enzymes I have to say something about what makes chemical reactions happen.

Take the simple case where you set fire to (oxidize) alcohol. This is not a reaction that normally occurs spontaneously; a cup of alcohol will not spontaneously burst into flames, but if you cause a little local heating with a lighted match the reaction proceeds vigorously and produces enough heat to keep itself going. This heat must come from within the alcohol molecule; in other words, more energy is stored in the chemical bonds uniting the carbon and hydrogen atoms in alcohol than is stored in the chemical bonds within the two products of the reaction, carbon dioxide and water. You can think of the reaction therefore as running downhill; if you wanted to achieve the reverse reaction and make alcohol out of carbon dioxide and water, you would somehow have to put energy into the process in order to drive the reaction uphill (if this were not so, you would have here the makings of a perpetual motion machine). To explain the role of the lighted match, there is an obvious, albeit somewhat imprecise analogy. If you carefully pour a bucket of wheat grains into a sieve with holes only slightly larger than each grain, a few grains may pass through but most grains will lie partly across the apertures and they will seldom shift their position and fall through the sieve. If, however, the grains are being bounced about slightly (which is exactly what heat does to atoms and molecules) the grains will all sooner or later fall through the sieve, and the faster they bounce (the hotter they are) the faster they will go.

To explain the mechanism underlying enzyme action, we can imagine placing a little device above each pore in the sieve that can temporarily hold one end of each grain of wheat until its long axis happens to

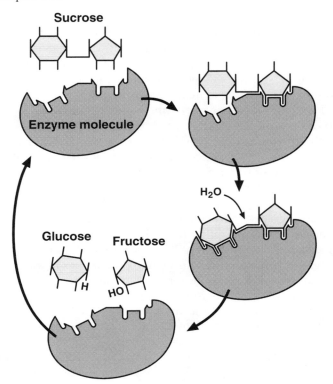

Figure 2.1. The action of enzymes. Enzymes are highly specific, each kind of enzyme accomplishing one particular kind of chemical reaction. Shown here diagrammatically is the action of the enzyme that splits the sugar sucrose into its two component parts. The enzyme contains a region that binds to a molecule of sucrose and subjects it to a slight change in shape so that the chemical bond that joins its two halves becomes more accessible to the surrounding water molecules and, in consequence, is quickly broken. The entire cycle, from binding to cleavage to release, takes less than 1/1000th of a second, which is many million times faster than the spontaneous rate of breakdown of sucrose at ordinary temperatures.

become directly aligned toward the pore and then let it fall. Such a device will hugely accelerate the passage of wheat through the sieve without itself expending any energy or itself undergoing any change. And that, more or less, is the mechanism of enzyme action (figure 2.1). Each particular enzyme molecule has a specific binding (orienting) site for a molecule of the starting material and holds it in such a constrained position that the desired reaction quickly takes place (e.g., so that one or more atoms in the molecule can react with oxygen). Of course, the whole process is on a very small scale and can proceed extraordinarily quickly. In the simplest chemical reactions, a single enzyme molecule can react with several thousand target molecules every second. The process is much slower when two large reactants have to be brought together by the enzyme, and for that reason very complex processes are often in the hands of a cooperating group of enzymes where, in a manner of speaking, one enzyme holds one end of the wheat grain, another holds the other end, and a third squeezes the grain and so on. (The ability to carry out such catalysis, as it is called, is not confined to enzymes, but is also shown by certain metals; for example, the incompletely oxidized products in automobile exhaust will quickly react with oxygen when they are absorbed onto certain metals such as platinum, and this is the basis for the catalytic converters that are now being fitted to most new cars.)

To summarize, the biochemists at the end of the nineteenth century had started to prepare an inventory of the types of molecule found in living systems, and most biochemists were prepared to believe that the chemical reactions going on in a cell are catalyzed by enzymes. The general feeling was that the proteins were the intelligent molecules, an opinion that was to gain strength over the next half century. Proteins were the molecules that made things. What made the proteins was not clear.

Evolution and the Beginnings of Genetics

Evolution is an old idea that goes back at least 2,000 years to the Roman poet Lucretius (who, incidentally, also produced an early version of the atomic theory). By the eighteenth century, it had become the fashion that anyone with leisure time should play at being an amateur naturalist and classifier of plants and animals. Gradually people discovered the huge diversity of living species, in particular the vast number of kinds of insects and other invertebrates. As a result, they came to see how well each living creature fits into its environment. Depending on your religious inclinations, you could take this as evidence for the precision of God's handiwork or as evidence for the operation of some mechanism in living creatures that allows each of them to match the demands of their environment. It was the belief in such a mechanism (for example, held very strongly by Erasmus Darwin, Charles's grandfather) that Voltaire was satirizing when he made Candide's foolish tutor keep saying "All is for the best in the best of possible worlds."

The main difficulty with the idea of evolution was in working out what were the rules governing change. Perhaps the most extreme idea (apart, of course, from the notion of a Divine Creation) was proposed by Jean

Baptiste Lamarck. He was a late eighteenth-century French botanist who had specialized in study of the invertebrates. He believed, like many other people, that the different species had evolved from common ancestors, but his fame (if that is the right word) rests on his idea that the driving force for such a process is an intrinsic ability of animals to produce heritable changes when there is a need (*besoin*) for change; it is not obvious what exactly he meant by besoin and rightly he has been criticized for his lack of clarity. The giraffe was born with a long neck as the result of the need of its ancestors to reach for leaves, the blacksmith's son has stronger muscles thanks to the efforts of his father, and so on. These ideas were ridiculed even in his lifetime, particularly by the great French palaeontologist Georges Cuvier. But it was some time before anyone produced a better explanation for the mechanism of evolution.

More and more people came to believe in evolution (divine or otherwise), thanks in part to the efforts of Cuvier who showed that many fossils are apparently early forms of creatures that are alive today. Indeed, you could take the existence of fossils as evidence for a Divine Creation if you postulated that the act of creation provided all separately created species with a mechanism for gradual "ascent" from primitive beginnings.

Early in the nineteenth century, geologists came to realize that the earth was not a few thousand years old (as implied by the genealogy given in the Bible) but, at the very least, tens or hundreds of millions of years and that fossils could be found that were unimaginably ancient. This discovery was an essential step in what was to follow.

The story of Darwin and Wallace is well known.[2] Their careers showed many similarities. Charles Darwin had been trained in geology and Alfred Russel Wallace had been a professional surveyor, both in their youth were enthusiastic collectors of beetles, both first came in contact with the profusion of tropical forests as the result of a trip to South America, and for both the moment of revelation was triggered by Malthus's description of the positive checks that control the population of primitive peoples. In 1838, Darwin had been back in England for two years after his trip halfway round the world on *The Beagle* and "happened to read for amusement Malthus on Population," and this set him on the long and careful task of assembling all the support for his idea; in 1858, Wallace was in Indonesia suffering from an attack of malaria when he suddenly remembered what Malthus had written. Within a week, Wallace sent off a manuscript to Darwin, and this pushed Darwin into publishing a companion paper.

What Darwin and Wallace proposed was, in essence, a mechanism for evolution. They supposed that there is some source of continual, heritable variation in all living creatures. Given this and the undoubted ability of all creatures to produce more offspring than can possibly survive, it is easy to imagine that the "positive checks" exerted by the environment will tend to kill the less well-suited variants. Thanks to such a process of natural selection, successive generations will tend to derive from the better suited variants, so every species of plant or animal will tend to become better and better suited to its environment.

Darwin had been slowly assembling a book that was to have been called simply *Natural Selection*.[3] But it would have been improper to hold back Wallace's manuscript, and so Darwin hastily added a brief note to accompany it and then set about producing a shortened abstract of his book, which was published in 1859 under the title "On the Origin of Species by means of Natural Selection, or the preservation of favoured races in the struggle for life." This was an immediate success and sold more than 1,000 copies on the first day.

Following on from the Copernican revolution, the theory of evolution removed *Homo sapiens* still further from the center of God's universe, and for this reason it is still opposed by many religious groups. For scientists, however, the chief difficulty was that the theory did not explain why creatures undergo heritable variation or what exactly it is that varies.

Mendelian Genetics

In 1856, while Darwin was quietly assembling the material for his book on natural selection, Gregor Mendel was starting on a series of crosses between several varieties of the garden pea, in the grounds of a monastery in Czechoslovakia. His experiments extended over a period of about eight years and the results were reported in a brief paper of a few thousand words,[4] which is now seen as the foundation of modern genetics (and, incidentally, of molecular biology). Like many complicated experiments, his are most easily described by starting with the conclusions and working backward from there (figure 2.2).

He deduced that the appearance of a pea plant is determined by units of inheritance (we would now call them genes) that it receives from its parents. There is a unit for height, a unit for shape of seed, a unit for arrangement of flowers, and so on. Each plant receives one of each kind of unit from each of its parents, and its cells therefore have two of each kind of unit. For example, in a cross between a tall plant (which we might define as having units called "T" for tall) and a short plant (which has not-tall units, which we can call "t"), all the hybrid offspring will receive a T from the tall parent and a t from the short; so their cells will be Tt. When these hybrids are crossed with each other (or allowed to self-fertilize), they can pass on either T or t to each offspring; so there

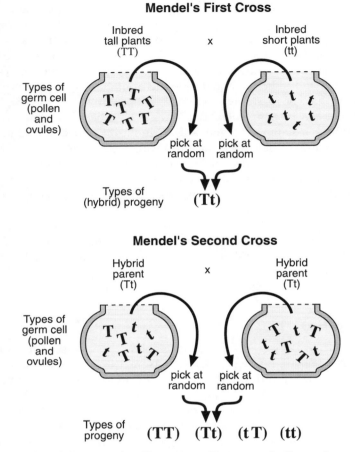

Figure 2.2. Mendelian genetics. Shown here diagrammatically are the results of (a) crossing a tall pea plant with a short pea plant to produce hybrid progeny, and (b) crossing the hybrid progeny of the first cross.

Every pea plant contains two copies of the gene for height, one having come from one parent and one from the other. If either of the copies is the version (T) that makes tall plants, the plant will be tall; if, however, both copies are the version (t) that makes a short plant, the plant will be short.

Each plant produces germ cells (ovules and pollen) that contain just one of the genes for height. So each progeny plant can be thought of as having picked, at random, one of its father's genes for height and one of its mother's. And it is that random choice that is illustrated here.

If we were to extend the diagram to cover, in addition, the inheritance of one of the other traits studied by Mendel (such as round vs. wrinkled, green vs. yellow, etc.), we would have to add *separate* containers for these traits, because the choice of genes for height is completely *independent* of the choice of genes for the other traits. In other words, classical Mendelian traits "segregate" independently of each other.

will be four kinds of offspring—TT and Tt and tT and tt (here I am adopting the usual symbolism that the character you get from your father is written on the left, and the one from your mother is on the right). Since it is pure chance which of the two units in a parent is passed on to each progeny, these four classes are equally likely (equally common).

Now, the behavior of these units determining height is such that a plant will be tall if it has either one or two Ts (i.e., is TT or Tt or tT), and it will be short if it does not (i.e., if it is tt); in Mendel's terminology, the unit called T is "dominant" and the unit called t is "recessive." (Note that this is a piece of descriptive terminology and it does not in any way explain the mechanism underlying dominance and recessivity; if you feel uncomfortable at having to accept these words unquestioningly, you can at least console yourself with the thought that you are going to be given a proper understanding within the next ten pages, whereas the world's geneticists had to wait 100 years.)

To continue with this backwards description of Mendel's experiments: knowing that T is dominant, we can work out which of the plants in that experiment were tall and which were short. All the progeny of the first cross (between the tall plants and the the short) were Tt, and therefore must have been tall. When they in turn were crossed, the offspring that were TT or Tt or tT must have been tall, and only the tt were short; in other words, out of every four offspring there were, on average, three tall plants and one short one.

The experiment can be continued for one further generation, by allowing these plants to self-fertilize; all the short ones (that are tt) will breed true; one-third of the tall ones (those that are TT) will breed true, and two-thirds of the tall ones (those that are Tt or tT) will behave like the progeny of the very first cross. Mendel also checked what happened when the different kinds of pea plants in these successive generations were crossed with the original tall (TT) and short (tt) varieties, and from what I have told you you can work out for yourself what he found.

So much for tallness. The six other characteristics studied by Mendel behaved in exactly the same way. For example, the unit responsible for producing a round pea-in-the-pod is the dominant unit and wrinkled is recessive. Knowing that, you can work out what happened when round was crossed with wrinkled. Just write R instead of T, and r instead of t, and you have it.

Mendel's experiments also showed, most importantly, that these different kinds of units (for height, for pea shape, and so on) behave *independently*. For example, imagine a cross between a tall round plant (TT-RR) and a short wrinkled plant (tt-rr). All the progeny will be tall-round (because they will be Tt-Rr, or tT-Rr, or Tt-rR, or tT-rR). When these tall-round progeny are allowed to self-fertilize, they produce the following kinds of progeny: tall and round (TT-RR, Tt-RR, tT-RR, TT-Rr, Tt-Rr, tT-Rr, TT-rR, Tt-rR, and tT-rR), short and round (tt-RR, tt-Rr, and tt-rR), tall and wrinkled (TT-rr, Tt-rr, and tT-rr) and short and wrinkled (tt-rr). Because these two types of unit behave independently during their passage from one generation to the next, these sixteen classes are equally common. Nine-sixteenths of the progeny are tall-round, three-sixteenths are short-round, three-sixteenths are tall-wrinkled, and one-sixteenth are short-wrinkled.

Such then is the essence of what is called Mendelian genetics, and I have described it in some detail because it was an important step in the history of molecular biology and, I think, is not easy to understand. I remember, as an undergraduate, that I found the argument irritatingly abstract, and it was only with the coming of molecular biology that I ceased to be baffled by the notion of dominance and recessivity.

To simplify the description I have confined myself to two features (height and pea shape), although Mendel looked at more than just those two characters. His rules of inheritance are straightforward: (i) Mendelian units exist as pairs, one member of every pair came from your father and the other came from your mother; (ii) it is pure chance whether your child receives from you the unit you got from your father or the one you got from your mother, and the outcome for each pair of such units is independent of the outcome for the other pairs; (iii) although the effects of these units will be temporarily masked if they are "recessive," the units do not disappear but persist unchanged from one generation to the next.

This is still accepted as a correct analysis of the fundamental mechanism of inheritance though there are, as in most biological phenomena, some complicated exceptions. For example, many of the more obvious features of a plant or an animal are under the control of several independently inherited units (we would now call them genes), and in such cases the results of breeding experiments can be difficult to analyze. Again, not all traits behave independently of each other (this is an important qualification and will be discussed later). Last, many traits are not either dominant or recessive, but something in between. Mendel himself went on to study inheritance in hawkweed (*Hieracium*), which was well known for producing stable hybrids that show no tendency to revert to the parental types, and he commented in a second paper[5] that the results with this plant were totally different from what he had found with the garden pea (*Pisum*).

For a long time, Mendel's work attracted little attention. But then, in the year 1900, several people who were doing the same kind of experiments discovered his paper and at that point Mendelian genetics became all the fashion. At first sight, there seemed to be little overlap between Darwinian evolution and Mendelian inheritance. The difficulty centered on the question of variation, or mutation, as it came to be called. Mendel never said whether he thought that units such as tall (T) and not-tall (t) had arisen from some change (mutation) in a common ancestral unit or were the result of Divine Creation. Early in the course of his experiments he had read a German translation of *The Origin of Species*, and there are at least some grounds for thinking that he was at heart a creationist and that he saw his results as disproving Darwin's ideas because his units of inheritance did not vary or blend with each other during the course of his experiments.[6] Darwin (who, it seems, never heard of Mendel's results and, for some reason, had not received a reprint from Mendel)[7] firmly believed that evolution was the result of a multitude of very small changes and that these changes (unlike the occasional mutations that occur in Mendel's units) somehow blend together with the passage of time. Wallace, who lived until well after the discovery of Mendel's paper, was insistent that evolution did not depend on the production of novel characters by mutation (which he referred to as "the fallacies of the Mutationists and Mendelians") but was the result of a multitude of small steps; Wallace took the word "mutation" as necessarily meaning some large change (such as "short" instead of "tall" in a plant, or the change that produces the commonest form of human dwarfism).

The argument can be seen most clearly if we consider the case of melanism in moths.[8] Around 1840, people in the sooty Midlands of industrialized England started to observe that certain species of moth had changed from brown to black, presumably because a black moth resting on the soot-encrusted bark of a tree was not as easily seen by birds as a brown moth. The Darwinians insisted that this change must have been the result of a gradual darkening of moths over many generations. The Mendelians believed that the change had occurred in a single step that produced a black moth (a "sport") which then survived and produced black offspring. As the English geneticist William Bateson pointed out, this was a test case that could have been resolved if someone had gone out into the countryside and looked for moths that were intermediate in color.

The conflict between the Darwinian and the Mendelian views of inheritance was a passing affair. During the early years of this century Mendelian inheritance attracted more attention, and Darwinian evolution went into a temporary decline. This may have been because the idea of evolution by the continual operation of natural selection had been adopted by the self-styled social Darwinists, many of whom sought to justify their own affluence (compared to the poverty of the masses) on the grounds that the quest for wealth quickly showed who were the fittest to survive; also, evolution is a rather abstract idea that is not readily tested experimentally. Mendelian inheritance, on the other hand, seemed politically neutral and was tested and shown to occur in many species of plants and animals; more important, it soon received some unexpected support from the microscopists.

Chromosomes

By the end of the nineteenth century, microscopes had greatly improved and it had become possible to see that nuclear division was a strangely elaborate process. For most of the time, the nucleus is a relatively structureless spherical region in the middle of the cell, bounded by a membrane just as the whole cell is itself enclosed within the cell membrane. Before a cell divides it duplicates its nucleus. At the start of this process, the contents of the nucleus can be seen to coalesce into thread-like structures which undergo some complicated movements before separating to form the two daughter nuclei. These structures were named *chromosomes* (literally, colored bodies, because they were very strongly colored by certain dyes). They seemed to behave in a very purposeful way. After they have become visible, the nuclear membrane disappears and the now-duplicated but still partially attached chromosomes line up in the middle of the cell. Finally, the members of each pair are drawn apart into the two regions of the cell that will become surrounded by new nuclear membranes to form the two daughter nuclei.

It gradually became clear that chromosomes are very important for the proper functioning of the cell. If a cell did not start off with a full set, it behaved in an abnormal way. For example, in the 1880s, the German microscopist Theodor Boveri found that he could mechnically disturb nuclear division during the early stages of development of an annelid worm, so that one daughter nucleus received too many chromosomes and the other was left with too few. He observed that all the descendants of these two cells inherited the abnormal chromosome number of their parents and underwent abnormal development. Because he also found that cancer cells often show abnormal numbers of chromosomes, he concluded that the affairs of each cell must in some way be managed by its chromosomes.

A closer study of the shape and number of chromosomes showed that each species has a characteristic number; the main cells in a plant or the body of an animal have one number and the germ cells (egg, and sperm or pollen) have half that number. For example, in 1902 an American microscopist, William Sutton,[9] reported that a species of grasshopper had eight pairs of large chromosomes and three pairs of small ones in the cells of its body (that is, twenty-two chromosomes in all) and half that number in its germ cells; therefore, at some point in the development of sperm and egg there had to have been a halving of the number of chromosomes (figure 2.3). Presumably each grasshopper started its life as a fertilized egg with a set of eleven chromosomes from its father and a second set from its mother (that is, eleven pairs or twenty-two in all). It was easy to imagine that it might be pure chance which member of each pair is chosen for each germ cell. Sutton saw that if that was so then chromosomes would be behaving exactly like Mendel's units of inheritance. He therefore proposed that chromosomes carry the determinants of heredity. (Actually, Sutton was not quite right, because he failed to see the two small chromosomes that determine the grasshopper's sex, but he was right in principle.)

The number of chromosomes varies enormously from species to species, in what appears to be a completely unsystematic way. *Homo sapiens* has twenty-two pairs of chromosomes plus two chromosomes that determine sex; the garden pea has seven pairs; the mulberry has about 300 pairs; and so on. These numbers are not worth remembering. But it is important to realize that it was obvious from the outset that there must be many Mendelian units within each chromosome. For example, the pea has only seven chromosomes, but it must have a huge number of Mendelian units that determine shape and size and all the other features of the plant.

Sutton's discovery, perhaps more than any other, marks the beginning of the science called genetics. Early this century, Mendel's units of inheritance came to be called *genes*, and the process of variation of these units which underlies evolution was called *mutation*. It is important to realize, however, that these words represented an abstraction; although they were very convenient, they were not in any sense an explanation of what was going on.

It remained to be determined how genes work, what they are made of, and in what way can they undergo mutation. First we will have to return to the chemical composition of the cell, for that after all must be what the genes are determining. But before moving into that subject I would like to interpolate a general comment. In this chapter on the history of molecular biology, the story has jumped about, from yeasts to pea plants, from them to worms and finally to grasshoppers and humans. And if I had been giving a full account rather than a minimal account of all the antecedents to molecular biology, many more creatures would have been mentioned, each of which, thanks to some physical oddity, made possible some important advance in biology.

Biologists naturally choose to study whatever creature is most convenient; no one would pick on an animal or plant that is exceptionally rare or extremely dangerous to handle, unless there were some other over-

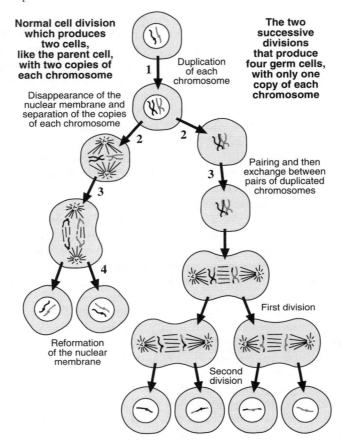

Normal cell division which produces two cells, like the parent cell, with two copies of each chromosome

Duplication of each chromosome

The two successive divisions that produce four germ cells, with only one copy of each chromosome

Disappearance of the nuclear membrane and separation of the copies of each chromosome

Pairing and then exchange between pairs of duplicated chromosomes

First division

Reformation of the nuclear membrane

Second division

Figure 2.3. The behavior of one pair of chromosomes during cell division. Humans have 23 pairs of chromosomes, and pea plants have seven pairs. Though their numbers are different, their behavior is the same. To simplify the description, the diagram considers the behavior of just one pair of chromosomes.

1. For most of the life of a cell, the individual chromosomes in its nucleus are not visible.
2. Shortly before division, the chromosomes become visible. By this time they have already been duplicated, but the two copies of each chromosome are still attached at a point near their centers, in an object called the centrosome.
3. The centrosomes now split in two, and the halves are pulled apart. This pulls apart the two copies of each chromosome.
4. The nucleus starts to separate in two, each half containing one copy of each chromosome.
5. Finally the cell divides, and the chromosomes in each nucleus once again disappear from view.

Figure 2.3 (*cont.*)

The production of sperm and egg cells (or pollen and ovules) occurs by a special program that makes progeny cells with only one chromosome of each kind, instead of the usual pair of chromosomes. This is achieved by one round of chromosome duplication followed by two successive cell divisions. Early in this elaborate program, the chromosome pairs come close together and undergo cross-overs. As a result, genes that are far apart from each other on their chromosome will segregate independently, as if they were not linked together at all. (For example, Mendel observed that seed color and flower color segregated independently of each other, but it is now known that they lie at opposite ends of one of the seven pea chromosomes.)

riding consideration that made it important or interesting. But the catholicity of taste shown by the founders of biology is saying something more important than that. Since the beginning of the eighteenth century, which was the heyday of taxonomy, it had been generally accepted that enough similarities can be detected in all living creatures to make possible a system of classification based on these similarities. You could believe this even if you were a creationist, and nothing has emerged that upsets the idea. Therefore the study of any plant or animal could, in principle, lead to a discovery that applies to all living creatures. People learned about enzymes by studying yeasts and about chromosomes from worms and grasshoppers. As we shall see, this process of extrapolating from the particular to the general has continued unabated throughout the twentieth century.

The Chemical Composition of the Cell and the Role of Enzymes

By the start of the twentieth century, a fairly complete list had been prepared of the types of molecule present in living systems. All the large molecules contain carbon—indeed, it is the ability of the carbon atom to form a huge array of different chemical compounds that makes it the basis for life as we know it. Fats are made out of carbon, hydrogen, and oxygen, combined together to make molecules that are not soluble in water (and are therefore suitable for making the boundary layers, such as cell membranes, that separate the different parts of a cell). Carbohydrates are water-soluble combinations of carbon, hydrogen, and oxygen that can serve as reserves of energy (e.g., the starch found in plant cells and the glycogen in liver cells). Another class of compounds discovered at the end of the nineteenth century were the nucleic acids because their highest concentration is in the nucleus; they contain carbon, nitrogen, hydrogen, oxygen, and phosphorus and were thought (incorrectly) to serve some structural function. Last come the proteins, which are made up of carbon, nitrogen, sulfur, hydrogen, and oxygen; some proteins are structural (e.g., keratin, which makes hair and the surface of skin, and collagen which makes tendons) and others function as enzymes.

That then is the list of the large molecules found in cells. At the beginning of the century, rather little was known about their exact size, but it was obvious that the biggest of the cell's "macromolecules" could be hundreds or thousands of times larger than a molecule like glucose (which itself is over 100 times heavier than a hydrogen atom). Each class of macromolecule appeared to be made up of a collection of building blocks that the cell had somehow assembled into the appropriate three-dimensional structure. The cell, of course, has had to manufacture all these building blocks—the various sugars that form the complex carbohydrates, the fatty acids that make up the fats, the twenty or so different "amino acids" in proteins (so-called because they all contain nitrogen, and nitrogen is the basis of ammonia, and ammonium salts were supposedly first isolated from the dung of camels and were named after the Egyptian god Amun). They were presumably made by a series of reactions brought about by specific enzymes, of which the cell therefore had to possess a huge array. (It so happens that some of the building blocks cannot be made by some animals—for example, *Homo sapiens* cannot make one kind of amino acid, and we and the guinea pig cannot make ascorbic acid—and these have to be obtained from plants; such essential building blocks were called "vitamins" because they were all thought to contain nitrogen and the name has stuck even though many, for example vitamin C, are now known to have no nitrogen.)

Some macromolecules, such as the protein called collagen and certain nucleic acids, were known to be long and thin and others were roughly spherical (for there are various physical ways to measure the average shape of molecules in solution, even when you cannot see them individually). Those proteins that functioned as enzymes obviously had to have something special about their shape that made each of them capable of binding one or two small molecules and then breaking them apart or joining them together; for example, the enzyme in yeast that breaks the sugar molecule in half (and thereby starts the process of alcoholic fermentation) carries out that one reaction and cannot do anything else; similarly, those special proteins called antibodies have the property of binding to and inactivating one particular kind of molecule (e.g., binding to some molecule on the surface of a bacterium); for instance, when you are immunized against tetanus you do not acquire immunity against anything else.

Because of the amazing specificity shown by antibodies, the idea gradually emerged that cells have a way of fashioning big molecules into the appropriate shape, much in the way that a sculptor molds a lump of clay.

In fact, this thought was taken even further. Until about the middle of the 1930s, many people believed that proteins did not have a well-defined internal structure; even though each protein might (as some believed) be composed of a single, unbranching chain of building blocks, it was obviously the outside of the protein that was important, not its inside. And because there was something magical about the action of enzymes, some people took an extreme position and argued that the protein part of an enzyme merely served as the carrier for some as-yet unidentified, magical component that brought about the enzyme's chemical action.

At this point it is necessary to say a little more about the energetics of synthesis. Ultimately the source of energy for life on earth is the radiant energy from the sun (which comes from nuclear fusion within the sun). When we burn wood or coal we are turning back into heat the energy (heat) that the leaves of the tree captured from sunlight and, as it were, locked up in the large structural molecules in the trunk of the tree. Plants have developed combinations of enzymes and light-absorbing pigments that capture the energy of sunlight. They use this energy to build simple chemical compounds that can then be transported through the cell and serve as the source of energy for building other compounds and allowing growth of the plant. These small carriers of energy are compounds that contain phosphorus and oxygen bound to carbon—a bond that contains a lot of energy. Crudely speaking, the carriers of energy are analogous to the small batteries we buy to serve as transportable sources of energy for various small electrical appliances we use in our everyday lives.

Animals do not have the machinery for photosynthesis and so our source of energy comes from eating plants and eating other animals. Our digestive enzymes break down the macromolecules of the plants we eat and we absorb the resulting smaller molecules, which are then either used by our cells as building blocks or are broken down (e.g., to carbon dioxide and water) in order to generate our cells' supply of energy carriers.

The main business of biochemists throughout the twentieth century has been to make a list of all the chemical reactions that occur in living cells, which together make up what is called *intermediary metabolism* (the word metabolism being taken from the Greek for "changing around"), and to try to discover what determines the shape and properties of the larger molecules, for example what determines the specificity of enzymes and antibodies. This has been a daunting task. Every cell contains thousands upon thousands of different proteins, each presumably having some particular function. A complete description of intermediary metabolism within one cell (that is to say, the comings and goings of all the players in that cell) would, I suppose, be about as complicated as a flow chart for all the factories in a large industrialized nation. But the flow chart has been worked out in part, and you now can see charts of intermediary metabolism hanging on the walls of biochemistry laboratories, where (as Aristotle said about great tragedy) they are no doubt meant to excite feelings of pity and terror.

The study of intermediary metabolism revealed dazzling complexities, but it left several mysteries untouched. How does a cell determine the shape of a molecule? It is one thing to make two building blocks and then join them together, but something much more complicated is needed if you are to make an object like an antibody molecule, which is perfectly shaped in three dimensions so that, like a lock that perfectly matches one particular key, it exactly matches the "antigen" with which you were immunized. Apart from this question of the shape of molecules, there was a horrible logical problem. If every chemical reaction in living cells is carried out by an enzyme specifically designed for that purpose, how was that enzyme made? Hardly by another enzyme, because that would trap the cell in an infinite regression. Last, none of the work on intermediary metabolism gave any hint how the cell knew what it ought to be doing or how it knew how to do it. My impression is that most biochemists believed that these things would never be understood. As we shall see, it was not until the 1940s that the solutions began to emerge. It all hinged on the nature of the gene.

The Gene

Most of the traits studied by Mendel were not easily interpreted in terms of the chemistry of the cell: if you do not know how a plant decides what its height and shape should be, you have no hope of understanding the action of the genes that determine characters like tall and short or round and wrinkled. There were, however, some rather simpler traits available for study. But before discussing these, I have to interject a note of apology. In what follows you may feel that I am needlessly jumping about among terms like Mendelian unit, gene, character, and trait when I could have stuck to one word; in fact, the terms are not completely interchangeable, but the distinction between them was not clear until the late 1950s. By not choosing to explain, I am at least giving you some sense of the confusion experienced by the early geneticists.

One of the most conspicuous forms of variation is in coloration. Plants and animals make pigments—for protection against radiation, for concealment from their enemies, or for advertisement in order to attract pollinating insects or potential mates—and occasionally variants arise that have a different color or are albinos. Early this century, the results of a set of crosses between mice of different colors persuaded the French geneticist Lucien Cuénot[10] that the color of a mouse's fur is determined by two enzymes that work on some unknown "chromogenic" substance manufactured by the cell; one enzyme converts the substance into a yellow pigment, and the other converts it into a black pigment. As a result the mouse is light or dark brown or black, depending on the ratio of the two enzymes; if the chromogenic substance is missing, the mouse will be an albino. This was just after Mendel's work had been rediscovered, and Cuénot realized that the two enzymes and whatever determines the presence of the chromogenic substance all behave like Mendelian traits. In order to be colored a mouse had to have received, from either or both of its parents, the ability to make the enzyme(s) that produced the chromogenic substance plus at least one of the other enzymes (the yellow-making or the black-making). So here we have the first statement of an important idea that the production by a cell of some particular substances requires more than one Mendelian unit. And in 1902, Cuénot proposed the generalization that each enzyme in a cell is the product of one particular Mendelian unit; he suggested the name "mnemons" for these units because he thought of them as mnemonics that allowed the cell to remember how to make each enzyme.

A little later, similar observations were made by the English physician Archibald Garrod, who was studying a rare defect in metabolism called alkaptonuria which results in the excretion of black urine.[11] He deduced that the defect was due to the loss of an enzyme involved in the breakdown of two amino acids (called phenylalanine and tyrosine), and he determined what were the normal steps in the breakdown process and what was the chemical nature of the intermediate that was excreted by people with alkaptonuria. The defect, he found, usually runs in families, and by going back over family histories he was able to show that it behaves exactly like a recessive Mendelian trait. In other words, the ability to break down tyrosine and phenylalanine is like tallness in a pea plant. Your urine will be normal (just as the pea plant will be tall) if you receive from either parent the functional gene for the enzyme (just as the pea plant will be tall if it receives from either parent the gene for tallness); if you do not have the enzyme, then you excrete the substance that the normal enzyme would destroy. Like Cuénot, he therefore suggested that each Mendelian unit determines one particular enzyme. In the next few years, he identified some of the other enzymes and Mendelian units that are involved in this metabolic pathway (figure 2.4).

Garrod's first paper, like Cuénot's, was published in 1902 (the year in which Sutton linked the behavior of chromosomes to that of Mendelian traits). For some strange reason, however, their work received little attention over the next forty years. Cuénot's paper may have been dis-

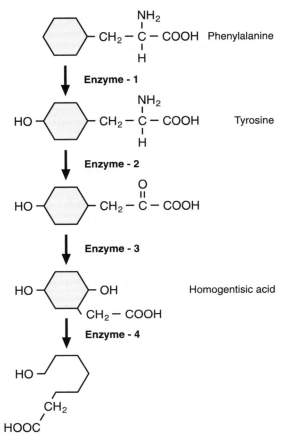

Figure 2.4. The pathway for breakdown of phenylalanine and tyrosine, and the basis for certain "inborn errors of metabolism" (Garrod 1909; see note 11). Phenylalanine and tyrosine are "amino acids" and are two of the 20 kinds of building blocks in proteins. They are therefore present in our diet, and their level in our body is controlled by enzymes in our liver and kidney that break them down to simpler compounds. The figure shows the pathway for this breakdown. Each step is in the hands of a specific enzyme (given here the numbers 1, 2, 3, and 4), and each of these enzymes is the product of a specific gene. If both of your copies of the gene for enzyme-4 is missing, you cannot break down homogentisic acid. This is a conspicuous (but not dangerous) defect called alkaptonuria. Because homogentisic acid slowly undergoes spontaneous oxidation to various dark black substances, your urine is black, and that is the main sign that there is something unusual about your metabolism. If both of your copies of enzyme-1 are missing you will, from an early age, accumulate abnormally high levels of phenylalanine, and this leads to mental deficiency. The frequency of this disease ranges between 5 and 200 per million births. Fortunately, it is easy to screen children for the condition and to control the disease by limiting the child's intake of phenylalanine.

regarded because he did not know much about the chemistry of the pigments, his analysis was obviously incomplete, and his symbolism was less clear than Mendel's; and I believe that Garrod made no impact because most geneticists were primarily interested in the results of experiments rather than in doctors' observations of rare diseases. (There is a certain snobbery in the biological sciences. I remember that the first time I met Max Delbrück, who is regarded by many as the father of molecular biology, he asked me about my background, and when I said that I was an M.D. he gave a gentle sniff and went to talk to someone else.)

There was, however, an added difficulty and that concerned the nature of each Mendelian unit, or gene, as it came to be called. William Bateson, who coined the word *genetics*, was an early champion of Mendel and was Garrod's source of inspiration, and he pointed out that "we do not know what is the essential agent in the transmission of parental characters, not even whether it is a material agent."[12] Was the gene that determined the production of an enzyme actually nothing more than the enzyme itself which somehow, if present, could be passed on from one generation to the next? If the gene was not the enzyme but something that merely ensured the presence of the enzyme, did it have to be embodied in an actual physical entity or was it more like that abstract thing that we call knowledge? When the enzyme (or whatever was the trait) was missing (a state that Mendel had represented by a lowercase letter), did this mean that the gene was missing, or merely present in some altered (silent or uninterpretable) form?

In the face of such a frightening list of questions, it is hardly surprising that biochemists turned their backs on the problem of the nature of the gene. The geneticists, however, had no option. They had to be content with a working symbolism like Mendel's that could describe the results of breeding experiments without implying any understanding of mechanism. As a result (as is so often the case), they became addicted to this habit of abstraction that had been forced upon them. (I remember, sometime in the 1960s, asking a famous geneticist whether she thought that the units she had named genetic regulatory elements were actual physical entities and she replied, "Certainly not!")

Fairly early in the century, it became apparent that the genes (whatever their nature) were arranged within each chromosome in a linear order, like a string of beads. Here I should explain briefly how this was found out. When the germ cells are formed, there has to be a cell division that halves the number of chromosomes, for example from twenty-three pairs of chromosomes down to twenty-three individual chromosomes so that when sperm and egg come together, the number of chromosomes is restored to 23 pairs. This "reductive" division is unusual because it is preceded by a step in which the members of each pair of chromosomes (the chromosome that came from the father and the one that came from the mother) come close together and undergo a process of exchange (you can think of this exchange as being like the frequent cross-overs between a pair of adjacent lines in a railroad marshaling yard). Obviously, genes that lie very close together in a chromosome are unlikely to have a cross-over between them; that is to say, they tend to stay linked together. If, for example, you inherited from your father his mother's copy of a particular gene (we will call it gene G), you will probably inherit his mother's copy of the genes (F and H) that lie close to G in the chromosome that carries G, rather than his father's copy; you are somewhat less likely to inherit the genes a bit further away on that chromosome (genes B and L); and when it comes to genes on other chromosomes, there will of course be no linkage at all and so you will be just as likely to receive copies of the genes that came to him in his father's chromosomes. Mendel had avoided this complication (perhaps intentionally) by working with traits of the garden pea that are inherited independently of each other (i.e., are not linked). But around the turn of the century people discovered many examples of linked genes that nearly always went together. By studying the inheritance of such traits that tend to be inherited together (i.e., are to some degree linked), you can work out what is called a *genetic map*, showing the linear order of the genes on each chromosome. The first such map was prepared by the American geneticist, Alfred Henry Sturtevant, in 1912 while he was still an undergraduate.[13] But since then, genetic maps have been prepared for many plants and animals, and they all show that genes are arranged within chromosomes in a linear order.

Returning momentarily to the nature of genes, in 1935 the subject of pigmentation was revisited, this time in Paris and Pasadena in a study by Boris Ephrussi and George Beadle of the genetics of eye color in the fruit fly *Drosophila*.[14] The normal red color of the eye appeared to depend on a sequence of enzymatic steps, like the sequence that Garrod had discovered for the breakdown of the amino acids tyrosine and phenylalanine. Like the hair of Cuénot's mice, the eyes of these fruit flies picked up whatever pigment was the end result of the pigment-producing enzymes present in the rest of the fly. Beadle then set to work to follow Garrod's footsteps and identify the enzymes and intermediates in this process, but it eventually occurred to him that "it ought to be possible to reverse the procedure we had been following and instead of attempting to work out the chemistry of known genetic differences we should be able to select mutants in which known chemical reactions were blocked."[15] So he and Edward Tatum set out to isolate variants of a microorganism, the bread mold *Neurospora*, that were defective in one or other of the enzymes required for synthesizing essential building blocks (i.e., that could grow only if fed the missing building blocks).[16] The experiments were laborious, because they involved hunting for mutants that could not grow in a simple, defined medium and then hunting for some specific nutrient that would allow the mutant to grow. But in the end they were successful, and as a result of their experiments they proposed what came to be known as *the one-gene one-enzyme hypothesis*.

But I am running slightly ahead of my story. It is now necessary to leave the origins of biochemistry and genetics, and give a brief description of microbiology and the simplest forms of life.

Unicellular Organisms, Bacteria, and Viruses

The history of molecular biology started, as we have seen, with observations on multicellular organisms such as peas, grasshoppers, mice, and human beings, plus the occasional microorganism such as yeast. But more recently, certain microorganisms have become the main dramatis personae, so I must introduce the reader to their characteristics and life-style.

The smallest totally self-sufficient creatures are the bacteria. They were studied and classified in the middle of the nineteenth century and, by the 1870s, certain species of bacteria were shown to cause various human, animal, and plant diseases. The importance of this discovery in bringing about the recent changes in human life expectancy has been discussed in chapter 1. Here we are interested in the role bacteria played in the twentieth-century revolution in the biological sciences.

Animal and plants cells are much larger than bacteria. A typical human cell is about a fortieth of a millimeter across and has a nucleus about one hundreth of a millimeter in diameter. The dimensioins of a typical bacterium are approximately ten times smaller. Many species of bacteria are absolutely free of any special nutritional requirement; in other words, all they require is a source of energy plus a mixture of inorganic salts to provide the various elements. Others have special requirements and, like us, can grow only if they have access to certain building blocks they cannot make themselves. Still others, such as the bacterium that causes leprosy, are so fastidious that they cannot be cultivated in the laboratory and will only grow inside the cells of their host (in the case of leprosy, which is really fussy, inside the cells of humans and armadillos).

Between 1875 and 1900, the most important bacterial causes of human disease were identified and methods were devised for separating the different species of bacteria and for cultivating them in the laboratory. This involved devising various sterile media on which the bacteria could be grown. When grown on a solid surface (for example, on the cut face of a potato or on various nutritious media made solid by the addition of either gelatin or agar), bacteria will multiply until they have made colonies visible to the naked eye, and the appearance of these colonies tends to be characteristic for each species.

The media used to isolate bacteria were sterilized by heat or by passing through a filter fine enough to hold back even the smallest bacterium. One way of showing that a disease was caused by a bacterium was therefore to show that infectious material (such as the sap of an infected plant or the pus from an infected tissue) could be freed of the infective agent if it were passed through such a filter. And this was how people discovered that certain diseases were caused by agents that were so small they could not be seen under a microscope and were able to pass through filters that would hold back all known bacteria. These "filterable agents," or *viruses*, as they came to be called, can be the cause of diseases in plants and animals. The first to be described was tobacco mosaic virus (discovered in 1892 by the Russian scientist Ivanovski) and the next was the virus of foot-and-mouth disease of cattle. Viruses were found in association with almost every kind of living cell; even bacteria had their viruses. Little was known about the exact size and shape of viruses until the invention of the electron microscope in the 1930s.

The essential difference between viruses and bacteria is that viruses are not self-sufficient and depend on the machinery of cells for their reproduction. For this reason, there used to be much argument over whether viruses should be classified as living creatures or as some kind of mysterious substance that made living cells produce more of the same substance. Naturally enough, geneticists tended to think of them as living creatures or perhaps more like wandering genes, whereas many influential biochemists regarded them as inanimate enzyme-like entities.

Although bacteria (and viruses), like the moths of industrialized England, could be shown to produce variants that had a survival advantage under certain conditions, many people felt that microorganisms were somehow separate from the mainstream of biology. As late as 1942, the English evolutionary biologist Julian Huxley wrote that "Bacteria (and . . . viruses if they can be considered to be true organisms) . . . have no genes in the sense of accurately quantized portions of hereditary substance; . . . That occasional 'mutations' occur we know, but there is no ground for supposing that they are similar in nature to those of higher organisms. . . ."[17] This quotation is very revealing because it shows what a muddle people were in about the nature of the gene and the real relationship between genetics and biochemistry. Imagine what it was like to have had to learn biochemistry and genetics in those days. As we shall see, it was the study of bacteria and their viruses that brought clarity.

The Origins of Molecular Biology

The story starts innocently enough. Before the invention of antibiotics, one of the major causes of death was pneumonia due to infection with a bacterium called *Streptococcus pneumoniae* or pneumoccus for short. This particular bacterium achieves its virulence by surrounding itself with a thick capsule of carbohydrate that protects it from attack by the defensive cells in our lungs. When there is no selection for such a protective covering, variant bacteria emerge that do not make any surface capsule and in consequence have lost their virulence. The capsulated virulent and noncapsulated avirulent bacteria can easily be distinguished because the capsulated ones make large greasy-looking, "smooth" colonies on agar and the noncapsulated make smaller "rough" colonies (figure 2.5).

Bacterial pneumonia is an infectious disease so it is often important to identify the source of each patient's infection. As it happens there are four main varieties of pneumococci (simply named I, II, III, and IV) that can be distinguished because the carbohydrates in their capsules are slightly different. So if you are tracing the spread of pneumonia through a community, you have to test every isolate to make sure it is the same variety.

So much for the background. Now to the story. In the late 1920s, Fred Griffith, an English bacteriologist, was studying the immunization of mice by inoculating them with smooth (virulent) or rough (avirulent) pneumococci.[18] Because injection of virulent bacteria kills a mouse, it was necessary to destroy their virulence and this was done by killing the bacteria by heating them to about 60°C (the process that is used for "pasteurizing" milk). At one point, Griffith happened to be doing an experiment in which mice were inoculated with a mixture of heat-killed capsulated (smooth) type II pneumococci and living avirulent (rough) type I pneumococci. No doubt to his great surprise, the mice promptly died and turned out to contain living, virulent capsulated type II bacteria (figure 2.6). It seemed that either the living rough type I bacteria were bringing back to life the heat-killed smooth type II bacteria or (as Griffith thought more likely) the heat-killed smooth type II bacteria were providing the rough type I bacteria with the means for making type II capsules and (amazingly) for continuing to make such capsules for ever afterwards.

This astonishing result was quickly confirmed by others. It was an upsetting discovery because it suggested that bacteriologists could not rely on the typing of capsules as a way of distinguishing the various strains of pneumococci. For this reason, the American bacteriologist Oswald Avery set about trying to determine what was going on. Initially, the exercise

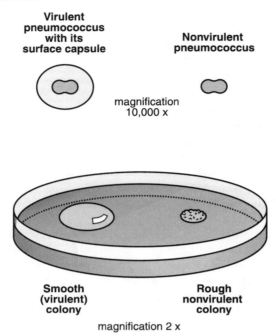

Virulent pneumococcus with its surface capsule

Nonvirulent pneumococcus

magnification 10,000 x

Smooth (virulent) colony

Rough nonvirulent colony

magnification 2 x

Figure 2.5. The characteristics of virulent and nonvirulent pneumococci. The bacterium called *Streptococcus pneumoniae* protects itself from attack by coating itself with a thick indigestible capsule made of complex carbohydrates. Different strains can be distinguished by the exact type of capsule that they make.

On prolonged cultivation in the laboratory, it tends to stop making a capsule, because it is not under any selection pressure to protect itself from attack and it can grow faster if it does not have to commit resources to making a capsule. Therefore it loses its virulence in the laboratory, as the result of accumulation of mutations in the genes responsible for making the capsule.

When grown on a nutrient agar plate, virulent strains make large shiny "smooth" colonies whereas non-virulent variants make smaller "rough" colonies.

was simply undertaken to defend the doctrine that bacterial species were as stable and distinct as the species of any other living creature.

The first questions to ask were what was the nature of the substance passing between the two kinds of bacteria and what was the direction of transfer. It was quickly determined that something was passing from the heat-killed smooth bacteria to the living rough bacteria, because an extract of the heat-killed bacteria would confer virulence on previously nonvirulent bacteria, and the substance in the extract was given the neutral name of *transforming principle.* The extraordinary thing, of course, was that the transferred substance made not only the recipient bacte-

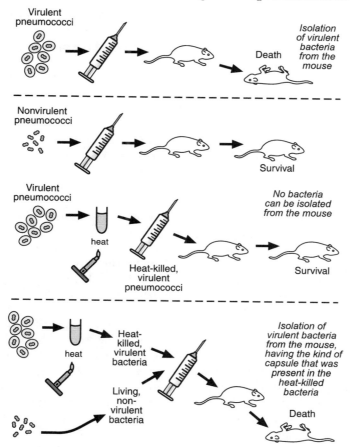

Figure 2.6. The phenomenon of bacterial transformation.

rium but also all its descendants synthesize the type of capsule originally made by the donor bacterium.

Over the next ten years, Avery gradually came to realize that what was being transferred was nothing less than the gene for synthesis of the bacterial capsule and that he was therefore determining the chemical nature of the gene.[19] To his surprise, "transforming principle" proved to be made of deoxyribonucleic acid,[20] or DNA for short (why it has this name I shall explain later). The result was unexpected. Although DNA was known to be a major constituent of chromosomes, its chemical composition appeared to be the same in all creatures and for this reason it had always been imagined to provide nothing more than a structural framework for whatever made up the genes. Indeed, for several years after Avery's report (which was published in 1944), some biochemists and geneticists believed that Avery was wrong and that transforming principle had to be a protein, hidden away among the mass of unimportant DNA.

Even if Avery was right his discovery was open to several interpretations. For example, three years later the Russian-American geneticist Theodore Dobzhansky wrote, "If this transformation is described as a genetic mutation . . . we are dealing with authentic cases of induction of specific mutations by specific treatments."[21] So obviously he, for one, was not clear about the meaning of the discovery. A few people did understand the significance of Avery's paper, but they were in a minority. Certainly, I can remember no rush of excitement spreading through the scientific community when the paper was published.

What settled the matter was an experiment by the American, Alfred Hershey, who was working with certain bacterial viruses. Like any other living organism these viruses undergo variation and the variant traits behave like mutations because they are inherited from one generation to the next. When a single bacterium is infected by two virus particles that differ in several traits, the virus particles that eventually emerge from the infected bacterium carry a mixture of the parental traits, but jumbled up together as the result of occasional exchange of traits, just like the exchanges (cross-overs) that can occur between pairs of chromosomes in higher cells. So it was possible for Hershey and others to work out a "linkage map" that showed the linear order of the genes within what might be called the virus chromosome (though, unlike ordinary chromosomes, whatever carried these genes was too minute to be visible). Once it was established that, in this sense at least, the viruses had genes just like those of any other creature, the exercise was to find out what part of the virus contained the genes. Since the virus particles were made up of about equal parts of DNA and protein, there were only two possibilities.

When these viruses infect bacteria their initial attachment to the bacteria is quite fragile, and they can be shaken off by violent agitation. If, for example, you have a liquid culture of the bacteria and you add a suspension of virus particles, you can interrupt the process of infection by buzzing the mixture in an ordinary kitchen blender. Hershey was able to show that if the moment of agitation were slightly delayed, it was possible to shake off virtually all the virus protein and leave the virus DNA still associated with the bacteria. Under these conditions, virus infection proceeded normally as if nothing had happened.[22] It followed therefore that the genes of the virus (which are passed on from one generation of the virus to the next) had to be in its DNA, not in its protein.

This experiment, the so-called blender experiment, was what finally persuaded people. There was no question in this case that the DNA was, as Dobzhansky had suggested, merely something that was causing a mutation. The genes of the virus and the genes of Avery's pneumococci were composed of DNA.

The Structure of DNA

Before embarking on the next episode in the story, I should say a little more about the properties of genes that seemed so strange. The first extraordinary thing about them was obviously their extreme stability. Certain species of animals and plants have not altered in appearance for millions and millions of years; somehow their genes have survived. Combine the gene's extraordinary stability with its need to be faithfully replicated (so that each cell can give its daughters perfect copies of every one of its genes) and you have a combination of qualities quite unlike that of any other complex substance. Last, and most important, the gene has to contain information; the genes of a pea plant or a fruit fly are, as it were, its instruction manual.

Although most geneticists were content to disregard these mysteries by treating the gene as a semi-abstract entity, several physicists, in particular Max Delbrück and Erwin Schrödinger,[23] had written about these problems. But no one could conceive what property would enable a molecule to escape the ravages of time. How one longs to have been able to whisper in their ear the thought that perhaps the gene is not endowed with a supernatural chemical stability and manages to persist unchanged because . . . But here I run ahead of the story.

The crude chemistry of DNA had been roughly understood since early in the twentieth century. It has four kinds of building block, the four *bases—adenine, guanine, thymine,* and *cytosine* (the names simply relate to the circumstances of their discovery); adenine and guanine each contain two rings made up of carbon and nitrogen atoms; thymine and cytosine each have only one such ring and in consequence are somewhat smaller. In DNA, each of the four bases is joined to a molecule of the 5-carbon sugar called *deoxyribose,* and these deoxyriboses are joined to each other by phosphorus and oxygen atoms to make a chain. The repeating unit is therefore one or another of the bases plus deoxyribose, coupled to some oxygens and a phosphorus atom; this unit is called a nucleotide. DNA therefore is a polynucleotide (figure 2.7). So far, there was nothing in this collection of facts to suggest that DNA was an important molecule.

The chemical composition of DNA had, however, been found to vary slightly from one organism to another, but the American biochemist

The Four "Bases"

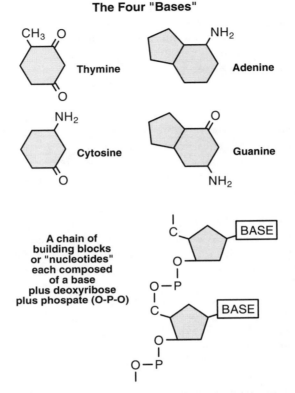

Figure 2.7. The components that make up DNA molecules. Deoxyribonucleic acid (DNA) is made up of a string of nucleotides joined together (i.e., it is a polynucleotide).

Each nucleotide contains a phosphate group (oxygen-phosphorus-oxygen) joined to a molecule of deoxyribose, which in turn is joined to a base—which can be either thymine (T), adenine (A), guanine (G), or cytosine (C).

Erwin Chargaff reported in 1950[24] that this variation followed a simple rule: the amount of guanine in any species of DNA was always roughly equal to the amount of cytosine, and the amount of adenine roughly equaled the amount of thymine. But this too did not have any obvious implication.

The elucidation of the structure of DNA, in England in 1953—by Watson and Crick, and Wilkins and Franklin[25]—is an oft-told tale. You have to know something about x-ray crystallography if you wish to follow what they did, but luckily that is not necessary if you simply want to understand the general outlines of molecular biology. The DNA molecule is made up of two polynucleotide chains (strands) that are wound round each other like the strands of a two-stranded rope; this makes it into what is technically called a double helix. The bases are in the interior of the double helix and the deoxyribose phosphate chains are on the outside, so that the bases form the rungs of a ladder that is twisted about its long axis. Each base in each of the strands is like a flat plate, lying sandwiched between the flat plates of the two adjacent bases in the strand, and is held in place partly because of the interaction with its neighbors and partly (and most important) because it is bonded to (paired with) the base that is opposite to it in the other strand.

The feature of DNA that most excited Watson and Crick was the rule governing such *base pairing*. Adenine (A) pairs with thymine (T), and guanine (G) pairs with cytosine (C); wherever there is an A in one strand there will be a T opposite it in the other strand (and vice versa); wherever there is a G there will be a C opposite it. This accounts for Chargaff's observation about the way the base composition of DNA varied between species. As I mentioned earlier, two of the four bases (A and G) have two rings and the other two (T and C) have single rings, but the two kinds of base pairs (A-T and G-C) are exactly the same size, so the width of a DNA molecule as you go up and down the double helix is not affected by which base pairs are present at each rung of the ladder (figure 2.8).

The DNA double helix has many beautiful features, but one stands out above all the others. Because of the rule governing base pairing, you can work out the sequence of bases in one strand if you are told the sequence of the other strand. To repeat: wherever there is a T in one strand there will be an A in the other, and wherever there is a C in one there will be a G in the other (and vice versa). If, for example, I tell you that one strand of a stretch of DNA has the sequence ACGTCATGTA, you immediately know that the other strand must have the complementary sequence TGCAGTACAT.

Sensing the need to signal the occasion with a quotable remark, Watson and Crick ended their paper with the words, "It has not escaped our notice that the specific pairing we have postulated immediately suggests a possible copying mechanism for the genetic material." As we shall see, their idea turned out to be absolutely correct. (If you are reading this story for the first time, it may be amusing for you to work out for yourself exactly what they had in mind.)

DNA Polymerase

As I mentioned earlier, it had always been hard to see how genes could, on the one hand, be complicated enough to serve the cell as a source of information and yet, on the other hand, be simple enough to be faith-

The Structure of DNA

The DNA molecule is made up of polynucleotide chains that are held together by base-pairing. Adenine pairs with thymine, and guanine with cytosine.

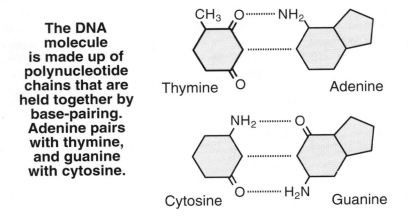

Thymine   Adenine

Cytosine   Guanine

Paired Polynucleotide Chains

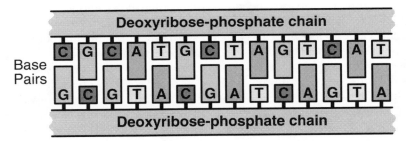

Base Pairs

The paired polynucleotide chains are twisted round a common axis to make a "double helix"

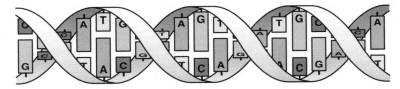

Figure 2.8. The structure of the DNA molecule.

fully copied by a mechanism that did not itself require a huge amount of information. As Watson and Crick realized, the structure of DNA seemed to provide the answer. For it was not too hard to imagine the existence of some enzyme (or cooperating group of enzymes) that could read the sequence of bases in a strand of DNA and join together, one by one, a succession of nucleotides to make a new strand that had the complementary sequence of the strand that was being copied. If that happened to both strands of a DNA double helix, you could end up with two double helices, each with the same sequence of base pairs as the original.

Of course, it is not always possible to predict how a biological process might work; often there prove to be constraints that we do not know about and things turn out to be much more complicated than expected. But in this case, the prediction turned out to be essentially correct. In 1958, the American biochemist Arthur Kornberg reported that he had isolated an enzyme from the bacterium *Escherichia coli* that, when given a strand of DNA (a *template* strand), could assemble nucleotide building blocks into a DNA chain that had the complementary sequence of bases.[26] In short, he had shown that enzymes do exist that can copy DNA. (DNA is what chemists would call a *polymer* so the enzyme that makes it is called a *polymerase*.)

At this point, I should give you a few more details about the structure of nucleic acids that are going to be important in the next chapter. They are, however, details of chemistry that are slightly peripheral to the overall narrative; some of you may prefer to skip the next two paragraphs.

As I said, the polynucleotide chains of DNA consist of a continuous alternation of deoxyribose (with one of the four DNA bases attached to it) and phosphate. Deoxyribose contains 5 carbon atoms, four of them (named C1, C2, C3, and C4)) in a ring which includes an oxygen atom, and the fifth (C5) in the form of a side group attached to the ring. The phosphates in the chain are attached to C3 and C5, so the sequence of atoms in the chain is: oxygen, phosphorus, oxygen, C3, C4, C5, oxygen, phosphorus, oxygen, C3, C4, C5, oxygen, phosphorus, oxygen, and so on. The chain is therefore not symmetrical but has a C3 at one end and a C5 at the other. This asymmetry is called *polarity*. Now, the two chains in the DNA double helix have opposite polarity. If we could lay a short piece of DNA across this page, one of the chains would have a C3 at the left end and a C5 at the right, and the other chain would be the other way round.

Synthesis of DNA by DNA polymerase occurs in one direction only. The precursors (nucleotides) used by the polymerase for DNA synthesis carry three phosphates on the C5 of their deoxyribose. The polymerase splits off two of the phosphates of the incoming nucleotides (which gives it the energy required for synthesis) and attaches the remaining, proximal phosphate to the C3 atom at the end of the growing chain. So growing chains of DNA grow (are synthesized) in the $5 \rightarrow 3$ direction.

To explain the importance of Kornberg's discovery, it may be helpful to turn to the analogy of a personal computer. My PC must have the space in which to store all that I want to put into it; but before it can serve that function it has to contain all the information for its various operations, and these must include an ability to make copies of all the information it contains (including, of course, the instructions on how to make copies). In other words, it has to be so arranged that only a small part of itself need be set aside for the machinery for carrying out the command "copy."

The requirement that genes could be copied had seemed an insoluble problem as long as they were thought to be made of proteins. Now, in one flash of understanding, the difficulty had vanished. Although I have not yet discussed how genes determine the synthesis of enzymes, you can see that the principle of "one gene, one enzyme" means that a single gene is sufficient to contain the information needed to make the Kornberg enzyme, and this enzyme should be sufficient to copy all the genes contained in the cell's DNA including, of course, the gene for itself. (In fact, it is somewhat more complicated than that because several different proteins turn out to be involved in DNA synthesis, but the idea is essentially correct that only a small amount of a cell's DNA needs to be set aside to deal with the task of copying all the DNA.)

DNA Replication

At about the same time that Kornberg was isolating the first known DNA polymerase, two postdoctoral fellows at the California Institute of Technology, Matthew Meselson and Frank Stahl,[27] were showing that the duplication (replication) of DNA double helices involves separation of the strands and the synthesis of a new complementary strand to convert each of the old strands into a double helix. In other words, every DNA double helix consists of one old strand and one new one (figure 2.9).

Some years later various people were able to photograph DNA molecules caught in the process of duplication and we could actually see the strands of the DNA molecule separating at the "replicating fork" and acquiring new complementary strands.

The experiments referred to in the last few pages all used bacteria or their viruses. However, the results were immediately applicable to all forms of life. We now know that each chromosome in higher cells contains a single DNA molecule which, like bacterial DNA, contains two strands of which one is new and the other has come from the parent cell. Bacterial DNA is circular and is duplicated at two replicating forks which start at one point on the circle and go in opposite directions until they

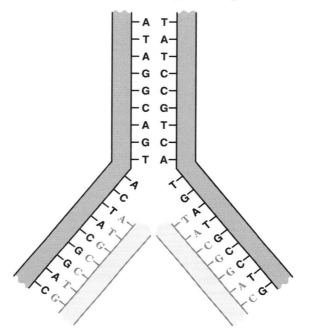

Figure 2.9. The duplication of genes; DNA replication. DNA molecules are duplicated by separating the two complementary strands and then synthesizing alongside each of them a new complementary strand. The enzyme that does this has to be able to read the sequence of strand it is working on; at each step, it has to be able to choose the right nucleotide; and it has to be able to join that nucleotide to the end of the growing chain. To assist in all this, cells have special enzymes that can unwind the parent double helix and then wind up each new daughter double helix. Despite the complexity of DNA replication, the process can go very quickly. In bacteria, the "replicating fork" moves at a rate of several hundred base pairs per second.

meet at the other side of the circle; the molecule in an animal cell chromosome is replicated at many replicating forks, each dealing with a small section of the molecule.

Here I should say something about rates of synthesis. Mammalian DNA is duplicated at a rate of about 100 base pairs per second and bacteria manage to duplicate their DNA ten times faster than that. These astonishing speeds are possible because cells have quite complicated machines for replication which include not only DNA polymerase but several other proteins concerned with unwinding the DNA, lining up the precursors and so on. (In fact, the synthesis of every kind of large biological molecule has turned out to be in the hands of some complicated machine; this is presumably because speed and precision are of the essence, and so evolution has kept adding more and more refinements; we will see in the next chapter that protein synthesis is particularly complicated.) The mammalian cell contains a huge amount of DNA and so, when it is duplicating its DNA, it has to use a large number of machines, but bacteria manage to duplicate their DNA with just one or two machines. The exact details of normal DNA duplication have been difficult to investigate because the duplicating machinery has to be handled very gently if it is to work in a test tube. In retrospect, it seems that Kornberg's success in isolating a DNA polymerase, that could act on its own in the absence of any complex supporting machinery, was the result of the existence of a much simpler, unexpected form of DNA synthesis, namely DNA repair.

DNA Repair

Genes are extraordinarily stable and can survive unchanged, from generation to generation, over hundreds or thousands of years. Obviously the bases in DNA are somewhat protected because they lie on the inside of the double helix, but this on its own is not enough to protect them from every kind of accident. Admittedly, DNA is more stable when it is dessicated (as it is in seeds and in the spores formed by certain bacteria), but even then it is still subject to a slow process of decay (which is why the grain found in ancient Egyptian tombs seldom germinates when planted).

There was one feature of DNA that gave a hint of what might be going on. Each of the four bases is distinguished from the other three in more than one way: no one type of chemical reaction will convert any of the four into one of the others. No matter what the nature of the damage, it should therefore be possible for the cell to identify any accidentally damaged base and, by looking at the undamaged base opposite, deduce what it was originally before it was damaged. It should therefore, in principle, be possible for cells to repair their DNA by cutting out any section of a strand that is damaged and replacing it with a strand complementary to the undamaged strand (figure 2.10).

Since the discovery of DNA and the elucidation of the mechanism of DNA duplication, many mechanisms for DNA repair have been identified. It seems that even the simplest cells possess an extensive armory of enzymes that are specific for certain kinds of DNA damage and can carry out several kinds of repair. There is no need for me to describe them in detail. But it is worthwhile considering what factors determine the optimum efficiency and precision of repair.

For any species, survival depends (among other things) on achieving the right balance between stability and versatility. At one extreme, for a virus that produces thousands or millions of offspring within each host

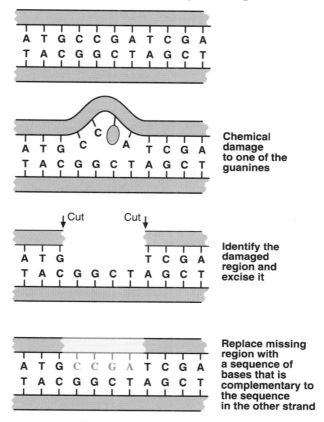

Figure 2.10. The repair of damaged DNA. There are many systems for repairing DNA and for correcting errors made during the synthesis of new chains. This diagram shows the system called short patch excision, which is found in nearly all kinds of cell and requires, minimally, the action of roughly half a dozen distinct enzymes (one for detecting the damage, one for cutting the damaged strand, one for peeling it back, one for filling in the gap, and one for joining the newly made piece to the undamaged end of the original strand).

that it infects, a fairly high level of variation (mutation) could be advantageous. For example, influenza virus is able each year to sweep through the human population because it produces variants at a very high rate that can escape the immunity we (its host) have built up as a result of previous epidemics; for such a virus, which anyway has very little nucleic acid at its disposal, it would be foolish to set aside much (if any) of this nucleic acid for genes determining the enzymes for repair. At the other extreme, a long-lived creature like *Homo sapiens* has to ensure that the large array of cells that make up the complete animal do not accidentally acquire any dangerous variants that are able to escape the proper controls and take over the whole system (the process we call cancer); for such an animal, even the best is scarcely good enough. So it is not surprising that long-lived animals have very precise systems for the replication and repair of DNA and therefore very low mutation rates.

The Information in DNA

DNA has the ideal properties for a repository of genetic information. It can be replicated relatively easily; because it has two complementary strands it can be repaired and this makes it, in effect, very stable; last, its sequence of bases, like the sequence of symbols in any written language, is obviously capable of containing information. In principle, the amount of information stored in a cell's DNA could be very large. The DNA in a typical bacterium contains a few million base pairs; its sequence of bases, if written down, would make up a book about as long as Tolstoy's *War and Peace*. The sequence of base pairs in a human cell is about a thousand times longer, or about as much as all issues of the *London Times* since the start of the twentieth century, or twenty sets of *The Encyclopædia Britannica*. The scale is daunting. Obviously, the "program" of the living cell must have a high level of complexity if it requires the cell's hard disk to have so many megabytes of space. And it is this thought, more than any other, that has taken the science of biology out of the reach of mystics and vitalists.

This new understanding of the nature of living things is not an abstraction. The objects and the numbers are real. These are things that are visible with modern microscopes (figure 2.11). As Bateson rightly fore-

On opposite page: Figure 2.11. Electron micrographs of DNA.

Top: The DNA double helix is not an abstraction. Here we see, at the top, a model showing the spiraling of the strands of a DNA double helix, and immediately below that, an actual photograph of a molecule taken by a scanning tunneling microscope (courtesy of John Baldeschwieler); magnification 10-million-fold. In the model the individual atoms are shown as solid spheres. The photograph shows the approximate external contours of a short section of a DNA molecule.

Middle: DNA replication is not an abstraction. Here we see an electron microscope picture of the DNA molecule of a bacterial virus, caught in the act of replication at a "replicating fork" (courtesy of Huntington Potter and David Dressler); magnification 10,000-fold. In this and the next picture, the molecule has been made easier to see by being coated with a thick layer of protein.

Bottom: Here we see part of the DNA molecule of a bacterium, caught spilling out of a breach in the bacterium's surface (courtesy of Huntington Potter and David Dressler). (A few small circular molecules can also be seen; this is the DNA of a small virus-like agent carried by the bacterium). Magnification 10,000-fold.

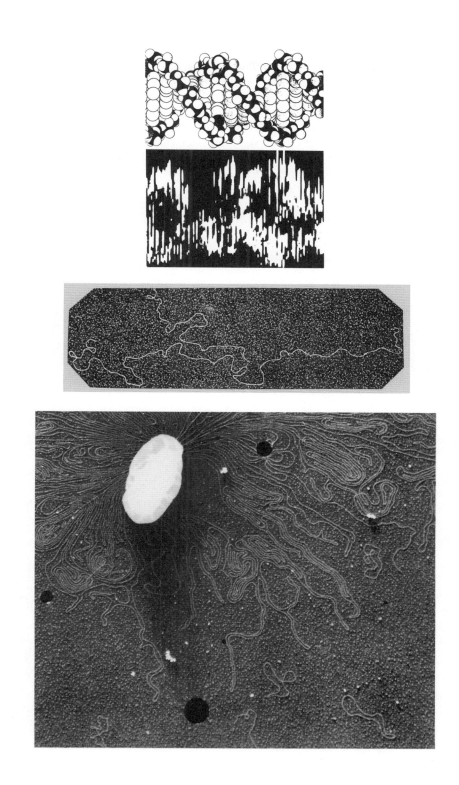

cast, in 1900, "An exact determination of the laws of heredity will probably work more changes in man's outlook on the world, and in his power over nature, than any other advance in natural knowledge that can be clearly foreseen."[28]

It remained to find out how the sequence of bases in DNA determines cell function. And that has been the happy occupation of a few thousand molecular biologists over the last forty years. A brief account of their discoveries is given in the next chapter.

CHAPTER 3

A History of Molecular Biology:
The Management of Biological Information

The discovery of the structure of DNA is now seen to have marked a turning point in the history of biology, rather like the publication of *The Origin of Species*. But unlike Darwin's book, which sold more than a thousand copies on the day it came out, the papers describing the structure of DNA did not provoke widespread debate and had little immediate effect on the average biologist. All those years spent learning to live with ignorance had produced a cast of mind that was not easily discarded. Several distinguished biochemists persisted in the belief that proteins are the only clever molecules. Others found it hard to accept that the structure of a molecule could tell you anything about the mechanism of its action or how it could be copied. And even if Watson and Crick's ideas were correct, it was not clear what was the next step. As it turned out, the next advance came from the study of proteins.

To describe what happened I must first go back to the period before anything was known about DNA. Although geneticists had created a science from studying the way genes pass from one generation to the next, the exact function of genes remained a mystery. Even the one-gene one-enzyme hypothesis did not really offer much clarification. It said that each gene was concerned with the production of a single kind of enzyme (or, perhaps more generally, a single kind of protein). When both copies of the gene for some particular enzyme were defective (i.e., both the gene inherited from your mother and the gene from your father), the enzyme activity would be missing. But this did not explain the exact role of genes in the production of enzymes. The word defective covered a multitude of possibilities.

The structure of DNA strongly suggested that every genetic defect would sooner or later be traced to some change in the sequence of the bases in the DNA molecule. This idea was a crucial retreat from the abstractions of genetics. But it did not say how DNA base sequence determined the activity of enzymes. When there is a genetic defect, does this mean that no enzyme molecules are formed or that the molecules are formed but are defective? At what level is the system operating? Is there, as it were, a direct, one-to-one relationship between DNA base sequence and protein composition, like the relationship between the letter keys on the keyboard of a PC and the messages stored within the PC? Or is it like the operation of the function keys on the keyboard, which influence the stored message in more complicated ways? Today, the answer to these questions is something learned in high school. Fifty years ago the answer was anything but obvious.

❧

The Structure of Proteins

Proteins are, in a sense, the workers. Whenever the cell has to do something, it usually entrusts the job to a protein made especially for that purpose. The enzymes that carry out the various chemical reactions going on in a cell are all proteins; antibodies are proteins; when a cell, such as a muscle cell, changes its shape it does so as the result of a change in shape of certain proteins. So proteins appear to have magical properties, and there would seem necessarily to be something magical about the process that gives them their shape and function. By the end of the nineteenth century, proteins were known to be made out of amino acids (the names and chemical properties of the twenty different amino acids will be given later, in figure 3.2). But it was not clear what determines the arrangement of the amino acids in any protein. How proteins were assembled and what determined the function of each kind of protein had long been thought of as one of the central mysteries of biology. Did the cell have a special device for shaping each particular protein so that it could act as an enzyme or an antibody molecule? If not, then how did proteins acquire their extraordinary properties?

The first step to resolving these questions came, quite unexpectedly, from an investigation of sickle cell anemia. This is a disease that is common in people of black African descent and is inherited as if it were caused by a recessive Mendelian gene; that is to say, people suffer from sickle cell anemia if they have inherited the sickle cell gene from both of their parents. In 1949, the American chemist Linus Pauling reported that sickle cell anemia is associated with a tiny change in hemoglobin (the red, oxygen-carrying molecule that is present in our circulating red cells); in other words, the gene concerned with hemoglobin synthesis must be responsible not merely for the presence of hemoglobin but for at least some of the fine details of its structure. I remember hearing Pauling lecture about this, some time in the late 1940s. He described the difference between normal hemoglobin and the hemoglobin from people with sickle cell anemia, but when asked what was found in the children of a cross between normals and sicklers he said he had not looked at that. I mention this because it shows that he was, at the time, more interested in the chemistry of proteins than the manner of operation of genes. Depending on how genes worked, one could imagine that the children of such a cross could produce either a mixture of the two types of hemoglobin or just the normal type.

When finally the paper was published, Pauling also reported that people with one normal and one abnormal gene have red cells that contain a mixture of the two types of hemoglobin. This was a satisfyingly simple result because it suggested that each of the genes we inherit from one parent operates independently of the corresponding gene that came from our other parent. Incidentally, sickle cell anemia is an extraordinarily interesting disease. The abnormal hemoglobin is somewhat less soluble than normal hemoglobin. If you inherit the abnormal trait from both your parents and all your hemoglobin molecules are abnormal, your red cells tend to be forced into abnormal shapes (like sickles rather than doughnuts) and therefore tend to become jammed in capillaries and break down (hence the anemia). But the trait can be advantageous, because red cells containing sickle cell hemoglobin are less readily parasitized by malaria. For this reason, the gene for sickle cell hemoglobin is much commoner in populations that have, since time immemorial, been subject to malaria.

Pauling's paper was enormously important because it showed, for the first time, that genetic defects could lead to abnormal proteins rather than simply the absence of some particular protein. Furthermore, in this case the abnormality was no more than a slight reduction in the electric charge of the hemoglobin molecule. Somehow the gene was responsible for some subtlety of the protein's structure.

There seemed to be two possibilities. The gene for hemoglobin might be simply determining the amino acid composition of hemoglobin or it might, in some more complicated way, be responsible for molding the final shape of the hemoglobin molecule after it had been made by some other (unknown) system in the cell. Pauling did not commit himself, but wrote that "we can identify the gene responsible for the sickling process with one of an alternative pair of [genes] capable, through some series of reactions, of introducing the modification into the hemoglobin molecule that distinguishes sickle cell anemia hemoglobin from the normal protein."

The next step forward occurred in the early 1950s. Shortly after the structure of DNA had been worked out by x-ray crystallography, ways were developed for determining the exact amino acid composition of each kind of protein. The methods were based on a technique known as *chromatography* (literally, writing in color), which separates small molecules such as amino acids according to their preference for one solvent over another or for a solvent versus adsorption to a solid surface. With this technique it became possible to determine the exact composition of any kind of protein by breaking it down into its constituent amino acids (which can be done by treating it with acid) and then separating these by chromatography.

There are twenty different amino acids, and each species of protein was shown to have a precise composition (1 of this amino acid, 3 of that, 5 of another, and so on, for each molecule of protein). What remained to be determined was how the hundred or more amino acids that make up a typical protein are arranged within the protein molecule and what determined the molecule's final shape.

All twenty types of amino acid have the same chemical composition in one part of the molecule, namely an *amino* group (-NH2) and a *carboxy* group (-COOH) separated by a carbon atom. But attached to this intervening carbon atom there can be any one of 20 different side groups, and it is these side groups that determine the properties of each kind of amino acid. So we can represent the general structure of amino acids as

$$H_2N - \overset{\overset{\displaystyle X}{|}}{C} - COOH$$

where X represents any one of twenty different combinations of atoms. Once again, I shall postpone naming the amino acids, because it is more important to know that proteins are made up of linear sequences of amino acids than to know their names. When amino acids are joined together to make a protein, the join is between the amino groups and the carboxy groups so that the amino acids form a chain. The join is called a peptide bond (because it is broken by the enzyme in our stomach that was named pepsin, after the Greek word for digestion), and the chain is therefore called a *polypeptide chain*.

$$H_2N - \overset{\overset{\displaystyle X}{|}}{C} - CO - HN - \overset{\overset{\displaystyle X}{|}}{C} - CO \ldots\ldots HN - \overset{\overset{\displaystyle X}{|}}{C} - CO - HN - \overset{\overset{\displaystyle X}{|}}{C} - COOH$$

(In passing, notice that the two ends of a polypeptide chain are different; the end shown here on the left is called the N terminus, the other the C terminus.)

In the mid-1950s, the English molecular biologist Fred Sanger devised a set of techniques for determining the order of the amino acids in proteins, and in this way he was able to show that the sequence of amino acids was constant for each kind of protein. Plainly, the business of making a protein required, at the very least, that the cell had some means for placing amino acids in the right order.

Proteins vary greatly in size. For example bovine insulin, the first protein sequenced by Sanger, has two chains, one of 30 amino acids and one of 21; hemoglobin is much larger and contains two kinds of chain, each of which is made up of several hundred amino acids. Using Sanger's techniques one of his students, Vernon Ingram, was able to show that sickle cell hemoglobin differs from normal hemoglobin in just one amino acid. The sixth amino acid from the N terminus of one of the chains was valine instead of the usual glutamic acid. (It is simpler if I give the names and properties of all twenty amino acids a little later in the chapter.) Since glutamic acid carries a negative charge on its side group whereas valine's side group has no charge, this change accounted for the charge difference observed by Pauling. In other words, Ingram had converted the one-gene one-enzyme hypothesis into what might be called the one-gene one-amino-acid-sequence hypothesis.

Although Ingram's discovery showed that genes determine amino acid sequence, it was still possible to imagine that cells possess not only the gene-determined mechanism for joining amino acids in the right order but also some additional mechanism that is responsible for coiling the chain of amino acids into the right three-dimensional configuration. For it is the final shape of proteins that surely determines their properties. If a protein can act as an enzyme it must be because it has a specially shaped region that binds its target molecule and then stretches or compresses it so that the desired chemical reaction takes place; if a protein is to act as an antibody it must have some surface feature that precisely matches whatever it is an antibody against. What determines how each chain of amino acids is folded up upon itself to give each protein its characteristic shape?

The Determination of a Protein's Shape

In the late 1950s, the American biochemist Chris Anfinsen was studying ways of modifying the three-dimensional structure of proteins. In the presence of certain solvents the chain of amino acids in a protein would completely unfold and lose all organization, and if the protein were an enzyme such unfolding completely destroyed its enzymic activity. But he found that if the unfolding solvent was gradually replaced with water, the original structure of certain enzymes would reform and the enzymic activity would return (figure 3.1). This was a very important result because

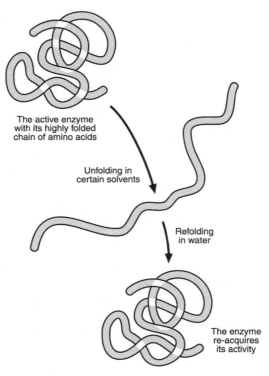

The active enzyme
with its highly folded
chain of amino acids

Unfolding in
certain solvents

Refolding
in water

The enzyme
re-acquires
its activity

Figure 3.1. The shape of a protein molecule is determined by its amino acids. The chain of amino acids in each protein molecule is intricately coiled so that the different amino acids can interact with each other and with the surrounding water. Proteins can be uncoiled by putting them into certain solvents, and the simpler proteins will assume their original structure when they are returned to water—showing that their shape is determined by their sequence of amino acids.

it meant that the three-dimensional structure of certain proteins is somehow an inevitable consequence of the sequence of its amino acids.

To explain how amino acid sequence could determine shape, I must describe some of the factors that determine the arrangement of molecules in solution. In part it is simply a question of solubility. Some things, such as sugar and salt, are soluble in water but not in liquids like benzene; others, such as fats and paraffins, are soluble in benzene but not in water. Some amino acids have side groups (marked X in the formulae given on page 92) that are water soluble and some have benzene-soluble side groups. (In DNA, the deoxyribose-phosphate chain is soluble in water but the bases are not, and that is why the bases are on the inside and the chains are on the outside.) Now, as every cook knows, oil and water do not mix. No matter how much you shake them up together, they will quickly separate as soon as you stop shaking. If, however, you add some suitable protein to the water (for example, the proteins in egg yolk), the oil droplets formed when you shake the mixture will become coated with the protein, because the side groups of some amino acids are more soluble in olive oil or butter fat than in water. This then leaves the side groups of the protein's water-soluble amino acids projecting into the water, and that has the effect of making the fat droplets compatible with water. And lo!, you have made a stable emulsion. (The recipes for such sauces usually require the addition of some vinegar or lemon juice, which makes the sauce rather acidic so that the proteins coating each droplet carry a positive charge, which makes the droplets tend to repel each other; but I do not want to burden the reader with a discussion of the factors that decide whether a molecule carries an electric charge, even though this is important in determining the shape and properties of proteins.)

The factors that determine the microscopic structure and stability of a sauce also determine the structure of proteins. In figure 3.2 the amino acids are listed according to the all-important properties of their side groups. The side groups of certain amino acids are not very soluble in water, and for this reason polypeptide chains tend to be coiled in such a way that these amino acids (like the olive oil in the sauce) end up on the inside, in the water-free interior. In contrast, the more water-soluble amino acids end up on the outside. Incidentally, the same forces determine the structure of DNA; the bases are inside, stacked on top of each other like a pile of pennies, while the two strands are on the outside. (There are other forces and interactions that serve to stabilize the structure of proteins and DNA, but they are not essential to what I have to say and thus can be left out of this ruthlessly simplified account.)

By changing to a solvent in which all amino acid side groups are equally soluble, Anfinsen had been able to uncoil the amino acid chain of a protein (an enzyme) so that it no longer had a tightly compact configuration. This part of the experiment was not at all surprising. But the astonishing thing was that, once the new solvent was removed and the protein was returned to its normal watery environment, the protein regained its enzymatic activity. Apparently, the order (sequence) of the different amino acids in the chain was sufficient to ensure that the chain would refold correctly, back into its normal configuration. In other words, it is enough for the cell to have genes that specificy the *sequence* of the amino acids in each protein, because that alone will determine the protein's three-dimensional structure. (Like almost every simple statement about biology, this one is not absolutely correct, because certain proteins have recently been shown to acquire their final shape as the

The Arrangement of (Three) Adjacent Amino Acids

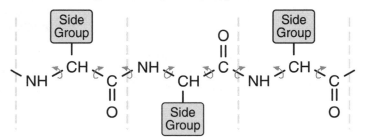

A chain of amino acids is made up of linkages between atoms that, almost without exception, are free to rotate. The exact three-dimensional arrangement of the chain is determined by the characteristics of the side-group of each amino acid in the chain.

The names (and abbreviations) of the 20 different amino acids, and the main properties of their side-groups, are listed below.

The Names of the 20 Different Amino Acids and Their Properties

Amino acids with water-soluble side-groups, which therefore tend to lie on the outsides of proteins.			Amino acids with water-insoluble side-groups, which therefore tend to congregate on the insides of proteins.	
Negatively charged amino acids	**Positively charged amino acids**	**Uncharged amino acids**	Glycine (GLY)	Phenylalanine (PHE)
Aspartic Acid (ASP)	Arginine (ARG)	Asparagine (ASP)	Alanine (ALA)	Tryptophan (TRP)
Glutamic Acid (GLU)	Histidine (HIS)	Glutamine (GLU)	Valine (VAL)	Methionine (MET)
	Lysine (LYS)	Serine (SER)	Leucine (LEU)	Cysteine (CYS)
		Threonine (THR)	Isoleucine (ILE)	Proline (PRO)
		Tyrosine (TYR)	*Cysteines have a special function because they can form a chemical (-S-S-) bond with each other, and so they can tightly link together different parts of an amino acid chain.*	
Because unlike charges attract each other and like charges repel each other, the charged amino acids affect the shape of each protein and the way it interacts with other molecules (including other, charged proteins).			*Proline has a special role because the bond with one of its neighbouring amino acids is not free to rotate, and so each proline forces a change of direction into the chain of amino acids.*	

Figure 3.2. The different amino acids and the chemistry of the join between amino acids.

result of being held by other molecules, called chaperones, while their amino acid chain is being assembled.)

About the time of the Anfinsen experiment, similar experiments using DNA were carried out by three U.S. scientists—molecular biologists Paul Doty, Julian Marmur, and Rollin Hotchkiss. Although the sugar-phosphate chains of DNA are water soluble and are on the outside and the insoluble bases have to be on the inside, the pairs of bases that lie opposite each other in the two strands are also being held together by hydrogen bonds in an absolutely specific way (A being paired with T, and G with C). When a solution of DNA in water is boiled, the forces holding the two strands together are weakened and the strands uncoil and separate. If you then drop the temperature quickly, each strand tries to move its bases away from the water and so ends up like a tightly tangled ball of string. In the early 1960s, however, it was shown that if you start with a solution of just one kind of DNA (e.g., the DNA molecules from, say, a million virus particles, all with the same base sequence), boil it to separate the strands, and then lower the temperature very, very slowly, each strand has a chance of meeting a complementary strand and aligning itself against that strand to reconstitute the original double helix, with each of its bases opposite the complementary base in the other strand. This process is called the melting and annealing of nucleic acids of complementary sequences, and in the next chapter I describe how it has provided a way for genetic engineers to purify particular regions of DNA (figure 3.3).

A Recapitulation of What Was Known in 1960

I have now taken the story roughly up to the end of the 1950s and this is an appropriate moment for a quick summary. Genes had been found to be made of DNA; DNA molecules proved to consist of two "complementary" strands, made up of a sequence of four kinds of building block (the four bases); DNA is easy to copy because each strand can act as a template on which a new complementary strand is formed, and the cell has enzymes that can assemble bases in the correct sequence so that they form a strand that is complementary to any given piece of single-stranded DNA. Proteins had been shown to consist of one or more polypeptide chains, made up of twenty kinds of building block (the twenty amino acids); there is one gene for every protein (or, perhaps, every polypeptide chain), and the gene's role is to determine the sequence of amino acids in each protein; last, it is its amino acid sequence that determines a protein's structure and function.

These discoveries about the structure and chemistry of DNA and proteins completely changed the way we look at living systems. Although

The "Melting" and Specific "Re-annealing" of Double-Stranded DNA

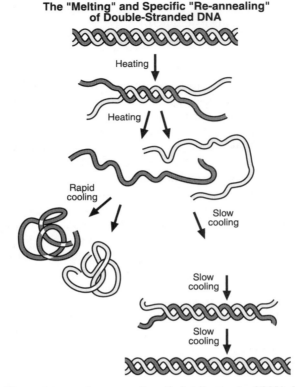

Figure 3.3. The melting and re-annealing (hybridization) of DNA. When a DNA double helix is put into boiling water, the two strands unwind from each other and separate. If they are then rapidly cooled, they do not have time to find each other and therefore each coils up on itself. If, however, a solution of DNA is "melted" by heating and then cooled very slowly, the complementary strands have time to find each other and reform a double helix. Even if the solution of DNA contains molecules with several different sequences, the individual melted strands will still find their appropriate partners, if they are given enough time.

cells and their component parts give the appearance of having been arranged and sculptured into complex three-dimensional shapes, it seemed clear, from about 1960, that this miracle is achieved using a conventional one-dimensional language, contained within the sequence of bases in DNA and expressed in the sequence of amino acids in proteins. Once the underlying operations of genetics and biochemistry could be expressed in such simple terms, there followed a torrent of discovery that continues even to the present day.

The task for molecular biologists has been made easier because, as it turns out, all forms of life on earth speak the same language (apart from what might be called occasional minor differences in dialect). Not only is the language the same, but many of the ideas are the same. Thus, all forms of living things prove to have some proteins that are so similar in amino acid sequence and genes that are so similar in base sequence that they must have descended from some common ancestor. For example, many of the genes involved in cancer play a central role in the control of cell behavior and are found throughout the animal kingdom, from humans down to single-celled creatures like the yeasts. Indeed, just as it is possible to work out the derivation of most of the major human languages by studying their similarities and differences, so is it possible to work out roughly the path of evolution by looking at the degree of relatedness of the genes in the different branches of the living kingdom.

Unfortunately, although the underlying principles are simple the actual conduct of the language of biology is surprisingly complicated and involves many hundreds of independent moving parts. Living systems have been evolving on this earth for at least 3 billion years, so perhaps we should not be surprised that today's forms of life are full of subtle interactions and adaptations. To make the next part of the story easier to assimilate, I will have to commit several oversimplifications and omit certain important qualifications.

Ribonucleic Acid (RNA)

From the early 1960s, the race was on to determine how base sequence is translated into amino acid sequence. At this point, however, I have to introduce another major performer in the affairs of the cell. Since the late nineteenth century, it had been known that there are two kinds of nucleic acid—deoxyribonucleic acid (which I have already described) and ribonucleic acid, or RNA. Indeed, cells have much more RNA than DNA.

Some viruses contain DNA and some contain RNA. This too had been known for many years, so the moment DNA was discovered to contain information, it seemed likely that the same would be true for RNA. But it was not clear why cells had to have a second class of informational molecule, still less why cells should have more RNA than DNA.

Two minor chemical differences distinguish RNA from DNA. First, the bases in DNA are adenine (A), cytosine (C), guanine (G), and thymine (T), whereas RNA contains A, C, G, and uracil (U) (which is the same as thymine but with an H instead of a CH_3 group). Second, as the names imply, the bases in RNA are attached to ribose whereas the bases in DNA are attached to deoxyribose (which is ribose without one of its oxygen atoms); so the building blocks of RNA are called ribonucleotides and the enzymes that make RNA are called RNA polymerases. Because of these two differences, DNA and RNA strands have slightly different physical properties, and they are readily distinguished in the cell by the various proteins that interact with nucleic acids (for example, cells have enzymes that break down DNA and other enzymes that break down RNA).

In the story of the discovery of the role of DNA it was necessary, at one point in the previous chapter, to introduce the reader to the biology of certain viruses that infect bacteria. In discussing the various roles for RNA we must once again return to the bacterial viruses.

Viruses and the Discovery of the Different Functions of RNA

As Hershey showed in 1952, certain DNA-containing viruses that infect the bacterium *Escherichia coli* start the process of virus infection by injecting their DNA into the host bacterium. This DNA then undergoes repeated rounds of replication and the 100 or more resulting molecules of DNA are then packaged into progeny virus particles by being rolled up and surrounded by new virus proteins made within the bacterium under instructions from the virus DNA. Finally, after about ten to twenty minutes, the bacterium bursts and liberates these new virus particles, which then go on to infect other bacteria. Viruses therefore represent an extreme form of parasitism. Each virus particle merely supplies the instructions, and it is left to the machinery of the parasitized cell to follow out these orders—namely, to produce multiple copies of the instructions and to see to it that these are safely packaged and handed on to other hosts. By studying the synthesis of proteins that are characteristic of the bacterium, the American geneticist Seymour Benzer was able to show that within a few seconds of infection by a virus the bacterium ceases to be able to make its own proteins; henceforth, it is totally (and fatally) occupied in making the proteins needed by the virus. It is as if, at the moment of infection, the slate is wiped clean and a completely new program starts to operate. This therefore is a good system in which to study the way information contained in DNA (in this case, the virus DNA) is translated into the sequence of amino acids in proteins (in this case, the virus proteins) using the machinery available in the bacterium.

Initially the role of RNA seemed completely obscure. The bases in DNA obey the simple rule that the amount of adenine equals the amount of thymine, and the amount of guanine equals the amount of cytosine. But the bases in RNA did not follow any obvious rule. To complicate matters still further, there appeared to be several different kinds of RNA. For example, roughly two-thirds of all the RNA in a bacterium is contained in particles called *ribosomes*" (literally, bodies containing ribonucleic acid); these are about the size of fairly large virus particles and are composed of several different kinds of protein as well as some RNA. Most of the rest of a bacterium's RNA is in small molecules which have come to be called *transfer RNA* or tRNA (for reasons that will become clear).

By exposing bacteria to amino acids marked with radioactive atoms, it was possible to show that incoming amino acids quickly become coupled to tRNA. A few seconds later, the amino acids start to appear in new polypeptide chains, and this early stage in the life of new proteins occurs in association with ribosomes, suggesting that the ribosome contains the machinery for making proteins.

But this could not be easily reconciled with the unexpected finding that a bacterium's ribosomes survive unchanged after virus infection. How can a ribosome, that was made by a bacterium before it was infected with a virus, know how to make the proteins needed by the virus? How can it be determining the actual sequence of the amino acids in these proteins? Surely, that information must come from the virus DNA. ·

Messenger RNA (mRNA)

The solution to the role of RNA, like so many discoveries in biology, was greatly assisted by a quirk of nature. The DNA of the bacterium *E. coli* contains roughly equal amounts of adenine-thymine and guanine-cytosine base pairs (i.e., it is 50 percent A-T and 50 percent G-C), whereas the DNA of the virus Hershey and Benzer were working with contains about three times as much A-T as G-C (i.e., it is 75 percent A-T and 25 percent G-C; the difference is due to what might be called word usage and will be understandable when I have described what is called the genetic code). A careful inventory of the different classes of RNA present before and after infection with the virus revealed one minor species of RNA, amounting to about one-twentieth of the total, that underwent a change in base composition at the time of infection—from being 50 percent G-C (like the bacterial DNA) to being 25 percent G-C (like the virus DNA). Furthermore, some of this RNA was found attached to DNA and some was associated with ribosomes. So it seemed to be acting as a go-between, carrying information from DNA to ribosomes, and therefore was called *messenger RNA* (figure 3.4).

Messenger RNA is made by an enzyme that copies the sequence of bases in one of the DNA strands into a complementary RNA strand (the only difference from the enzyme that copies DNA is that this one uses bases attached to ribose); in other words, where there is a guanine in the

The Transcription of DNA into mRNA

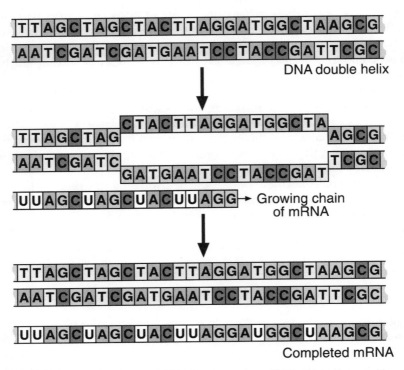

Figure 3.4. The transcription of DNA into messenger RNA. This diagram shows, in a highly stylized way, the copying of a stretch of DNA into an RNA molecule with a sequence that is complementary to one of the DNA strands.

DNA it puts a cytosine in the new RNA (and vice versa), where there is a thymine it puts in an adenine, and where there is an adenine it puts in a uracil. The information that lies within the sequence of bases in DNA is therefore being faithfully transferred to mRNA. This process has been called *transcription* because one kind of base sequence is being written across (transcribed) into another. (In a moment, I will describe how base sequence is turned into amino acid sequence—a process that, for obvious reasons, is called *translation*.) Unlike molecules of DNA, which can be enormously long and contain millions of base pairs representing many, many genes, mRNA molecules usually contain only a few thousand bases, and each molecule represents the base sequence of just one or two genes.

The final property of mRNA I want to mention is, in some ways, the most important. Unlike DNA, which is a conspicuously stable molecule, mRNA molecules usually survive for only a few minutes in bacteria and a few hours in animal or plant cells, after which they are destroyed. At once we begin to see the strategy. A molecule of DNA is made up of many hundreds or thousands of genes, joined end-to-end; we can think of it as being like the succession of articles in an encyclopedia. At any moment, a cell (or a virus), like any reader of an encyclopedia, is wanting to be guided by only a small part of the total information available; for example, we know that every one of our cells must have the gene for making hemoglobin but only one of the many kinds of cell in our body is actually making hemoglobin. Furthermore, the needs of a cell will surely change from moment to moment, so cells must have a way of stopping the expression of any gene and turning on the expression of others. The use of a special form of RNA (messenger RNA) as an unstable intermediary gives the cell exactly that kind of versatility. To control which genes are in use at any moment, all the cell has to control is the choice of which genes it is transcribing; whenever it wants to stop using a particular gene, all it has to do is stop transcribing the gene and wait for that gene's mRNA to be destroyed.

An obvious analogy leaps to mind. A personal computer stores information on magnetic disks (hard disks and floppy disks), which retain this information even when the computer is not working. But it takes some time to find and retrieve (to access) any piece of information that is stored that way, so the computer has a separate system (random access memory, or RAM) which can be read quickly because it is based on transistors and depends on the continual flow of electric current (and therefore operates only when the power is on). Apart from those moments when information is moving in or out of the magnetic disk, the speed of the system is determined by the speed of operation of RAM, but the versatility of the system is achieved by having many different programs and files stored in the magnetic disk, which can be retrieved into RAM as the need arises.

In these terms, the virus studied by Hershey and Benzer behaves like a floppy disk that, among other things, contains the information needed to stop the cell referring to the program in the cell's magnetic disk and to substitute the virus's own program. Following virus infection, the power supply remains the same as do all the mechanical parts, and the language is the same, but the program changes. Actually the analogy goes deeper than this, because the logical requirements for a virus that takes over a cell are very much like the component parts of rogue programs designed to spread through interconnecting systems of computers, and for that reason such programs have been called viruses.

Before describing how a cell determines which genes should be transcribed into mRNA, I must describe how the base sequence in messenger RNA molecules is translated into the amino acid sequence of proteins.

The Genetic Code

From the first few known amino acid sequences it was clear that each of the twenty amino acids could be next to any other. This suggested that genes determine the placing of amino acids in the right order, one by one rather than in groups. So there had to be some "code" that relates base sequence to amino acid sequence (like the code that relates the dots and dashes of Morse to the letters of the alphabet).

Given an alphabet of four letters (A, G, C, T in DNA, and A, G, C, U in RNA), you can write sixteen different two-letter words and sixty-four three-letter words. So it was clear from the outset that some or all of the twenty kinds of amino acid had to be represented by words of at least three letters. But there were many possibilities. For example, it was not clear whether all words were the same length and whether the adjacent words in each message lay next to each other or were separated by a symbol representing the spacer we put between our words. One subtle experiment, which I will not describe, had strongly suggested that the genetic code was a spacer-less, three-letter language.

Various ingenious schemes were devised for cracking the code. For example, the substitution of valine for glutamic acid in hemoglobin, which is responsible for sickle cell anemia, suggests that the words for these two amino acids probably differ by only one letter. One could imagine collecting other such examples and, given a little luck, reconstructing the code that way. But in the end the problem was solved by the biochemists, in the following way.

If a cell is broken open carefully its contents will, for a time, continue to carry out the synthesis of proteins, and if you feed such a system radioactive amino acids it will make radioactive polypeptide chains. Furthermore, if you give it, for example, the mRNA from cells that are making hemoglobin, it will correctly translate that message into hemoglobin. In 1961, the American biochemist Marshall Nirenberg prepared RNA molecules in which every base was uracil. When given this artificial mRNA (which we can call poly-U), cell extracts proceeded to make a little protein in which every amino acid was phenylalanine. It seemed likely therefore that the code (or one of the codes) for phenylalanine was UUU. Using mRNA containing a mixture of various proportions of U and C led to the formation of little proteins containing various proportions of phenylalanine, leucine, proline, and serine. So the code for one of these amino acids could be CCC, and for the others some combination of U and C.

It soon became possible to prepare short stretches of RNA of precisely known sequence, and this disclosed the meaning of other triplets. Finally, a collaborator of Nirenberg's, Philip Leder, found a way of testing

The Genetic Code

AGA									
AGG									
GCA CGA						GGA			
GCC CGC						GGC		AUA	
GCG CGG AAC GAC UGC GAA CAA GGG CAC AUC									
GCU CGU AAU GAU UGU GAG CAG GGU CAU AUU									
ala	arg	asn	asp	cys	glu	gln	gly	his	ile

UUA				AGC						
UUG				AGU						
CUA			CCA UCA ACA					GUA		
CUC			CCC UCC ACC					GUC		UAA
CUG AAA		UUC CCG UCG ACG					UAC GUG			UAG
CUU AAG AUG UUU CCU UCU ACU UGC UAU GUU										UGA
leu	lys	met	phe	pro	ser	thr	trp	tyr	val	stop

Figure 3.5. The genetic code. A four-letter alphabet can produce 64 different three-letter words. This table shows the meaning of each of the 64 words. As you can see, there are several synonyms for some amino acids. Three of the 64 words serve the function of the word "stop" in a telegram. (As explained on page 81, nucleic acid chains possess a direction, "polarity"; thus the RNA triplet GCU is distinct from the triplet UCG.)

the coding properties of individual triplets, and by 1965 the code had been cracked. The complete table is shown in figure 3.5.

There are sixty-four possible three-letter words and, as you can see, most amino acids are represented by more than one word. Three of the sixty-four triplets (UAG, UAA, and UGA) do not code for any amino acid and these are used by the protein-synthesizing machinery as stop signs, signifying the end of an amino acid sequence. One triplet (AUG) is both the word for the amino acid called methionine and the signal for the start of an amino acid sequence. What happens if the cell does not want a protein to have its amino acid sequence start with methionine? The answer is that it cuts off the methionine after the protein is made.

For practical purposes, the genetic code is the same for all animals and plants. With the coming of genetic engineering it has become plain that all forms of life really do speak the same language. A gene from an animal will nearly always work perfectly well if put into a plant and will lead to the synthesis of the same protein that was made in the animal from whence it came. (That incidentally is why the immunity you can acquire against a virus like yellow fever, which has multiplied in your cells and stimulated your immune system to produce antibodies against it, will later protect you against the virus particles that grew in the cells of the mosquito that bites you.) So it has become a common practice, in the industry of biological products, to move genes into bacteria where the gene products can be produced more cheaply. (A few minor differences in the code have recently been found in some creatures, but they need not concern us here.)

Once the genetic code was known, you could deduce the meaning of any sequence of bases. Given such a sequence, the first thing was to decide how to read the sequence (i.e., which of the three possible "reading frames" should be used). So you would look for an AUG that led straight into a long string of meaningful triplets (sense codons), uninterrupted by any of the three stop signs (nonsense codons). Such a sequence is called an *open reading frame*.

Mutation

With the code in front of us, it becomes possible to discuss the consequences to be expected from the various types of possible change in base sequence. Most single base changes will result in a change in protein sequence, one amino acid being replaced by another; for example, sickle cell anemia was the result of the change of a glutamic acid in the hemoglobin molecule into a valine—that is, a change in the mRNA of an A to a U, converting GAA or GAG for glutamic acid into GUA or GUG for valine. Some single base changes will convert a sense codon into a stop codon, and this is usually disastrous because it will prematurely terminate the amino acid sequence of the protein. Equally disastrous is the loss or gain of a single base (or any nonmultiple of three) because such frameshift mutations destroy the reading frame and totally alter the sequence of amino acids downstream of the frameshift; if you are reading the code from left to right, a frameshift will totally alter the meaning of the sequence to its right and will probably quickly lead to a stop codon within the garbled message.

I can illustrate this using a rather whimsical sentence borrowed, with a slight modification, from a child's reading primer written by the poet Housman. The message written in a spacer-less code is SHESAWTHE-NUNINACABOHOFIEBADNUN. With spaces put in, it reads SHE SAW THE NUN INA CAB OHO FIE BAD NUN. After a single base change it might become SHE SAW THE NIN INA CAB OHO FIE BAD NUN, which is obscure but not totally meaningless. After loss of a base it would become SHE SAT HEN UNI ACA BOH OFI EBA DNU N, which is a disaster.

Larger scale changes can produce more complex effects, like the result of shuffling the pages of an instruction manual for the assembly of some complex piece of equipment. The effects of such changes will become obvious when I have described the general logic of gene control.

Most of the single base changes that arise in DNA are thought to be primarily due to errors made at the time DNA is copied by DNA polymerase. For long-lived animals, the rate is about one mistake for every billion bases that are copied. But the rate can be greatly increased by exposure to X-irradiation, ultraviolet light, and certain chemical mutagens that interact directly with the bases in DNA and force the polymerase to make errors when trying to copy these damaged bases. All but the very simplest of creatures have developed ways of identifying and repairing the commonest forms of DNA damage, and these systems for repair go a long way toward protecting us against the hazards of our environment. The subject of mutagens will come up again in chapter 4 which is on cancer. Now we must continue with the history of molecular biology.

Having introduced messenger RNA and the genetic code, I can now describe the mechanism used for translating base sequence into amino acid sequence, and then describe what determines when each open reading frame (each gene) in DNA should be used and when it should be kept in abeyance.

Translation

So far we have followed the movement of information from DNA into mRNA and out from the nucleus of the cell into the cytoplasm, where the message has to be translated into protein. Obviously, the mechanism responsible for translation must know the genetic code because it has to be able to convert base sequence into amino acid sequence.

It turns out that this is a very elaborate procedure which requires a sizeable investment of the cell's total resources. The process is extraordinarily complicated, and some readers may choose to skip the next four paragraphs. For, I do not think it is necessary to remember the intricate details of translation in order to have a rough understanding of molecular biology.

As I mentioned earlier, there is a third variety of RNA called transfer RNA (tRNA). These are small molecules containing about eighty bases. A cell will have many kinds of tRNA, each of which recognizes one of the sixty-one coding triplets shown in figure 3.5. (Remember, there are sixty-four possible triplets, but three of them represent stop signs.) Each tRNA molecule is folded back on itself to form what has been picturesquely described as a clover-leaf structure, because the RNA strand forms three loops. At the tip of the central loop of each kind of tRNA, three bases protrude outward, and these bases are complementary to one of the sixty-one coding triplets. (If we call the triplets in mRNA *codons*, then the triplets of tRNA can be called *anticodons*.) The two ends of the RNA molecule are in the stalk of the clover-leaf, and to one of those ends is attached the amino acid that is appropriate for the anticodon in the loop. This attachment is achieved by amino acid activating enzymes, each of which specifically recognizes one of the twenty amino acids and one kind of tRNA. So the RNA acts as intermediary in the *transfer* of information between DNA and amino acid sequence.

The actual process of protein synthesis is conducted by the ribosomes. As mentioned earlier, these are large particles present in the cell's cytoplasm, and they have the ability to attach to one end of a mRNA molecule and then progress along it, selecting and joining together the correct sequence of amino acids. In other words, they pick the tRNA molecules whose anticodons match the codons of the mRNA, then join together the amino acids attached to these tRNA molecules, and at the same time disconnect the tRNAs once they have served their purpose. Each step in the manufacture of a protein therefore requires several things to happen; the correct activated amino acid has to be chosen (and this means that the ribosome has a way of distinguishing the correct tRNA out of the sixty-one possible kinds of tRNA); the amino acid has then to be joined to the growing end of the protein polypeptide chain and, at the same time, be severed from its tRNA; and finally the mRNA molecule must be moved along by the length of three bases.

The process of translation makes considerable demands upon the cell's resources. Each cell has to have 61 genes for the 61 kinds of activating enzymes and 61 stretches of DNA to be transcribed into the 61 species of tRNA, and roughly 200 genes for the 200 different kinds of protein that are present in ribosomes, plus the stretches of DNA that are transcribed into ribosomal RNA, and a few other proteins that help the ribosomes move along mRNA molecules. For a small cell like a bacterium, which has just a few thousand genes, this investment in the hardware for protein synthesis takes up 5 to 10 percent of its DNA and even more of its capital investment because the total mass of the ribosomes makes up almost a quarter of the weight of each bacterium. But, despite its complexity, the system is extraordinarily efficient. Less than one in a thousand of the amino acids in proteins is incorrect, even though each polypeptide chain is built up at a rate of about forty amino acids per second.

It is natural to ask how a mechanism as elaborate as this could have evolved from simple beginnings. As it is presently constituted, the system uses several hundred separate ingredients and every one of these has to be present for the system to function properly. The goddess Minerva may well have sprung fully armed from the brow of Jupiter, but it is difficult to see how several hundred gene products could have arisen simultaneously. This is one of the issues that will be discussed in a later section that deals with the origin of life.

So far, this introduction to molecular biology has concentrated on the flow of information from the base sequence in DNA to the amino acid sequence in proteins. Now we must consider how large collections of genes are controlled so that, at each moment, the cell contains just the right mixture of proteins for whatever it wants to do.

The Regulation of Gene Expression

The simplest example of gene regulation is seen in the way bacteria choose the best source of energy out of a mixture of several sources. If *E. coli* is offered, for example, a mixture of the two simple carbohydrates glucose and lactose, it eats the glucose first; glucose is a normal ingredient in its own biochemistry, so it does not have to make any special enzymes in order to use any glucose it receives from the environment. Not until it has eaten all the glucose does it start on the lactose. But lactose (the main sugar in milk) is not a normal part of the bacterium's environment, and to deal with it the bacterium has first to make a special enzyme called β-galactosidase which cuts the lactose molecule in half (into glucose and galactose), and a special protein called lactose permease which sits on the bacterial surface and assists in the transport of lactose into the bacterium. In the absence of lactose, there is negligible synthesis of β-galactosidase and permease, which is sensible because it is obviously a waste of effort and resources to make proteins that are not needed.

As mentioned earlier, the primary method of regulation of gene expression is by control of transcription. When a protein is needed, the gene for that protein is transcribed into mRNA which is then translated into protein; when this particular class of protein is no longer needed, transcription stops, the existing mRNA is broken down, and the protein ceases to be made.

The system used by cells to regulate transcription was worked out in the 1950s and 1960s by Jacques Monod and François Jacob at the Pasteur Institute in Paris. They were trying to lay bare the logical system that determines cell behavior, and I think it was appropriate that this exploration should have been undertaken in the land of Descartes, where logic is admired above all else. The first step was to isolate bacterial mutants that showed abnormal regulation of the synthesis of the lactose-cleaving enzyme β-galactosidase—for example, mutants that could not switch on synthesis in the presence of lactose or that synthesized the enzyme the whole time whether lactose was present or not. To describe how these mutants were analyzed, I have to say something about genetic *maps* (namely, the order in which genes are arranged in the DNA molecule), although it is not necessary to understand the technology of genetic mapping in order to understand how genes are regulated, so you may choose to skip the next two paragraphs.

In the previous chapter I briefly mentioned the phenomenon of recombination, which is the process of exchange that can occur between identical or almost-identical DNA molecules. A lot of recombination (between the paternal and maternal members of each pair of chromosomes) occurs during the formation of our germ cells, and this ensures that new genes (new sequences arising by mutation) are not only tested in combination with the neighboring genes in their chromosome of origin but also have a chance of being tested in combination with whatever genes are in the corresponding chromosome that came from the other parent. Bacteria have only one copy of each gene (contained within a single chromosome), so they have to use other methods to put new gene combinations to the test. One way is by a version of sexual reproduction, in which one bacterium (the male) passes over a copy of his chromosome to another (female) member of the same species; this chromosome then undergoes recombination with the female's chromosome. In addition, some strains of bacteria can take up DNA from dead cells and, if it proves to come from their own species, will allow this DNA to recombine with the appropriate region of their own chromosome. (This is the phenomenon of bacterial transformation which allowed Avery to discover that genes are made of DNA.) A third route for transfer of genes between bacteria is via certain bacterial viruses that can package bits of bacterial DNA along with or instead of their own DNA. Some of these viruses have developed a complex form of symbiosis with their bacterial hosts, and they are the villains that spread around the genes for antibiotic resistance among the bacteria that infect humans. Each of these forms of gene transfer—bacterial mating, bacterial transformation, and transfer by viruses—can be used to work out the exact order of the genes within a stretch of DNA.

For example, the complete transfer of an entire chromosome, from a male *E. coli* to a female, takes about 2 hours. At any time during this period, vigorous shaking will separate the mating couple when only part of the chromosome has been transferred. By shaking at different times after mating, it is possible to determine the order of the genes on the bacterial chromosome. If a pair of genes are seldom separated by shaking, they must lie close together in the bacterial chromosome. For example, if you interrupt mating between a male who is resistant to some antibiotic and is able to use lactose and a female who is sensitive to that antibiotic and is unable to use lactose (e.g., because of a mutation affecting her gene for β-galactosidase), you might find that every female who acquires antibiotic resistance also acquires the ability to use lactose, and you would then know that the two genes must be fairly close together; alternatively they might never go across together, or they might prove to be partially linked. In this way, by looking at lots of different genes, it is possible to build up a rough map of the bacterial chromosome. For the finer details, you would turn to the transfer of genes by small bits of DNA or by viruses. For example, if the gene for antibiotic resistance and the gene for lactose fermentation usually went together in a bacterial transformation experiment you would know that they must lie very close together on the bacterial chromosome, because the pieces of DNA used in such experiments are only about one-thousandth the size of the whole chromosome.

Using such techniques, Jacob and Monod were able to produce an accurate map of the region of the *E. coli* chromosome concerned with the use of lactose as an energy source, which is known as the *lac operon*. This allowed them to dissect the system into its component parts and find out how it worked (figure 3.6).

As mentioned earlier, when lactose is present *E. coli* makes β-galactosidase and lactose permease. The genes for these two proteins lie next to each other, and their positions were worked out by determining the map position of mutations that affected one or other of these two enzymes. The two genes are transcribed (by the RNA polymerase) into a single mRNA molecule, which starts at the left end of the β-galactosidase gene and extends beyond the right end of the permease (again, it is customary, in simple cases like this, to arrange the diagram of a gene and its surroundings so that the gene, like our writing, is shown as being transcribed from left to right). The ribosomes translate this message in the same direction, but occasionally drop off as they pass the stop signs at the end of the β-galactosidase open reading frame; as a result, the cell makes more β-galactosidase than permease—a very sensible arrangement because it does not need as much permease.

Just to the left of the start codon for the β-galactosidase gene there is a region (a sequence of about forty base pairs) that binds RNA polymerase and sets it up to start transcribing the sequence to the right of it into mRNA. Mutations in this region, called the *promoter* region, therefore prevent both genes from being transcribed. (There is also a terminator region quite a way to the right of the permease gene which stops mRNA synthesis, but the features of that region are not important for this story.)

Transcription is regulated by the product of another gene, called the *repressor*, which is just to the left of the regions I have been describing. The repressor gene is responsible for the synthesis of a protein, called the *lac* repressor, which specifically binds to a twenty base pair sequence, called the *operator* region slightly to the right of the promoter region. This blocks transcription because it stops the RNA polymerase from getting onto the DNA. The repressor protein is able to act as a controlling element because it has a special binding site for lactose. When this site is occupied by a lactose molecule, the protein changes its shape slightly and as a result is no longer able to attach to DNA; this then exposes the promoter region and allows the RNA polymerase to make messenger RNA. To repeat, in the absence of lactose the repressor protein blocks transcription; in the presence of lactose, the repressor binds lactose, changes its shape, and falls off the DNA. So the repressor controls the synthesis of β-galactosidase.

As I mentioned at the outset of this section, there are two requirements for the synthesis of β-galactosidase—the presence of lactose and the absence of anything better (namely glucose). This second level of control is achieved by another controlling protein (called the CAP protein). Unlike the repressor protein, which exercises a *negative* control because it inhibits transcription when it is bound to DNA, the CAP protein has a *positive* effect. In the absence of glucose it binds to a region of about twenty base pairs just to the left of the promoter region, and its presence in some way helps RNA polymerase to bind to the promoter. Of course, lactose is just one of many sources of energy that the bacterium will not bother to use if glucose is present. So *E. coli* has put a CAP protein binding site just to the left of the promoter for each of the many genes involved in the use of these other sources of energy.

What then controls the transcription of the genes for the repressor and the CAP protein gene? Who controls the controllers? The answer is that they are not controlled but are transcribed at a slow and steady rate which, in the case of the repressor, is sufficient to give each bacterium an average of about ten molecules of repressor protein at all times. This concentration of ten per bacterium is enough to ensure that, in the absence of lactose, the operator region is blocked by one or another of the repressor molecules nearly all the time so that RNA polymerase very seldom gets the chance to leap in and produce a mRNA molecule. This is an extremely efficient system; in the absence of lactose, there is occasional transcription and as a result the average *uninduced* cell contains a few molecules of β-galactosidase; in the presence of lactose and absence of glucose, transcription occurs at a high rate and the induced cell quickly acquires several thousand molecules of β-galactosidase.

I have given here just the bare bones of what is a beautifully designed system of control. As was so often the case in the history of molecular

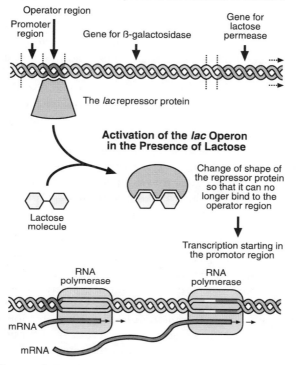

Repression of the *lac* Operon in the Absence of Lactose

Figure 3.6. The regulation of expression of the genes of the *lac* operon (which is concerned with the use of the sugar lactose). When an RNA polymerase transcribes the genes coding for the proteins that handle lactose it starts at a special sequence ("the promoter region") just to the left of the genes, and it moves from there along the DNA transcribing one of the strands into messenger RNA. In the absence of lactose, it cannot attach to the promoter sequence because a regulatory protein (the *lac* repressor) is bound to a special sequence (the operator region) just to the right of the promoter region. But when lactose is present, it alters the shape of the *lac* repressor so that the protein is no longer able to attach itself to the operator region, and this then allows the RNA polymerase to attach to the promoter region and start transcription. So the control of transcription depends on an "allosteric" change in shape of the repressor brought about by lactose.

biology, the detailed study of a single phenomenon (in this case, the control of lactose utilization) enormously increased our understanding of the behavior of all living things. For example, we can now see why, when a cell has two different copies of a gene, one of them may be dominant (as Mendel put it) and the other is recessive. Consider a cell that has two entire copies of the system I have just described (usually bacteria have only one copy, but they can be made to have two). If one of two copies of the gene for β-galactosidase were damaged by mutation, this mutation will hardly be noticed (will be "recessive") because the other copy would still be there, ready to be induced by lactose. Similarly, if a mutation damaged one of the repressor genes so that it could not bind to the operator region, this too might not be detected (would be recessive) because the other copy would still be there, and so the cell would still contain enough repressor to control both copies of the system. However, a mutation in the operator region of one of the β-galactosidase genes that stopped it interacting with repressor would be dominant because it would prevent the blockage of transcription, so the cell would make β-galactosidase whether lactose were present or not. Similarly, a mutation in the repressor gene that stopped the repressor from interacting with lactose would be dominant, because such a repressor cannot be pulled off the operator by lactose, so the transcription of both copies of the β-galactosidase gene would be blocked. Those few examples show that if you understand any given system of gene control and the function of the gene that is being controlled, it is easy to work out which mutations will be dominant and which will be recessive. At last Mendel's words dominant and recessive cease to be daunting abstractions and instead become perfectly straightforward descriptions of the various types of interactions that can occur in gene regulation and expression.

The other piece of illumination to come out of the study of lactose utilization in *E. coli* lay in the behavior of the repressor. Here we have a protein whose function depends on its ability to assume two shapes. In the absence of lactose, it binds very strongly to a particular base sequence in DNA (the lactose operator sequence); but a different part of the repressor can bind a molecule of lactose, and this results in a change in a slight shape of the protein so that it can no longer bind to the operator. The repressor protein is therefore acting as a communicator (*signal transducer*), allowing the cell to respond appropriately to the presence of lactose. Jacques Monod called this switch of a protein between two possible shapes *allostery*, from the Greek words meaning changing shape.

Since then a huge array of allosteric effects have been observed (figure 3.7), sometimes affecting (as in this case) the binding of proteins to DNA, sometimes the activity of enzymes, and sometimes just the choice between binding one thing and binding another. Hemoglobin very sensibly binds oxygen most efficiently when the concentration of carbon dioxide is low, but it slightly changes its shape and releases the oxygen when it meets the carbon dioxide and lactic acid produced by muscle cells. The physical movement of proteins is achieved by allosteric changes; for example, as I type this chapter, the myosin molecules in my muscle cells are undergoing a repetitive cycle of change in shape. The

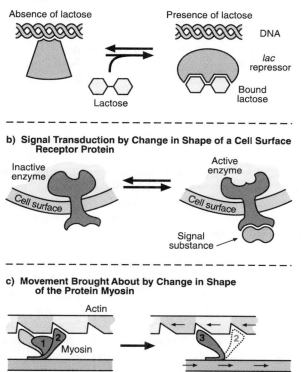

a) Gene Regulation by Change in Shape of the *lac* Repressor Protein

Absence of lactose   Presence of lactose

DNA

lac repressor

Bound lactose

Lactose

b) Signal Transduction by Change in Shape of a Cell Surface Receptor Protein

Inactive enzyme

Active enzyme

Cell surface

Cell surface

Signal substance

c) Movement Brought About by Change in Shape of the Protein Myosin

Actin

Myosin

Figure 3.7. Functions mediated by the changes in shape of certain proteins.

a. As described in the previous figure, the *lac* repressor controls expression of the genes concerned with the use of the sugar lactose by the bacterium *Escherichia coli.*

b. Signals can be transmitted to the interior of cells as the result of interaction between substances arriving at the cell surface with proteins that extend from the outside to the inside of the cell. For example, when insulin binds to the insulin receptor, the receptor changes shape and its inner section becomes an enzyme that can produce subtle changes in many intracellular proteins.

c. The protein called myosin is responsible for all movements of cells and of objects within cells, because it has three possible shapes and is able to act like a ratchet. The energy for its back-and-forth movement comes from its other activity, as an enzyme that breaks off a phosphate group from molecules of adenosine triphosphate.

myosin molecule is able to do work because the oscillation in its shape is achieved by binding a nucleotide triphosphate and then cutting off the terminal phosphate and liberating the disphosphate, so that part of the energy contained within this chemical bond is converted into movement. Much of the communication of cells with their environments is achieved by the allostery of certain proteins on their surface. Single protein molecules can extend right across the cell membrane; the inner aspects of these proteins, inside the cell, function as enzymes, and the outer parts act as the sensor for the presence of certain small molecules in the surrounding medium (just as the lactose repressor is a sensor for lactose-like molecules) and so any sudden change in the concentration of circulating signal substances will quickly be communicated to the inside of the cell, without the signal substance having to enter the cell.

Many other regulatory systems have been studied since those early days at the Pasteur Institute, and it turns out that the regulation of lactose utilization is somewhat exceptional in using a negative regulator (a protein that inhibits transcription). Much more common is positive regulation (like the regulation by the CAP protein), in which the regulatory protein actually helps the RNA polymerase start transcribing the regulated gene by slightly altering the configuration of the promoter region so that polymerase can bind to it more easily. When you come to think of it, negative regulation would be impossibly expensive in a cell as large as a mammalian cell, which can be 10,000 times larger than a bacterium; if *E. coli* needs ten lactose repressor molecules per cell to control the production of β-galactosidase, a mammalian cell would need 100,000 repressor molecules for each gene that had to be repressed.

Another factor comes into the design of gene regulation. The regulation of β-galactosidase synthesis is a simple issue; the bacterium makes it when lactose is present, unless there is something better to eat. But there are many genes that have to be under more complex control, and this is achieved by having, just to the left of the promoter, several binding sites for regulatory proteins; these regulatory proteins are often capable of interacting with each other so that each strengthens (or weakens) the other's bonding to DNA. This kind of elaboration is carried to great lengths in higher cells, where there are many more genes and a need for more complex systems of control: "Transcribe - this - gene - during - winter - especially - when - the - temperature - is - very - low - unless - of - course - you - have - recently - experienced - an - increase - in - light - (although - these - rules - must -be - overridden - whenever - there - has - been - DNA - damage)." Given the need for multiple layers of control, it is not surprising to find that the regions of DNA devoted to the control of many of our genes are much longer than the actual coding regions (open reading frames) that are being controlled.

At the moment we can be only dimly aware of the kinds of restraint imposed on the way cells preside over the expression and interaction of their many thousand genes. Here it is sufficient for me to mention one problem. Cells have to be prepared for good times and bad times, and for everything in between. Sometimes food is plentiful and then the race is on to grow as fast as possible. Eventually the population will find that food is running out. Every cell then starts to wind down its metabolism and settle into an existence where there is little gene expression, while it waits for the return of nutrients. Obviously the winding down (and later the winding up) of the expression of a multitude of genes has to occur in the right order. Furthermore, since starvation can come in many forms (being starved for energy, or starved for one or another of the essential nutrients, and so on), there has to be a right order for every occasion. And none of these orders must pass through any stage where the system is unstable. This last requirement may seem a bit obscure, but it is a problem that is well known to people who design computer software programs. Every new program will occasionally plunge the user into a totally unexpected limbo from which there is no return. As a result, for the first year or two the software manufacturer has to keep adding to the program various *ad hoc* controls that block off entry to these limbos. As more and more controls and refinements are added, the software becomes larger and larger.

This is presumably why all living creatures are so similar in the general design of their metabolism, the amino acid sequence of their proteins, and their systems of gene regulation. Once even the smallest level of complexity was achieved, a few billion years ago, there was no going back. I mention this level of subtlety as a way of emphasizing that, though we may know an astonishing amount about the general molecular biology of cells, we certainly cannot claim to be at all near to having the complete picture. That may come, once the DNA sequences of *E. coli* and of *Homo sapiens* have been determined, but I do not think it is going to come very quickly. For example, the virus that causes AIDS has only about 10,000 bases, but its whole program has not yet been deciphered in its entirety. If 10,000 bases can defeat the analytical skills of several billion dollars' worth of scientist-years, the million times as many bases present in a mammalian cell promise to occupy molecular biologists for a long time to come.

Returning to the present, the exact base sequence of the region of DNA concerned with *E. coli*'s use of lactose is now known. Already the rules governing protein synthesis are well enough known that any molecular biologist could look at that sequence, pick out the open reading frames and tell you the amino acid sequence of the proteins for which the region is responsible. In a few years, we will no doubt understand the rules that determine the exact shape and function of proteins from their amino acid sequence. At that point, it might be possible to deduce the function of the entire region (and the way it is controlled) simply from its base sequence.

   E. coli needs about 7,000 base pairs of DNA to allow it to use lactose as an energy source in a regulatable way; that is about half the number of words in this chapter. In total it has about 4 million base pairs and has genes for more than 4,000 different proteins, although at any moment it will probably be sampling less than 1,000 of these. The sequence of all this DNA could be known by the time I have finished this book. And in principle if not in practice we should be able, one day, to deduce exactly how *E. coli* works and lay bare all its skills, strategies, and capabilities. Certainly we can feel comfortable with our present, limited understanding of *E. coli* and of simpler creatures such as viruses. We are not at the moment confronted with any biological phenomenon that requires us to invoke the mysterious operation of the kind of vital force that was central to the beliefs of nineteenth-century biologists like Pasteur. Even though higher cells and multicellular organisms are vastly more complicated than bacteria, we know enough about genes and their regulation and their control by signal-sensitive proteins to feel that even the most complex systems, such as the mammalian brain, may be nothing more than a great elaboration of the various kinds of processes found in bacteria.

   This account of the mechanisms of molecular biology describes what had been discovered by about 1970. To summarize: The sequence of bases in DNA is transcribed into unstable mRNA molecules and from there is translated into the sequence of amino acids that make up each protein and uniquely determine its shape and function. To do all this, the cell has enzymes that can read and copy the base sequences of nucleic acids; it also has proteins that can read base sequence and thereby interact with nucleic acids and control the expression of genes and ensure that the various macromolecules of cells (nucleic acids and proteins) do not contain too many errors. Molecular biology, in short, is a clever way of converting a system of information in one dimension (stored in DNA) into a complex, continually changing three-dimensional system that responds appropriately to changes in the cell's environment and, most important, is capable of reproducing itself. The whole edifice had been deciphered, virtually in its entirety, within the space of a mere twenty-five years. Or so it seemed.

Certain Complications and Exceptions

During the early 1970s, techniques had been devised for determining the sequence of bases in long stretches of DNA, and out of this and the study of certain mammalian tumor viruses arose the astonishing discovery that the open reading frames of the genes of mammalian cells (and of some of the genes of their viruses) contained several long stretches of DNA that did not match the sequence of bases in their mRNA (or the sequence of amino acids in the resulting proteins). These extra stretches of DNA were called *introns* (because they had apparently been introduced from elsewhere) and the intervening stretches of coding DNA were therefore called *exons*. So the process of transcription in these cells turns out to have an extra step. Before a newly made mRNA is exported from the nucleus into the cytoplasm, all its introns have to be cut out (spliced out is the usual term, even though a splice is usually the act of joining rather than taking out). This step is carried out by small particles (spliceosomes) in the cell nucleus which, like the much larger ribosomes of the cytoplasm, contain both protein and RNA. (Interestingly, introns are present in the genes of higher nucleated cells but are very rare in the genes of bacteria and their viruses; perhaps bacteria, in their rush to grow as quickly as possible, have been under selection pressure to discard their introns, whereas nucleated cells were under pressure to become more and more complex and versatile.)

Naturally, there has been much speculation over the evolutionary advantages of such a system. It seemed to be an expensive luxury, because introns are usually much bigger than exons and so the cell is perpetuating sequences in its DNA that, at first sight, appeared to have no function. It is now clear, however, that proteins evolved into their present forms by the shuffling around of a limited number of blocks of amino acids, coded by exons and moving about by insertion between noncoding introns whose ends mark the sites for splicing. Such a system of modular construction has great versatility, as any architect will tell you. Once a useful stretch of amino acids has evolved, its coding sequence of bases can spread and bring an added role to the sequences for many different proteins. Indeed, we can see the residue of this history being re-enacted during embryogenesis, because the pattern of splicing of certain genes is known to change as cells in the embryo take on their adult form. Changes in the pattern of splicing are seen at their most extreme in the behavior of AIDS virus RNA. Although this virus contains only about 10,000 bases (i.e., is about half the length of Shakespeare's *Macbeth*), it manages to code for a wide range of different proteins because its pattern of splicing keeps changing, and furthermore it uses all three possible reading frames as well as both complementary sequences, one read in one direction and the other in the opposite direction.

The second surprise came in 1981, when certain mRNA molecules found in a protozoan were shown to undergo spontaneous splicing in a test tube, in the absence of any added protein. This led to the even more astonishing discovery that some quite small RNA molecules (in particular, the intron in the self-splicing mRNA) can act as enzymes. Some of them cut RNA molecules at specific sequences, some move nucleotides from the end of a chain and put them onto another chain, some can take free nucleotides and add them to an existing RNA molecule, and some can join amino acids together. Indeed, as the final *volte face*, it now seems likely that the assembly of amino acids into proteins is actually being accomplished by the RNA within each ribosome.

Among other things, this unexpected discovery goes a long way to solving a problem that had been looming large since the very beginnings of molecular biology. How on earth (and I mean this both literally and figuratively) could anything as complicated as the present system for protein synthesis have come into being? More than 200 different proteins are required, most of which appear to be absolutely essential if the system is to work at all. How could all these different kinds of protein come into existence at the same time?

The Origin of Living Systems

About 4 billion years ago the earth stopped being continuously bombarded with planetary debris and acquired a climate that was sufficiently benign to be compatible with living systems. The most ancient fossils found so far are bacteria dating from about 3.5 billion years ago. This suggests that the entirety of the molecular biology that I have described in the previous pages originated over a period of less than a billion years. This is a rather disturbing conclusion. I for one would have guessed that the jump from nothing to bacteria should have taken much longer than the jump from the age of bacteria to the emergence of mammals. But I suppose it is imagineable that the early stages occurred relatively quickly, and then the whole process slowed down as it came up against the instability of the earth's climate. (The alternative idea—that life actually originated somewhere else, before the earth came into being—is an easy way out, but its very easiness should make us unwilling to embrace it without a bit of a struggle.)

Numerous experiments have shown that, before the first appearance of life, the earth's surface would already have contained a fairly rich mixture of the building blocks for nucleic acids and proteins. If you prepare a mixture of substances like hydrogen cyanide, ammonia, formaldehyde, and so on (all of which are likely to be present in any environment containing carbon dioxide and nitrogen), and bombard the mixture with electric discharge (to simulate lightning), this will lead to the formation of several kinds of amino acids plus the bases found in nucleic acids. So the main question about the origin of life concerns the jump between this and the first self-replicating molecule. Until some molecule originates that can reproduce itself, nothing has been accomplished.

As long as replication was seen as the sole preserve of polymerases made of protein, it was really impossible to imagine any way of getting life going. Two classes of protagonists had to be invented at the same time, each of which could exist only if the other had already been created. But as soon as enzymatic RNA was discovered, the problem was greatly simplified. The jump from a solution of nonliving precursors to a solution that contains a small self-replicating RNA molecule is still difficult to imagine (and certainly has not been re-enacted in the laboratory) but it definitely is not unimaginable.

For a molecule to have some complex property such as the ability to replicate itself, it has to have a well-determined shape. Enzymes work because they have specially shaped sites of attachment for their target molecules, and their function depends on their shape. Because the interactions between the side groups of the different amino acids are not very strong, chains of amino acids do not readily coil up into stable three-dimensional structures unless they are quite long. (The main exceptions to this rule are found in the small polypeptides of about two dozen amino acids that are used by multicellular organisms as signaling substances which pass between neighboring cells. In these cases it is usual to find a high concentration of the amino acid cysteine, which helps to hold the chain in a tight coil because cysteines in different parts of the chain are able to make a chemical bond between their sulfur atoms.)

Because of the structural instability of the average short chain of amino acids, it seems very unlikely that any protein large enough to have the definite structure required for enzyme activity could arise by the chance joining together of just the right sequence of amino acids. By comparison, even quite short nucleic acid strands can fold back on themselves and make stable three-dimensional structures; after all, tRNA molecules contain about eighty bases but this is enough to give each of them a unique shape that can be recognized by the enzymes that join the right amino acids to the right tRNA molecules.

At the moment, it is not clear what is the smallest length of RNA that could have a chance of managing its own replication. The best characterized naturally occurring RNA enzyme has 377 bases, but probably only a small minority of these are specifically required for its enzymatic activity. The search is on for smaller molecules that can act as enzymes, and several people have set up artificial systems that generate random sequences and then test them for biological activity. You can think of these as experiments designed to recapitulate one of the steps in the origin of life, and they may eventually show us what was the most likely path followed when life first originated.

Once the first self-replicating nucleic acids had arisen, the process of natural selection would ensure the continual addition of more and more refinements that increased the efficiency and speed of the process. Other species of molecule (such as sequences of amino acids) might have been found to contribute some special attribute to the overall process, and at this point it becomes easy to imagine that parts of now rather long RNA molecules would become concerned with replication while other parts were attached to accessory molecules (made by the RNA) that increased the efficiency of the whole process. For example, the ability of a self-replicating RNA to join amino acids together would confer an advantage to that RNA if the proteins it made were able to cooperate in any of its activities (this would be the origin of the ribosomal RNA which, to this day, remains responsible for the synthesis of all proteins). Thanks to the need to perform several different roles, RNA would come to be divided into coding sequences and self-replicating sequences, and this could account for the origin of exons and introns. Once an enzyme emerged that could copy a sequence of ribonucleotides into a complementary strand of deoxyribonucleotides and subsequently copied the DNA back into RNA, it might bring some survival advantage simply because polymers made of deoxyribonucleotides are more stable. And at that point, DNA would have been invented.

The Origin of Structure

One major, and much later, step in the evolution of complex forms of life was the invention of compartments. The rate of any chemical reaction depends on the concentration of the ingredients taking part in the reaction. An enzyme whose function is to join substance A to substance B has to wait until it can grab hold of a molecule of A and then has to wait for a molecule of B to come within reach. The higher the concentration of A and B, the faster it will work. The rate of synthesis of a molecule like RNA will be greatly slowed down if any one of the four precursors (the four bases) is in low concentration. This principle would apply to all the chemical reactions going on in the earliest self-replicating systems. As the systems became more complicated, the number of essential ingredients increased. Each of these ingredients had to be in reasonably high concentration in order for the system to grow fast enough to outstrip the natural rate of degradation of the self-replicating molecules. So there would be a huge advantage for any system that somehow managed to contain all the ingredients within a limited space.

As soon as compartments were invented, biology could become much more complicated because living systems could maintain within these small compartments an adequately high concentration of all the ingredients for a multitude of different chemical reactions; exactly the same principle is used in the cylinders of an automobile engine, which compress the mixture of gasoline and air before igniting it, to ensure that the resulting explosive interaction between gasoline and oxygen proceeds at the greatest possible rate.

For a cell as small as a bacterium (which weighs about one-millionth of a millionth of a gram), the concentration of all ingredients is high enough to ensure that everywhere in the bacterium all reactions can proceed fairly quickly; for example, as mentioned earlier, ten molecules of the lactose repressor are enough to ensure that the operator region of the β-galactosidase gene keeps bumping into repressor molecules and is therefore repressed almost all the time. But when cells became much larger, the cost of maintaining every chemical reactant at a high concentration everywhere in the cell became too high (as pointed out earlier, ten repressor molecules is a fairly inexpensive way of controlling a gene, but this kind of negative regulation would be a huge investment for a cell 10,000 times larger). As cells became larger and more complex they had to compartmentalize themselves.

The most obvious compartment is the cell nucleus, which contains the cell's DNA. It is in the nucleus that the cell keeps all the ingredients for gene regulation, for DNA replication and repair and transcription, and for the excision of mRNA introns. Quite separate from all this is, as it were, the factory floor (the cytoplasm) where all the enzymes and structural components of the cell are made as well as all the precursors for every kind of synthesis.

But this division of larger cells into two major compartments was not enough to resolve the problem of size. Inevitably, in any large space, the chances that several reactants (e.g., enzymes and their targets) should all come together in a short space of time is rather small—which is why complex biological processes tend not to work very well when asked to perform in a test tube. So we find the emergence of another highly effective solution to the problem, namely a reduction in the number of dimensions.

There is an entrancing topological theorem which shows that a pair of objects moving about in a two-dimensional space will meet sooner or later, but they may never meet if they are in a three-dimensional space. This rather abstract vision becomes clearer if we consider the game of billiards. In one dimension there could be no contest; in two dimensions, it is a good game; in three dimensions, it would be almost impossible to score. It is therefore not surprising to find that larger cells have developed a folded internal membrane (called the endoplasmic reticulum) that creates a folded two-dimensional space, and it is within this space that the ribosomes conduct protein synthesis.

Later in evolution, cells acquired a more and more elaborate internal structure, made up of an ever-increasing number of separate, specialized

compartments. The next step was, of course, the development of collaborating groups of cells, and then finally the specialization of individual
cells within the group, which is found in most of today's multicellular
organisms.

The more recent steps in this sequence are not much in doubt. The
outlines of the family tree that connects the different forms of life present on the earth today are now fairly obvious. Similar enzymes made of
almost identical sequences of amino acids can be found scattered
throughout all branches of the living kingdom, and by looking at the way
variations in the sequence of bases and amino acids of similar genes are
distributed among today's species, it is possible to start figuring out how
the different orders and species are related to each other. The exercise
is just like working out the evolutionary tree for the different branches of
the Indo-European family of languages from the relationships of words
and grammatical construction, or working out the past migrations of
populations around the Mediterranean from the frequency of the different blood groups.

The absolute time scale for these events has been derived in a variety
of ways. The simplest to understand is the process of dating by radioactive decay. For example, one common radioactive element is potas-
sium-40. This has a half-life of 1,300 million years and decays into argon-
40, which is stable. When molten material in the earth congeals into
rock, it will not initially contain any argon, because argon is a gas and will
have been expelled from the molten material. But it will contain some
potassium-40, and the argon formed by the decay of this potassium will
be trapped in the rock. Therefore you can determine the age of a rock
by measuring the amount of potassium and argon contained within it. If
you find a fossil in this rock, it must represent a creature that existed
before the rock congealed. On a shorter time scale, the age of biological
materials can be determined by measuring what proportion of their carbon is carbon-14, which has a half-life of about 6,000 years and therefore
is gradually lost with the passage of time.

Measurements like these give us a rough chronology for the various
components of the earth's surface, including its fossils. The more recent
parts of the family tree (phylogenetic tree) of the living creatures on the
earth's surface had been roughly worked out by the end of the nineteenth century, simply by looking at the similarities in form, but the fine
details of the family tree are now known much more precisely thanks to
the study of the sequence changes in proteins and nucleic acids that
have occurred. Some common proteins or parts of proteins have turned
out to be insensitive to changes in amino acid sequence, and the regions
of DNA coding for these proteins accumulate base changes at a steady
rate of about one per billion base pairs per cell division (or one amino

acid changed per protein every 200,000 years). If you compare the amino acid sequence of proteins found in, say, humans and chimpanzees, you can get a fairly good idea of how many hundreds of thousands of years have elapsed since the life and times of our shared ancestor. And this kind of analysis can be extended to show that all living creatures are part of a single family tree.

Summary

Because molecular biology is so complicated, I have had to abandon in this chapter the historical approach used in the previous chapters and just lay out the facts as clearly as I can. For this reason, I have not given references within the text. Anyone who wants to know more can easily go straight from this book into a textbook such as *The Molecular Biology of the Cell* by Alberts and others (Garland Press, London 1994).

Inevitably, I have given many of my readers rather more than they feel they need to know, and this is because I know perfectly well that it is common practice to skip rather than read every paragraph from beginning to end. But even the most casual flip through this chapter should leave the reader with two important ideas: We now more or less understand how living systems work, and we are beginning to understand how life originated. Naturally, many of the pieces are missing and astonishing discoveries are no doubt just around the corner. But it seems likely that within the next fifty years someone will have found a way of re-enacting the origins of life under laboratory conditions. We can choose to give one or more gods the credit for creating the universe. But that may be all. Once our universe existed, it can be argued that origin of life was inevitable.

～～

The molecular biology that I have described in the last two chapters was worked out almost entirely by studying unicellular creatures such as viruses, bacteria, and yeasts. Judging from certain fossilized bacteria, unicellular biology had emerged within about a billion years after the earth cooled down. During the next 3 billion years, evolution produced more complicated forms of life, in particular the multicellular systems of plants and animals. The basic molecular biology remained unchanged, but now there were opportunities for specialization and collaboration between different types of cell within a single organism. Complex systems evolved that put each cell's behavior partly under the control of the other members of the group. In the last twenty years or so, we have started to understand the molecular biology of cell-cell interactions, and this is coming about in much the same way that the molecular biology of single cells was worked out. In chapter 2, I described how the study of human pneumonia seventy years ago led eventually to the discovery that genes are made of DNA. History is now repeating itself. In the last twenty years, the study of cancer cells has shown how cells communicate with each other and (more important) how signals from a cell's neighbors can modulate its entire pattern of behavior, even down to the level of the activity of its enzymes. So the next chapter looks at the subject of experimental cancer research.

CHAPTER 4

Cancer and the Molecular Biology of Multicellular Systems

In 1970 I found myself having to learn about cancer research. The reason was somewhat unusual. For five years I had been director of The Cold Spring Harbor Laboratory in Long Island, at the time of its greatest financial insecurity. Although the combined efforts of several people managed to extricate the Laboratory from its mountainous debts and set it up with a reasonable cash reserve, the struggle had left our family with no house and with capital of only a few thousand dollars. Our two sons had graduated from college and now wanted to go to medical school, and our daughter needed support for graduate work in statistics at the London School of Economics. Because the cost of higher education is far less in England than in the United States, we moved across the Atlantic and I accepted a job with The Imperial Cancer Research Fund in London.

As a result of the decline in the infectious diseases at the end of the nineteenth century, cancer has become a major cause of death and an important target of research. Already by 1970 the literature had become enormous. As it happened, 1970 was about the time the subject was invaded by the molecular biologists, and so my position at the Imperial Cancer Research Fund gave me a ringside seat for the clash between the old and the new.

Any account of experimental cancer research written in the 1990s will no doubt have the same kind of inadequacies as accounts of infectious disease written at the beginning of the twentieth century. Even so, the subject is the natural continuation from an introduction to molecular biology, because it deals with the next level of complexity. Classical molecular biology was concerned with the behavior of individual cells; cancer research is concerned with defects in the special mechanisms that control the interactions of cells in multicellular creatures.

❧❧

Cancer

In a sense, cancer is a fairly straightforward disease. Most cells in the body are capable of rapid multiplication when called upon, but normally they are under strict control. Occasionally, however, a cell arises that manages to evade its controlling network of instructions, starts multiplying, and produces a little localized family of abnormal descendants. This level of abnormality is fairly common. By the time we reach old age, most of us will have acquired a fairly extensive patchwork of visible defects such as freckles and warts (our internal organs contain similar abnormalities, but we are unaware of most of these). Very rarely, a cell and its descendants acquire the ability to grow out beyond the confines of their normal territory and to spread throughout the body. When this happens the abnormal cells are said to have formed a cancer. Fortunately, this next level of abnormality is much less common.

The forces of natural selection have ensured that each species, including *Homo sapiens*, is fairly well protected against cancer for the duration of its usual life-span, and it is only when life-span is unnaturally extended that cancer becomes a major hazard. Animals in the wild seldom get cancer because they do not live long enough. But when they are domesticated or kept protected in a zoo, they survive into old age and then cancer becomes quite common. Roughly one-third of all humans who reach old age will have produced a cancerous family of cells at some time in their life, and this is now the cause of about 20 percent of all deaths in the long-lived populations of the world.

The disease is such an oppressive threat at the end of our lives that most biologists must have wondered at some time whether their own work would illuminate the nature of cancer. Many advances in the biological sciences have been hailed as a possible contribution to its cure, but so far the results have not matched people's expectations. In fact, the flow of information has usually been in the other direction, from cancer research into general biology. One of the most remarkable features of experimental cancer research has been the way it has, in the past 100 years, repeatedly opened up fields of research that are interesting in their own right. At the end of the nineteenth century, it was the study of certain infectious tumors (for example, the kind of warts that are common in children, and an infectious leukemia of chickens) that led to the discovery of some of the first viruses known to infect animals. Microscopic studies of cancer cells revealed that they often contain abnormal chromosomes; since cancers grow because each cancer cell hands on its abnormality in behavior to its descendants, this was one of the important pieces of evidence, discovered early in the twentieth century, that inherited characteristics are carried by chromosomes. Attempts to transplant tumors from one animal to another (or from one human to another) were largely unsuccessful, but this failure led to the discovery of the special section of the immune system, called cellular immunity, which protects us from certain infectious agents and from being invaded by other people's cells; and this in turn led to the discovery of blood groups which, in turn, made blood transfusion possible. Attempts to breed lines of mice with raised susceptibility to various kinds of cancer led to the discovery of the genes for what are called histocompatibility antigens, and this has made organ transplants possible.

This flow of information from cancer research into basic biology has continued all through the twentieth century. Although study of the molecular biology of cancer has not yet laid bare the causes of most cancers or produced a cure, it has enormously increased our understanding of the molecular biology of mammalian cells. Indeed, many of the techniques used in what is called genetic engineering were originally developed for the study of cancer cells.

The previous chapter described how the 1960s saw the gradual beginnings of the understanding of gene regulation. Before the coming of molecular biology, no one had the slightest idea how cells knew what they should be doing; indeed, many biologists felt that this would never be known. But by the 1970s it had become clear that the behavior of cells is primarily governed by control of gene expression and the interactions of proteins.

It should have been obvious to everyone that cancer represents a defect in the functioning of the genes concerned with the regulation of cell growth and territoriality, and that an understanding of cancer would require an understanding of gene regulation. But cancer research was predominantly in the hands of the medical profession, who knew little molecular biology or experimental embryology, and it was not easy for them to accept the idea that the study of gene regulation and the control of cell division in creatures like bacteria and yeasts could illuminate the behavior of cancer cells. I well remember the scorn that was heaped on our heads when we introduced into our cancer research laboratories a group studying the social interactions of an ameba. As the quotation from Julian Huxley indicates (page 72), unicellular animals were regarded as inferior beings and not capable of telling us anything about the organization and diseases of higher animals.

Before tracing the sequence of discoveries that showed which genes are involved in the formation of cancers, I should first discuss the rules that govern the behavior of the individual cells within a multicellular animal.

The Development of Multicellular Creatures

The characteristic form and behavior of a complex multicellular creature is achieved by the precise programs that govern the way its cells multiply and take on specialized functions. This is particularly evident in plants. Each species of plant has a characteristic type of leaf and a characteristic arrangement of leaves on its branches. In one species the leaves come in pairs, in another they may alternate or be arranged in a spiral around the branch. Because the roots and branches of plants are created by the multiplication of a few cells at the tip (apex) of each growing shoot, the precise form of each plant is a reflection of the rules that govern the multiplication and development of these *apical* cells. In one species the cells undergo several divisions and then produce a specialized, leaf-forming daughter cell to the left, quickly followed by another to the right; this whole program is then repeated again and again so that the leaves arise opposite each other, with a space between each successive pair of leaves. Other plants have different programs. Look at any plant and you can deduce what, roughly, must have been its program.

Plants are therefore showing us that cells have fairly precise ways of counting divisions and of timing the production of descendants with specialized functions (a process called *differentiation*). In fact, such programs do not just cover division and specialization, but also involve what is called *programmed cell death*. A tree is able to drop its fruit because a ring of cells around the stalk are programmed to die when the fruit is ripe. In autumn, deciduous trees withdraw much of the nutrients in their leaves and then shed the leaves by a similar mechanism. These are active processes. A tree that dies in summer does not drop its fruit or shed its leaves.

Like plants, animals develop by a combination of cell division, cell differentiation, and cell death. The process tends to be less conspicuous, because so much of our form is determined before we are born. The dividing cells in plants tend to be near the growing tips of leaves and shoots, and as a result of their repeated cycles of cell division they are pushed farther away from the main body of the plant, leaving behind their descendants (figure 4.1b); so the past cell lineage of a plant remains permanently on display. (The grasses are an exception; their dividing cells lie at the base of the leaf, and that is why grass can survive being continually cropped by grazing animals.)

The dividing cells in an adult animal lie beneath the surface, and it is not them but their descendants that are pushed away (and are eventually discarded) (figure 4.1a). But animals can turn on a display that is quite as exotic as anything achieved by plants. For example, feathers and hairs have been molded by selection to serve a multitude of purposes—

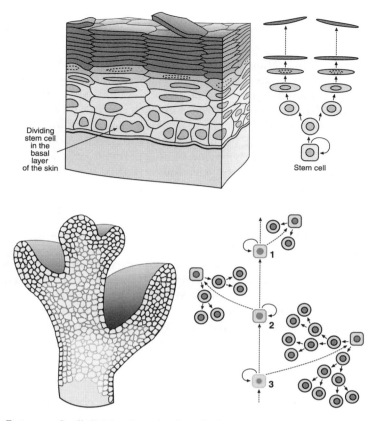

Figure 4.1. Patterns of cell division in animals and plants.

Top: In the simplest form of animal skin, cell renewal is the result of division of cells in the deepest layer of skin. This pushes daughter cells up into the more superficial layers. There they embark on their program of development, which consists of loss of their nucleus and the synthesis of the insoluble proteins of skin (keratin). Finally, the cells are reduced to thin flakes of keratin and are shed from the surface. Each dividing cell in the deepest layer contributes to a single column of developing cells.

The arrangement of cells in the skin is shown on the left. A diagram of the lineage is shown on the right, where the founder cell or local matriarch (called the "stem" cell) is shown as a square and its developing descendants as circles. Each time the stem cell divides, one of the daughter cells undergoes development and the other takes on its mother's role as the stem cell for the next division.

Bottom: The growth of plants is the result of the division of a group of special "stem" cells in what is called the apical meristem, which lies just below the growing tip. The direction of growth is, in a sense, the opposite of that in skin because here it is the stem cell that is pushed outward by the accumulation of its descendants (the grasses are an exception because their stem cells lie at the base of the leaves, which is why grass can survive being continually cropped by grazing animals and mowing machines).

The arrangement of the growing tip is shown on the left, for the simplest case, where the leaves alternate between left and right; usually the program is much more complicated than this, with the plane of division of the stem cells steadily rotating, so that the petals, leaves, and stalk form a complex three-dimensional array. A diagram of the kind of lineage that could produce a simple left-right arrangement is shown on the right. For a pattern like this to arise, it is necessary that the apical meristem can count the number of divisions it has undergone and is aware of the three-dimensional arrangement of its surroundings.

aerodynamics, insulation, flotation, camouflage, advertisement—and consequently they come in a bewildering variety of shapes and sizes. Each feather was extruded as the result of the multiplication of cells in the feather follicle, deep within the skin; each survives for a few months or years, serves its function and then, like a leaf in autumn, is thrown away. The precise form of a feather is therefore a reflection of the program that governed the behavior of the pigment cells and growing feather cells in the feather follicle. Knowing this, it is hard not to be overwhelmed by the complexity of even the simplest of feathers, let alone the perfectly ordered arrangement of all the different kinds of feather that are present in a bird's wing.

I have picked these everyday examples to make the point that we can learn a lot about patterns of gene expression just by looking around us. Although the discoveries of molecular biology were made in a microscopic world not visible to the naked eye, they have totally changed our way of looking at the visible world. When we now consider the lilies of the field or the fearful symmetry of the tiger, we have the added pleasure of knowing that the lilies and the tiger are giving us a glimpse of how they grew and came to be arrayed like this.

The Generation of Diversity

We can think of the development of a human being as a huge family tree that starts off with a single progenitor, the fertilized egg, and ends up with about 10 million million cells, comprising hundreds of types of cell. Studies of the development of certain simple multicellular animals have shown that each new type of cell tends to arise in a predetermined part of the animal's family tree and at a fixed time in the growth of the embryo. It is as if at various moments in embryogenesis, certain cells decide to undergo a permanent change in behavior and appearance (i.e., decide to undergo a drastic change in their pattern of gene expression).

Instances are known where such decisions seem to be the result of some strictly internal program; to take an extremely simple example, the progenitor cell of a microscopic, freshwater animal called *Volvox* undergoes four divisions, to make sixteen cells, and then one of these becomes the progenitor for the next animal, while the other fifteen go on to make the hundred or so cells that comprise the body of the current animal. Usually a cell's decision to differentiate seems to be triggered by some stimulus coming from outside. In other words, it is attributable to nurture rather than nature—to something in the cell's environment rather than its birthright—and in a moment I shall mention some examples in vertebrate development where the behavior of cells is plainly being determined by signals coming from their neighbors.

The molecular biology of differentiation is understood in only a few very simple cases. For example, when the going gets tough certain species of bacteria form impervious spores that, like the seeds of many plants, are encased in a hard container which protects the bacterium's DNA from even the most hostile environments. The process of spore formation starts with an asymmetric division which produces two bacteria. One of the daughter cells undergoes an inversion of a stretch of its DNA that puts a powerful promoter just upstream of a special set of normally silent genes whose products are used to make a spore.[1] As a result of this inversion, the cell will eventually die, but before it dies it produces all the proteins needed for spore formation, and these are then passed over to the unchanged sister and turn her into a spore, which will live to grow another day.

Equally drastic processes may be going on during the development of animals; for, in a few simple cases where it has been possible to analyze the entire family tree of an embryo, some steps in the build-up of the embryo are seen to be accompanied by the programmed death of one of a pair of sister cells. Nevertheless, it is clear that many of the cells present in multicellular animals retain a virtually complete and accessible set of the genes that were present in the fertilized egg. This is obviously true for many plants, as anyone will tell you who has grown a plant from the peelings of a potato or from a leaf stuck into the ground, but it has also been shown to be true for the cells of vertebrates. For example, if you replace the nucleus of a fertilized frog egg with a nucleus taken from the circulating red cell of an adult, the egg will develop normally at least up to the stage of making a tadpole.[2] So not only are all, or nearly all, the genes of a frog still present in the frog's red cell, but they are capable of being summoned back into action when returned to the conditions of early embryonic life.

The main way that cells are stimulated to embark on specialized programs is as the result of signals coming from their neighbors. The most obvious instance of this is the formation of identical twins. This results when the first division of a fertilized egg produces a pair of cells that happen to separate instead of staying next to each other; apparently, the lack of a companion makes each cell (or perhaps the first few descendants of each cell) temporarily block development and proceed to take on responsibility for making the entire embryo.

Numerous experiments have shown that when groups of cells are grafted from one part of an embryo to another, they tend to take on the behavior that is appropriate for their new location. This shows that their development is responding to *positional information*. For example, when the skin overlying the developing legs of embryonic chickens and ducks are exchanged, the grafted cells produce the kind of skin and claws that are appropriate for a foot, but the presence or absence of webbing between the toes proves to be determined by the deeper cells underlying

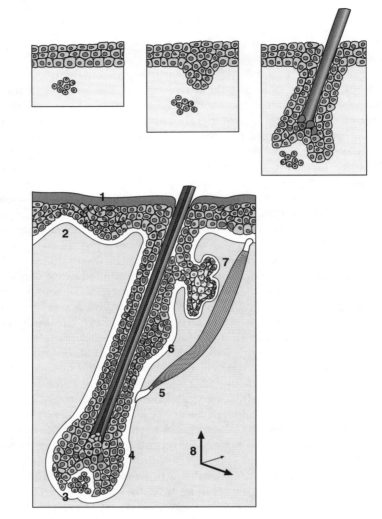

Figure 4.2. The development of a human hair.

Top: A small group of cells (the dermal papilla), underlying the skin, stimulate the overlying skin cells to grow inwards toward the papilla and then undergo a special program of development that produces the hair and various other structures.

Bottom: The final arrangement of the hair and its various appendages is dependent on the availability of *positional information*. Although the precise signals that convey this information are not known, we can deduce what kinds of information must have been present at some time or other during the formation of the hair, and these are numbered in this diagram.

1. The skin cells must be receiving signals from their immediate neighbors, because they will grow sideways and replace any lost areas of skin.
2. The ridges of the skin are determined by signals coming from beneath the skin, which is why you cannot permanently file away your fingerprints.
3. The cells in the dermal papilla apparently do not multiply during our adult life, but their presence (i.e., the signal they produce) ensures the existence

Figure 4.2 (*cont.*)

and periodic replacement of the hair follicle. If you kill the overlying skin with x-irradiation and then carry out a skin graft, the new skin will reform the kinds of hairs that were originally present.

4. Early in its development, the hair follicle must have been a source of signals, because it has to be colonized by pigment cells and nerve fibers migrating out from the nervous system.

5. Early in its development, the hair attracts muscle cells which then make a tiny muscle that attaches the hair to the skin. The muscle then receives a nerve fiber, and this allows your hair to stand on end when you are frightened.

6. A small group of cells on the muscle side of the follicle are set aside, and their role is to be the stem cells for the later replacement of the follicle and perhaps the nearby skin. These are probably the cells that are involved in the early steps leading to skin cancer.

7. A little further up the shaft of the hair, the skin cells are somehow stimulated to form the little sebaceous gland that accompanies every hair.

8. Last, this whole structure is oriented correctly with respect to the axes of the body; for example, the hairs on the backs of your hands and fingers all point toward the tips of your fingers or the little finger side of your hand. Because all tissues have to be aware of their orientation within the body, the three axes (up and down, fore and aft, starboard and port) are shown in the diagram.

the skin. In other words, the programmed death that removes the skin between the toes (the webs) of chickens must be the result of some signal sent by the underlying tissues of chickens (but not ducks) rather than a decision originating within the skin cells themselves. Incidentally, this experiment also shows that although the cells of ducks and chickens differ somewhat in their intrinsic programs, they can understand the instructions produced by each other's underlying cells.

Many of our surface features are determined by orders coming from deeper tissues. The transparency of the cells overlying the eye is developed as the result of signals coming from the eye as it buds out from the underlying brain. The arrangement of hairs and bristles, claws and feathers, is in the hands of special groups of underlying cells, even though the exact type of claw or feather is determined by the skin itself. The signals reaching these skin cells are apparently determining not only how much the cells are allowed to multiply but also which combination of proteins they make and, perhaps, which signals they themselves send forth (see figure 4.2).

To summarize, the generally accepted picture of the development of animals and plants is that the specialized behavior of each cell has been determined partly by its nurture (what signals it receives from its neighbors) and partly by its nature. For example, because it is in a particular point in the lineage of the cells in the bone marrow and position in the body (its nurture), the red cell precursor makes hemoglobin; because it is a duck cell (its nature), it makes duck hemoglobin, not chicken hemoglobin. For the purposes of cancer research, the most important rules of cell behavior are obviously those that govern cell division and territoriality.

Programs of Cell Division and Cell Death

Some cells in the body are not allowed to multiply at all. In the first few years of our lives, our nervous system has to adjust itself to match our environment, but this is done not by growing more nerve cells but by killing off the cells for which there turns out to be little or no use, and by enlarging the connectivity of those that are most used. Much of the wiring of the nervous system is therefore not developed until we come face to face with the outside world and discover what skills we are going to need and what skills we should put aside. It is because of this additional wiring and not because we gain any extra nerve cells that our brains increase in size during the first few years of our life. Similarly, muscle cells, once formed, are prohibited from any further multiplication; if you exercise regularly you will increase the size of your muscle cells, but you cannot increase their number. (It is perhaps because nerve and muscle cells do not multiply after we are born that adult humans never develop cancer of neurons or muscle.)

The cells in some internal organs such as the liver and our various endocrine glands retain the ability to divide but they do not do so unless the organ has been damaged and it is necessary to replace what has been lost. So the production of cancers in these organs usually requires some prolonged stimulus for the cells to divide.

The maintenance of many parts of the body involves a continual process of cell division and cell death. We are separated from the outside world by the layers of cells that coat our skin and gut wall, and these protect us from our surroundings partly because the cells directly exposed to the environment are all destined to be thrown away; in both skin and gut, the most superficial cells are being displaced outward and discarded as the result of the continual division of underlying cells. As an additional protection, the surface layers of skin cells (like the sister of the bacterial spore) are carrying out their own lethal program of development. As they approach the surface, they destroy their nucleus and devote their energy to making an insoluble protein called *keratin*. As a result, our skin is covered with an impenetrable, insoluble layer of protein that protects the underlying cells from physical and chemical injury. Similarly, the cells of the gut make their own kind of protective layer that stops the underlying cells from being destroyed by the digestive enzymes in our gut.

The other main sites of *cell turnover* are our blood-forming tissues (bone marrow and lymph nodes). These are responsible for producing a continual stream of cells that briefly circulate in the bloodstream and are then discarded or destroyed. Like the nervous system, our immune system is continually learning from experience. Unlike the nervous system, it does this by producing a new crop of special cells to cope with each new challenge from our environment; for example, the production of each new class of antibodies, made during our lifetime, is due to the selective proliferation of whichever family of immune cells makes the best antibody for dealing with each new challenge.

In each adult human, about 100,000 cells divide every second and 100,000 cells are destroyed. Not surprisingly, the majority of cancers arise among the populations of cells that are proliferating. We therefore have a particular reason to be interested in factors that alter the rate of this proliferation.

Cell-to-Cell Signaling

From a few simple facts, many of which are fairly obvious when you come to think about it, we can deduce a lot about the control of cell division. For example, we know from personal experience that when an area of our skin is destroyed by injury, the surrounding skin is immediately stimulated to grow and to cover over the exposed area. This tells us that the capacity of skin cells to multiply is somewhat held in check by signals coming from their close neighbors; when a skin cell's neighbors are lost it will set about replacing them. For skin, therefore, the controlling signals are local in origin.

In an organ like liver, however, it is not just the local arrangement of the liver cells that is important but also the total quantity of liver; if you remove most of the liver of an animal, the remaining liver cells start multiplying. This shows that liver cells are sensitive to signals that are somehow responding to the total size of the liver, not the local concentration. Similarly, the cells of the bone marrow increase their rate of division following blood loss, so they too are responding to some system that monitors the blood itself. The cells that produce hormones such as insulin and thyroxin are clearly subject to this kind of control. For example, if your diet is lacking in iodine, the thyroid cannot make the hormone thyroxine (an iodine-containing compound related to the amino acid tyrosine); certain cells in your pituitary detect the shortage of thyroxine and send out a signal for the thyroid cells to multiply, and that is why iodine deficiency gives you a goiter.

The easiest signals to study are those that circulate through the bloodstream. The first of these to be identified were called hormones, from the Greek word *hormôn* (meaning urging) because they are substances that urge cells into action. Some of the signals circulating in the bloodstream affect the behavior of many kinds of cells; growth hormone (from the pituitary gland), insulin (from the pancreas), thyroxine (from the thyroid), and the sex hormones (from testis and ovary) belong to this class. Other circulating hormones, such as the signal that triggers liver regeneration and the signal that regulates the production of red cells in the bone marrow, have specific targets; in other words, only a few kinds of cell carry on their surfaces the specific receptors for these signals.

But hormones are just the tip of the iceberg. By now, a very large number of local signal substances have been identified. Their precise chemistry is perhaps of less interest than their general manner of operation. In certain tissues, neighboring cells actually make connections (called gap junctions) that traverse their touching surfaces and allow small chemicals such as calcium atoms to pass directly from cell to cell. In the nervous system, cell-cell communication is achieved by brief bursts of signal substances that are released into the small space immediately surrounding the connections (synapses) between nerve cells; several such signaling substances are used, some of which have a positive effect on the recipient cell and some a negative effect, much in the way the output of a transistor or vacuum tube may affect positively or negatively the activity of the next one down the line.

Many signals are somewhat localized but work over rather longer distances. This is conspicuously true during the growth of the embryo. Cells, deep beneath the skin of the embryo, give forth signals that determine the behavior of the overlying skin. If you graft embryonic skin from one part of the embryo to another, it will proceed to develop according to the signals that come from the underlying tissues. For example, the nerve cells that are going to form the eye somehow tell the overlying skin cells to develop the special properties needed to make the lens of the eye. The kind of hair made in hair follicles (whether it is thick or thin, straight or curly) is determined by groups of cells deep beneath the skin that acquired their ability to instruct hair follicles quite early in embryogenesis. As I have mentioned already, during the development of a bird's foot the decision on whether it should keep or remove the skin between the digits (i.e, whether or not it will have webbed feet) is determined by signals sent to the skin cells by the underlying tissue.

Signal substances come in many forms, ranging from single atoms (such as calcium) and small molecules (such as nitrous oxide) to medium-sized molecules (such as the hormone thyroxine) and even full-sized proteins (such as insulin). When the spread of a signal is by diffusion and has to extend over long distances, the signaling cell may have to emit a very large number of signal molecules. For reasons of economy, therefore, long-range signals tend to be small molecules (e.g., a moth seeking a mate by means of a pheromone cannot afford to fill the forest air with very large molecules). When a message has to be continually changed or revised, the signal substance is arranged to be unstable. For example, the endings of signal-transmitting nerve cells produce various small molecules, and as soon as these have acted on the recipient cell they are destroyed by an enzyme so that, within a small fraction of a second, the receiving cell is ready to receive the next burst of signals. (Similarly, the searching moth must continually clear its receptors so that it can keep judging its progress.)

Perhaps the most important feature of chemical signaling is that it conveys *positional information*. The moth finds its mate by flying up the *concentration gradient* of pheromone, toward the source. It was thanks to the local concentration gradient of some signal substance that the cells in your developing arm knew which was the head end of the embryo, and that was why your arm developed the right way round. Our pigment cells (melanocytes) developed within our nervous system and migrated out from there to colonize our entire surface, and they were able to do this because they were programmed to move to regions with the lowest concentration of their own signal substance; this antisocial habit of pigment cells may perhaps contribute to the exceptionally rapid spread of the cancer called malignant melanoma.

The idea that chemical gradients control the spatial arrangement of the different parts of the body had been around for a long time. But it was hard to imagine how the concentration of just one kind of signal substance could determine the multitude of decisions that are needed to make something like a leg or a wing. And the mystery deepened with the discovery of certain extraordinary mutants of the fruit fly, *Drosophila*. Early in development, the fruit fly embryo, like the human embryo, becomes partitioned into segments. When the *Drosophila* larva develops into the adult fly, certain cells in each segment are responsible for producing the appropriate part of the fly—antenna, eye, wing, leg, and so on. Astonishingly, it turns out that the distinction between the segments depends on the functioning of very few genes (called *homeotic* genes). For example, if a fly has a defect in one of these genes (named antennapedia), it develops perfectly formed legs in place of its antennae; a defect in another gene makes the segment just behind the wing produce a second wing; and so on. The dozen or so homeotic genes (or, rather, the proteins that they encode) are somehow managing to control the exact pattern of behavior of all the millions of cells in their segments—how these cells will be arranged in space, how much they will multiply, and what proteins they will make. As it turns out, this is not a peculiarity of the development of insects. A similar limited set of homeotic genes is now known to control the development of mammals, and even of plants. Here, therefore, we are getting a glimpse of something unexpected about the molecular biology of multicellular creatures. If asked, I would have guessed that the distinction between a leg and antenna, or a petal and a leaf, would be rather like the difference between the word-processing program in a computer and the graphics program, and that the programs for leg and an antenna, petal and leaf, would each have to be assigned a large amount of disk space. But it seems that it is not like that. The products of a few special genes are somehow able to make a whole set of appropriate adjustments to the behavior of many different kinds of cell. Just in the last few years, the molecular biology of this kind of control has started to become clear, as the result of work on the molecular biology of cancer cells. But I am running ahead of myself, and I must postpone the rest of the story until later in the chapter.

This is an appropriate moment to summarize this section of the story. Thanks to the production of various signal substances early in development, each cell in the developing embryo is made continually aware of its orientation (which way is up and down, fore and aft, larboard and starboard) as the result of signals coming from its immediate neighbors; thanks to other signals, some of which work through homeotic genes, it has already been told what part of the embryo it is occupying, what structure it and its neighbors have to make, and what rules will govern its growth and division. In addition, it is monitoring its own internal environment and the integrity and proper functioning of its component parts; for example, it is constantly checking the integrity of its DNA. The response to this continual stream of information allows it to modulate its behavior, partly according to pre-set programs and partly to adjust for any unprogrammed chance events.

I have described the control of cell behavior in terms of the signals that pass between cells, but that was not the kind of introduction to cancer research given in most textbooks in the 1960s. Like the early studies of zoology and botany, or biochemistry and biophysics, cancer research had produced a huge array of undigested facts. Fifty years ago, textbooks of biochemistry gave a detailed description of intermediary metabolism, but could not say how enzymes worked or how cells knew which enzymes to make and how to make them. Thirty years ago, textbooks on the microscopic anatomy and pathology of human cancer could be inches thick, yet tell the reader almost nothing about what underlies the behavior of cancer cells. The experimental study of cancer had generated its own equally voluminous literature. These days, few people have the time to work their way through all this stuff. But I think there are often lessons to be learned from the histories of the various sciences. So I will now give a brief recapitulation of the early days of cancer research.

The History of Cancer Research

The first attempts to produce cancers in animals were based on what little was known about the causes of human cancers. The Industrial Revolution had resulted in large numbers of people being exposed to toxic substances that are not part of the normal human environment, and by the end of the nineteenth century, factory workers who were continually exposed to tars and oils had been observed to develop cancer in the exposed areas of skin. So it was natural to test the effects of these substances in animals. Most animals, however, have much thicker skins than humans, and the results were negative until the experimenters used rabbits and mice.[3] In the meantime x-rays, discovered by the German physicist Wilhelm Röntgen in 1895, had been shown to cause cancers in rats.[4] By the time of World War I, the list of procedures known to produce cancer in animals consisted of infection with certain viruses,[5] x-irradiation, and prolonged exposure of the skin to coal tar.

The emergence of the science of genetics quickly led to the suggestion that cancer, like the variegation of certain plants, is the result of mutations[6] arising during the cell multiplication that normally occurs in many tissues (somatic mutation as compared with the heritable germline mutations in the cells that give rise to sperm and egg). This view was strengthened when x-rays were shown to cause mutations in the fruit fly *Drosophila*[7] (at the time, the best animal for research in genetics). But it was not clear how chemicals and viruses cause cancer. Remember that I am now talking about the 1920s. In those days, the disciplines of biochemistry and genetics had little common ground, and neither had much contact with cancer research, which was in the hands of the medical profession. Since cancer is such a fatal disease, the experts on cancer were surgeons and pathologists.

But techniques were available for working out the exact chemical structure of fairly large organic (carbon-containing) compounds. So a concerted effort was made to determine the structure of the compounds in coal tar that cause cancer,[8] in the hope that an understanding of their chemistry would lead to an understanding of mechanism. Thirty years later it was the discovery of the structure of DNA that started a scientific revolution. This time, however, a knowledge of structure carried no obvious message. Coal tar contains a huge array of organic compounds, some of which are carcinogenic and some not. Many of the compounds were quite toxic when fed to animals, which was a little surprising because most of them are not soluble in water and are very stable (which is what you would expect of substances that have survived many million years of decomposition). It appeared to be a general rule that the carcinogenic compounds were flat (i.e., the atoms were arranged in a two-dimensional array, like a plate) whereas the noncarcinogenic compounds were buckled (i.e., the atoms did not all lie in the same plane). We now know that the compounds have to be flat because only then can they slip in between adjacent base pairs in DNA and cause errors (mutations) during DNA replication, but no one could possibly have deduced that in the 1930s.

I mention this episode in cancer research because I think it has an important message. Many people devoted their whole careers to the study of the structure of carcinogens in the hope that it would tell them what exactly was going on during the creation of a cancer. But the solution came from outside the field, first in the discovery of DNA (which came from the study of microorganisms), and then in the study of chemical mutagenesis (also in microorganisms). Without this infusion from microbiology and genetics, there would still be little understanding of the nature of cancer and the mechanisms of carcinogenesis. The moral of the story is that the problem you wrestle with today may not be solvable until much more is known about seemingly unrelated subjects. A lifetime of effort may take you no nearer the answer.

World War II stimulated research on chemical weapons (I can remember my own forearms being used in a test of agents that might protect against the burns produced by mustard gas). Out of that kind of work came the discovery, initially in *Drosophila*,[9] that certain chemicals cause mutations. This was quickly extended to some of the carcinogens found in coal tar.[10]

Unfortunately, there often seemed to be little correlation between the potency of a chemical as a mutagen and its potency as a carcinogen. But in the mid-1930s the English chemist Dick Boyland suggested that the more toxic compounds found in coal tar may be changed (detoxified) in the body by being oxidized by enzymes in the liver,[11] and the active ingredient in the production of a cancer might not be the substance you are giving to the animal but rather one of the intermediates formed from the starting chemical during its detoxification in the liver. Whether a compound is carcinogenic or not could therefore depend on whether it is converted in the body into a mutagenic intermediate and whether that intermediate reaches a tissue that can give rise to cancer cells.

This idea turned out to be correct and is one of the reasons why a compound can be carcinogenic for one species but not for another. For example, early in the 1960s, a chemical called 2-acetyl-aminofluorine (2AAF) was shown to be carcinogenic in mice but not in guinea pigs. The explanation was that guinea pigs do not possess the enzyme that converts 2AAF into the oxidation product N-hydroxy-2AAF, which is the actual proximate carcinogen and is equally carcinogenic for mice and guinea pigs.[12] Inherited differences like this might explain why some species are more susceptible to certain forms of cancer than to others. Similar differences in biochemistry might be important in determining individual susceptibilities in human populations.

As soon as genes were shown to be made of DNA, it was natural to suppose that the carcinogenic coal tar derivatives produce cancer because they (or the intermediates formed during their detoxification) are damaging DNA, especially since they could be shown to interact with DNA.[13] Curiously enough, this idea was initially ridiculed by the cancer research establishment.[14] Even as late as 1963, ten years after the structure of DNA was worked out, the party line was that cancer is the result of damage to proteins.[15] However, as the list of experimental carcinogens became longer and longer and nearly all were shown to cause sequence changes in the DNA of bacteria and animal cells, the arguments gradually died down.[16] By now it is absolutely clear that certain chemicals are carcinogenic because they cause sequence changes (mutations) in DNA.

Quick tests for mutagens were devised, and the public came to believe that these tests would allow scientists to identify and eradicate the main causes of cancer. Unfortunately, the fact remains that the causes of most human cancers are still not understood, and there is certainly no a priori reason why they should be attributed to the chemical mutagens that are in our diet and environment.

The Succession of Steps in the Making of a Cancer

So far this has been a greatly simplified account of the history of research into the production of cancer by chemicals, and I have left out an important complication. A conspicuous feature of cancer is that it takes a long time to develop. When experimental animals or humans are continuously exposed to some carcinogenic stimulus, such as cigarette smoke or some of the chemicals used in the aniline dye industry, a large fraction of their lifetime may have to pass before they start to develop cancer. Obviously, we could not claim to understand the process that makes a cell form a cancer until we had worked out why cancer takes so long to develop.

One very early suggestion, dating from the 1940s,[17] was that the well-regulated behavior of normal cells is, in effect, a Mendelian dominant character (or, if you prefer it, that the mutations that lead to cancer behave like Mendelian recessives). In other words, we could imagine that each cell has one particular gene that controls its behavior, and that both copies of this gene (the one you inherited from your father and the one from your mother) have to be mutated before the cell can grow and form a cancer. Obviously it takes longer to do two things than to do one, and this might explain why the production of cancer requires prolonged exposure; to be precise, if two genes have to be mutated, the probability of having cancer should tend to increase as the square of the duration of exposure to whatever is the cause of the mutation. However, here too the idea that cancer was a matter of mutation was not accepted by the establishment[18] who did not wish to see their subject being turned into a branch of genetics. In fact, the hypothesis that some cancers are caused by recessive mutations languished unnoticed for about thirty years before being resuscitated as a description of certain familial cancers.

There is visible evidence that the development of human cancer is usually a long, drawn-out process, involving many steps. For example, it is now clear that the early stages in the development of human cervical cancer are very common and usually do not progress any further. For this reason it is customary, in order to avoid unnecessary surgery, to monitor women who show these precursor stages and only intervene if the abnormalities persist and progress. As a result, what might be called the natural history of cervical cancer is now well understood (figure 4.3). The condition usually begins with the appearance of a group of abnormal cells occupying a small patch of the surface layer of cells in the uterine cervix (the cervical epithelium); these cells are behaving as if they are insensitive to some (but not all) of the signaling that is going on in the epithelium because they do not show the ordered organization that is characteristic of the normal epithelium. The next step in the progression to cancer occurs when the abnormal cells start to spread sideways and take over a larger and larger area of the epithelium. Next they break through into the underlying tissue. Finally, some of them may penetrate into the bloodstream and colonize distant sites such as the liver. The time course of these events usually extends over many years. Luckily, each of the steps in the sequence (except possibly the last) represents the exception rather than the rule; in most cases, the abnormal population dies out and is replaced by normal cells, and the epithelium resumes its normal appearance.[19]

This sequence of events occurring in the cervical epithelium looks like the familiar Darwinian combination of variation plus natural selection, where selection is for the variants that produce the greatest number of progeny. The cells in a normal epithelium are continually responding to the restraining signals emanating from their neighbors and, as a

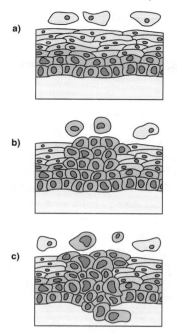

Figure 4.3. Stages in the development of cancer of the uterine cervix.

a. The surface epithelium of the normal cervix shows an orderly arrangement of cells, with the more superficial cells being considerably flattened (though not as much as in skin). The cells that are shed from the surface are uniform in size.

b. The earliest sign of abnormality is the appearance of a family of cells that are not undergoing the normal process of development. They do not flatten as they approach the surface, suggesting that they are not sensitive to the signals that normally tell cells when they have left the deepest layer and are being pushed outward. The cells that are shed are therefore more solid looking than normal shed cells. (Usually this level of abnormality undergoes spontaneous regression or, perhaps, the abnormal cells just disappear because normal cells compete better for the available space.)

c. The abnormal family sometimes undergoes a progressive increase in abnormality. The cells become more variable in size (suggesting that their division is less well controlled) and they start to invade the underlying tissues and may eventually spread to other tissues and into the bloodstream.

result, are not in competition with each other. The unrestrained behavior of cells in the early stages of progression to cancer suggests that they have become, to some extent, insensitive to the presence of their neighbors and this allows them to multiply and undergo natural selection for a more extreme departure from normality. Fortunately, there must be some advantage in a collaboration with your neighbors, because sooner or later the normal cells usually supplant the abnormal family. But if they do not win, the abnormal cells can continue their own life of unrestrained growth and may eventually produce a variant that can invade the surrounding tissues and kill the patient.

More is known about the natural history of the early stages of cervical cancer than that of other human cancers because it is so accessible to observation, but this kind of gradual progression seems to be a general phenomenon. Given that there is competition between precancerous cells and the normal cells they are trying to supplant, one would expect that any physical disruption of the tissue might create greater opportunities for the abnormal cells; this would be analogous to Darwin's observation that when plants or animals are put into the kind of abnormal environment that comes with domestication, there is a much higher chance that variants survive and flourish. Certainly a combination of exposure to a mutagen plus physical damage has proved to be a particularly effective way of producing experimental cancers.[20] The same may be true for some human cancers; for example, cancer of the mouth resulting from chewing betelnut commonly occurs at a site of continual irritation, such as on the inside of the cheek next to an old broken tooth.

The simplest way to look at all this, as I have already said, is in terms of mutation and Darwinian selection, in an environment where competition is normally not allowed. And here I cannot resist a brief digression. The living world evolved and gained complexity as the result of continual mutation and selection; any heritable change that improves your chance of leaving viable descendants will tend to be preserved; any change that lessens that chance will tend to be lost. At first sight one might suppose that Darwinian selection applies to all forms of life, throughout the entire universe. But the invention of the multicellular organism created a haven in which natural selection is somehow held in abeyance; among groups of collaborating cells, altruism seems to be the rule. There is, however, the risk that mutation may make a cell no longer reachable by the normal controls so that it ceases to behave in an altruistic way. Such a cell would have great survival advantage compared to its normal neighbors. Fortunately, because there is a great redundancy in the controls, this is a very rare event; even though each human being contains, at any moment, about ten million million cells, most of us manage to survive for almost 100 years without producing a fully fledged cancer cell. (Interestingly, late in evolution multicellular creatures developed two sophisticated systems of cells that operate by breaking the rule of altruism; the cells of the immune system compete with each other to make the best antibody and only the winner is allowed to multiply; similarly, during the development of the nervous system, nerve cells can behave as if they are competing with each other, though in this instance the fruits of success do not include the right to multiply.)

The changes that occur when a cell becomes cancerous can, to some extent, be studied in populations of cells cultivated in the laboratory. Many of the kinds of cell present in mammals will multiply if taken from the body and put into a suitable medium. After growth on a solid surface such as the bottom of a glass dish, the cells form ordered arrays, and as soon as they have covered the whole surface and are touching each other they stop growing. When such populations are exposed to carcinogens such as coal tar derivatives a few of the cells start to behave in a disordered way. They change their behavior and keep growing, piled up on top of each other, and eventually they take over the whole culture,[21] suggesting that they have become cancerous. Indeed, if these piled up cells are removed from the culture vessel and injected into an animal they will form lethal cancers. This process is called *in vitro transformation* (literally, transformation in a glass container) and has made it possible to categorize some of the differences in behavior between normal cells and their cancerous derivatives.

Typically, normal cells stop multiplying in vitro when they have used up the available space and are starting to come in contact with each other,[22] whereas transformed cells are not "contact-inhibited" in this way. It is as if cancer cells are deaf to the signals of their neighbors. Part of this deafness may be the result of their failure to form what are called gap junctions. When normal cells lie in close contact with each other, they develop holes in their surface membranes that allow direct connection between the contents of the cells and these serve as channels of communication with each other. Transformed cells do not make such connections, either between themselves or with their normal neighbors. If you inject a dye into a normal cell it will quickly spread to all the neighboring cells, but there is no such spread between cancer cells or between them and their normal neighbors[23] (figure 4.4).

In this highly compressed account of classical cancer research I have described the problem in terms of the restraints in cell behavior due to the signals that pass between cells. But it was not until the late 1960s that it became conventional to describe cancer in these terms. Apart from the circulating hormones and the specialized systems of communication between nerve cells and between nerves and muscles, virtually nothing was known about cell signaling until fairly late in the 1970s. Nobody knew what was the chemical nature of most signals or how they were received or (perhaps more important) how they then influenced the behavior of the receiving cell. Although natural and experimental cancers appeared to be the end result of a sequence of steps, it was hard to see how the

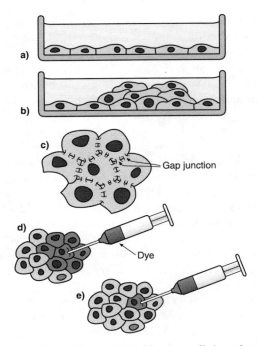

Figure 4.4. The interaction between neighboring cells in culture.

a. When normal cells are cultivated in the laboratory, they stop growing when they come in contact with each other. If they are growing attached to the bottom of a glass dish, they stop growing when they have covered the surface with a single layer of cells. In other words, normal cells are said to be subject to "contact inhibition."

b. When cancer cells are cultivated, they do not stop growing when they come into contact with other cells. So if a population of cultivated cells contains a few cancerous cells, these can be easily identified because (unlike normal cells) they form heaped up colonies at the bottom of the container.

c. Contact inhibition is achieved, in part at least, because normal cells communicate with each other by forming connecting channels that allow small signaling molecules to pass from each cell to its neighbors. These channels are called "gap junctions."

d. When a normal cell is injected with a dye, the dye can be seen to spread to all the cell's normal neighbors.

e. When a cancer cell is injected with dye, there is no spread to neighboring cells.

exact molecular biology of these steps could ever be determined. Certain rare human cancers were always associated with particular genetic changes; for example, since 1960 it had been known that the cells present in one kind of leukemia always showed a specific, microscopically visible change in their chromosomes.[24] But there was no obvious way of identifying the genes involved.

Just as molecular biology had originated in studies of the simplest organisms (the bacteria and their viruses), here too the solution came from a study of the precise molecular biology of a few simple examples. As is often the case in biology, the odd behavior of certain living creatures offered the experimentalist a novel way of solving a problem that previously had seemed totally inaccessible.

Cancer Viruses and Oncogenes

Since the turn of the century, many viruses have been shown to produce cancer in animals. Some are an important cause of death (for example, viral leukemia is a common disease in domesticated cats). Others were discovered by accident, when cancer cells were being transferred in the laboratory from one animal to another and it turned out that cell-free filtrates of the cancer would work just as well.

The amount of nucleic acid (i.e., genetic information) contained in these viruses is roughly one-millionth of the amount in a human cell. If a virus with only a few thousand bases of DNA or RNA knows how to turn a cell into a cancer, we should be able to find out how it does it. One particular group of viruses, the so-called retroviruses, were instrumental in opening up the molecular biology of cancer. (A separate group led to the discovery of RNA splicing, but that is another story.)

One of the first retroviruses was discovered in 1911 by Peyton Rous, working at the Rockefeller Institute.[25] The Rous sarcoma virus (RSV) can cause cancer in a wide variety of animals and also will transform cultured cells (sarcoma is the name for the cancer that arises in the supporting cells that lie beneath surface sheets of epithelial cells). Its nucleic acid consists of two copies of a single-stranded RNA molecule, and its most unusual life-cycle was gradually worked out by an American virologist, the late Howard Temin.[26] After the virus enters the cell, a special enzyme (contained within the virus particle) copies this RNA into a complementary strand of DNA and then copies that DNA into another strand of DNA, to produce a double-stranded DNA molecule. (The virus is called a retrovirus because, instead of the normal flow of information from DNA to RNA, it is able to reverse the flow by having a gene that codes for a reverse transcriptase which transcribes RNA into DNA.) The newly made viral double-stranded DNA then moves to the cell nucleus and becomes incorporated at some random point into the cell's DNA. (If you think of the sequence of bases in a cell's DNA as being like the text of a book, then this act is the equivalent of inserting into a book a few extra pages of perfectly readable but essentially alien text.) The viral sequence contains a strong promoter for transcription, so the cell's machinery for transcribing genes into RNA will now start transcribing the viral DNA into messenger RNA. Some of this viral mRNA is then translated to give the viral proteins needed to make new virus particles and the rest becomes packaged into the particles, which then leave the cell and repeat the whole process in other cells.

Very rarely, the cell becomes transformed into a cancer cell and produces a family of tranformed descendants that multiply without restraint and, furthermore, produce virus that infects and transforms neighboring cells. That is why RSV is a tumor virus.

Variants of RSV were known to arise that are able to infect and multiply in cells but never transform them. These variants all proved to contain changes in sequence in one of the open-reading frames in the virus's RNA (a gene that came to be known as *src*, pronounced "sark" because it is the gene that is responsible for the sarcomas). The secret of transformation by RSV was therefore to be found in the function of *src*. Soon after this, other cancer-causing retroviruses were discovered and they too turned out to have their equivalents to the *src* gene. A large number of such genes are now known and they are called *oncogenes* (from the Greek word *ogkos*, meaning tumor).

For the present purposes, it is sufficient for me to mention two other oncogenes. A gene like *src* was found in a virus that causes sarcomas in rats, and it was named *ras*. Another was found in a virus that causes a kind of leukemia in mice that is called myelocytomatosis, and it was given the name *myc*.

Once you know of the existence of a gene, you can use nucleic acid hybridization (see figure 3.3) to ask if there are other genes with similar sequences. And it was not long before homologs of *src* and *ras* and *myc* were shown to be present in the DNA of many, if not all, animals. At first, these cellular oncogenes (initially termed *c-onc*, as opposed to the equivalent *v-onc* in the virus) were seen as evidence of infection of the animal's ancestor by a tumor virus. But gradually people came to realize that this was not at all the right way to look at it. The truth of the matter is as follows:

1. When retroviruses go through their life cycle (i.e., convert their nucleic acid sequence into DNA, insert it into the host's DNA, and then have it transcribed back into RNA) they occasionally pick up part of the host's sequence as the result of an accidental rearrangement of the DNA. (Incidentally, this phenomenon, called transduction, had been

discovered in the mid-1950s as something that occasionally happens when certain bacterial viruses infect their host,[27] and it had proved very useful for fine scale genetic mapping.)

2. Retroviruses contain strong promoters that ensure that their genes, when integrated into the host's DNA, are transcribed at a high rate by the host's transcription apparatus. So any cellular gene that by chance finds itself captured within the sequence of a retrovirus will be overexpressed when the virus passes it on to the next cell (it may also undergo mutation, because the replication of RNA is rather error-prone).

3. Now, when an animal is infected with a retrovirus, hundreds of millions of cells (each with its hundred thousand genes) are supporting the growth of virus, and in some of these the virus accidentally picks up a stretch of host sequence. So we can think of infection by a retrovirus as asking the following question. Do these cells contain any genes that, when overexpressed (by being placed accidentally next to a virus promoter), will make the cell behave like a cancer cell? The answer is yes. And the retroviruses, because of the peculiarities of their life cycle, are identifying those genes.

It was not clear, however, that the retroviral oncogenes were relevant for human cancers. For one thing, overexpression of a retrovirus-carried oncogene seemed to be sufficient to make a cell cancerous, whereas human cancer is seldom if ever caused by a single change. Indeed, when normal cells are fused with cancer cells (to make a cell with double the normal number of chromosomes, and four copies of each gene instead of the usual two), the genes that are responsible for the abnormal behavior of the cancer cell behave like recessive Mendelian traits because their effects are hidden in the presence of their normal, dominant counterparts. So there was a mystery here. The oncogenes of retroviruses behave like Mendelian dominants, whereas the genes responsible for most cancers seem to behave like Mendelian recessives.

The next step in the story came from a totally different set of experiments.

Transformation

As mentioned in chapter 2, certain bacteria are able to take up DNA from their surroundings and join it up to their own DNA; it was the study of this phenomenon in the 1930s and 1940s that opened up the whole subject of molecular biology and led to the discovery of DNA. Early in the 1970s, ways were found for making cultured mammalian cells do the same thing,[28] and one of the first traits shown to be transferable was the cancerous state. Raw DNA, taken from cells transformed by Rous sarcoma virus (RSV) and transferred to normal cells, will transform a few of the recipients into cancer cells. Their DNA will in turn transform other cells.

To make this clearer, I should describe the experiment in a little more detail. You extract the DNA from a few million cancer cells, fragment the molecules into pieces of a few thousand base pairs (which you can do by putting a solution of the DNA into an ordinary kitchen blender), and then feed these pieces to a few million normal cells in culture. Only perhaps one in a million of the DNA fragments contains the cancer-causing sequence, but the cell that receives that particular piece will become transformed. This one cell then stands out from all the others because it can form a colony of transformed cells that continue growing when all the other cells have stopped. Thus the experiment works simply because you can detect the presence of the very rare transformed cell. (It is just like the transformation of bacteria, discovered by Griffith in 1928; here too only a tiny minority of bacteria picked up the crucial bit of DNA, but these bacteria could be detected because they had acquired virulence and would multiply when put into a mouse.)

Initially, this example of DNA-mediated transformation of mammalian cells must have seemed a rather unexciting technical development, because it was already clear that the crucial piece of DNA had to be the bit containing the RSV sequences (in particular the gene called *src*). But then, at the end of the 1970s, certain human tumors were discovered to contain sequences that behaved just like *src* because the cells' DNA would transform cultured mouse cells.[29] Unfortunately, there did not seem to be any obvious way of determining which of the 100,000 or so genes in a human cell were responsible. Few people could have had any inkling of the surprise in store.

When almost everywhere is dark, the only places where you can look for your car keys are the few areas that happen to be lit. In 1982 several groups in the United States virtually simultaneously reported that one transforming sequence, present in the cells of a human bladder cancer, was none other than the human version of *ras*, and that the cancer cell's *ras* was transforming the recipient cells because it had undergone one base change, of a GC base pair to a TA base pair that changed the twelfth amino acid in the *Ras* protein from glycine to valine.[30] (It is a convention in many branches of biology that genes are given names of three letters in lowercase italics, and the proteins they code for have the same names with the first letter in uppercase). In other words, mammalian cells contain a gene called *ras*; this gene is presumably concerned with some aspect of control, because it can lead to cancer if it undergoes a change in sequence. The rat version of the gene was picked up by a retrovirus of rats and underwent a mutation that made it into a dominantly acting oncogene, and this converted the virus into a tumor virus (of rats), which was then studied by experimentalists. The mutation in the human equivalent of the gene occurred in one of the patient's bladder cells and this was presumably a crucial step in the development of the patient's bladder cancer.

If that were not enough, 1982 brought another equally startling discovery. I mentioned earlier that some cancers are associated with chromosomal rearrangements. The obvious thought was that these rearrangements result in abnormal neighbors for the genes next to the junction points and that this could be leading to overexpression (or underexpression) of some gene that is important for the regulation of cell behavior. (Earlier in this chapter I mentioned the example of the genes for spore formation in bacteria, which are activated by just such a rearrangement involving a nearby promoter sequence.)

To take one example, Burkitt's lymphoma (a rare cancer that occurs in African children) affects the antibody-forming cells of lymph glands, and it is common to find that in this cancer the end of one of the copies of chromosome 8 in the leukemia cells has been exchanged with the end of chromosome 2, 14, or 22[31] (chromosomes are given numbers, starting with the largest, and humans have 22 pairs of chromosomes plus the sex chromosomes, named X and Y). In 1982, the human *myc* gene was shown to be just next to the breakpoint on chromosome 8, and the rearrangement was putting *myc* under the control of regions in chromosome 2 or 14 or 22 that normally stimulate the expression of genes involved in antibody synthesis.[32]

So now there were two examples of human cancer apparently being caused by changes in the very same genes that are picked up by retroviruses when these viruses become capable of producing cancers in animals. The first example involved a change in sequence of the *ras* gene; the second involved overexpression of the *myc* gene.

The final discovery, in this miraculous year of cancer research, concerned the interaction of different oncogenes. The mouse cells that could be transformed by the mutant *ras* gene from the human bladder cancer had been cultivated for some time and were already slightly abnormal. When normal mouse cells were used, nothing happened. This meant that the GC-to-TA mutation in one of the copies of the *ras* gene is not sufficient on its own to make a normal cell cancerous. It turned out, however, that normal cells could be transformed if they were also given a *myc* gene that was overexpressed through being next to a viral promoter.[33] So here at last was the first worked out example of *multistep carcinogenesis*. Actually, it was clear that a third step was required to make a fully fledged cancer, because most of the tumors produced by mutant *ras* and overexpressed *myc* eventually underwent regression, presumably as the result of the kind of programmed cell death that occurs when the cells have gone through repeated divisions. Only when the cells were "immortalized" by inactivation of a gene for programmed cell death would the change in *ras* and overexpression of *myc* produce an endlessly proliferating line of cancer cells.

The generality of the *ras*+*myc*+immortalization case was strengthened by the discovery that certain DNA tumor viruses carry genes that are analogous in function (though not in sequence). Thus two quite dissimilar viruses, called polyoma and adenovirus, were found to contain genes that could do what mutant *ras* and overexpressed *myc* were doing. Normal cells would be transformed if they received mutant *ras* plus either a gene from polyoma called *large-T* or a gene from adenovirus called *E1a*. So polyoma *large-T* can pinch-hit for overexpressed *myc*+immortalization; similarly, a gene in polyoma virus called *middle-T* can substitute for mutant *ras* plus immortalization.[34]

This was an important turning point in the history of cancer research. The fact that just two particular cell functions are involved in the formation of certain natural human cancers *and* in the tumorigenicity of several totally different kinds of tumor viruses implied that when cancers arise it is as the result of defects in a limited number of weak points in the control of cell behavior.

Since 1982, the itemizing of these weak points has progressed very rapidly. By now, more than 100 such genes have been identified, in which a change in sequence or in level of expression can be one of the steps in the development of a human cancer. That may seem a large number, but the genes turn out to belong to a limited number of families. The normal function of these families of genes is to control cell behavior. The genes were discovered as the result of their involvement in cancer, but obviously the cell does not have them in order to expose itself to the risk of becoming cancerous. So the genes are now called proto-oncogenes to distinguish, for example, the normal proto-oncogene called *ras* from the mutant *ras*, which is a cancer-producing oncogene. Mammalian cells have several copies of *ras*-like genes and of the other major classes of proto-oncogenes, each of which is presumably under somewhat different regulatory control. Each class of cell apparently uses only a few of these. So the cancers arising in one type of cell tend to show changes in one particular member of the *ras* family.

The three genes I have mentioned (*src, ras,* and *myc*) are oncogenes because, when mutated or overexpressed, they can (directly or indirectly) deregulate cell division; one altered copy of the gene is enough to disrupt the cell's controls, and therefore the abnormal version of the gene behaves like a Mendelian dominant trait.

Other equally important genes have been discovered where, by contrast, one normal copy of the gene is enough to control cell behavior (i.e., an abnormal version of the gene behaves like a Mendelian recessive). They are therefore called tumor suppressor genes or simply *suppressor genes.* The first example to be identified was a gene involved in the formation of a rare tumor of the retina seen in young children. The tumor arises when both copies of the retinoblastoma gene (*rb*) have been inactivated by mutation.[35] This can happen in one of two ways;[36] either the child inherits a mutated gene from one of its parents and acquires the second mutation during the growth of the retinal cells, or (more rarely) one of the child's retinal cells acquires mutations in each of the genes (other kinds of cancer are more common in people who inherit a mutant version of the *rb* gene, but the main effect is in the retina, presumably because these cells are crucially dependent on a properly functioning *rb* gene). Similar suppressor genes have been found to be commonly involved in breast and colon cancers, and an inherited defect in one of the copies of these genes greatly raises your risk of developing breast or colon cancer (as the case may be).

Certain suppressor genes are apparently crucial for the proper functioning of many kinds of cell in the body. For example, about half of all human cancers show mutations in a gene called *p53* (so named because it codes for a 53,000 molecular weight protein).

So far I have avoided any mention of what these oncogenes and suppressor genes are actually doing in the cell. This might have been difficult to find out, because it is not yet possible to determine the exact function of a protein by looking at its amino acid sequence (unless of course it happens to be similar in sequence to a protein whose function is already known). So a certain amount of luck was required. But the whole exercise was really made possible by the development of all the procedures used in what is called genetic engineering. Although I have tried, in this book, to avoid any discussion of the technologies of science, I have to say something about the way genes can be manipulated, because this is going to be so important in the years to come.

A Brief Introduction to Genetic Engineering

For the last 10,000 years, *Homo sapiens* has carried out programs of selective breeding. These have produced plants and animals that are far removed from their natural ancestors. Most of the crops and animals that support us could not survive in nature but for our protection. For example, many a famous variety of apple arose just once, in some ancient garden in the past, as an abnormal branch on a tree which since then has had to be propagated by grafting.

At first all selective breeding had to rely on choosing the best combination of the genetic traits that arose by spontaneous mutation. But the process could be speeded up once ways were found for raising the rate of mutation (e.g., by x-irradiation). For example, when the antibiotic penicillin was discovered, one of the first steps toward mass production was to isolate mutant strains of the mold *Penicillium* that produced abnormally large amounts of penicillin. And because these were not easy to find in nature they were produced in the laboratory by mutating the mold with x-rays.

Of course, our overuse of antibiotics quickly led to the appearance of bacteria that were resistant to these antibiotics. Surprisingly, this resistance usually turned out to be due to infection of the bacteria with what are now called resistance transfer factors (RTFs). These are circular pieces of DNA that, like viruses, control their own replication and can take up permanent residence within a bacterium and pass from one bacterial generation to the next. Obviously it is not to the bacterium's advantage to have to support an extra piece of DNA, unless that DNA contains some useful information. But when, through human intervention, many species of bacteria suddenly find themselves under attack from certain fungal antibiotics, there is strong selection pressure for the spread of any DNA that carries genes for resistance to these antibiotics.

I think that this was the first example where genes were found being transferred between species. But it had been known since the 1940s that some genes are able to move around from chromosome to chromosome within the same organism. Indeed, the variegation of many plants is usually caused by the movement of such mobile genetic elements.

It is easy to see that the existence of systems for moving genes between species will speed up evolution and therefore, once invented, will tend to be preserved by natural selection (incidentally, it was presumably from such systems that all viruses arose). Just as each cell has a battery of enzymes that look after the repair of its DNA, so a whole armory of enzymes has arisen concerned with the shuffling of genes. This in turn has led to the evolution in microorganisms of enzymes that protect against invasion by alien DNA.

With the aid of all these enzymes, it is now possible to conduct genetic engineering in the laboratory, pick out the gene you want, and then move it from one species to another. Before describing some of the techniques, I should remind you of one of the extraordinary properties of DNA, that was illustrated in figure 3.3. The strands of the DNA double helix are held together by the hydrogen bonds between the complementary bases in the two strands. The strength of these bonds is greatest at low temperature. If you put double-stranded DNA into boiling water, the strands unwind and separate. That is hardly surprising; chemical bonds are weaker at high temperature (which is why, when we can, we wash in warm water). But, amazingly, these separated strands will gradually come back together again (re-anneal) if they are kept at just the right intermediate temperature.

You can think of the phenomenon in the following way. The bonding between noncomplementary bases is far weaker than the bonding between complementary bases, so you can imagine that there is a temperature where complementary sequences will stay together but noncomplementary ones will not. If two separate, single-stranded pieces of DNA, that are being held at this temperature, happen to bump into each other they will not stay together unless they happen to be complementary in sequence and, by luck, happen to meet with their sequences correctly aligned in register. It may seem unlikely that such a rare event would ever occur, but events happen with extraordinary rapidity at this submicroscopic scale; sooner or later, complementary sequences do find each other, and when they do they quickly zipper up together and reform a DNA double helix.

The ability of complementary sequences (either of DNA or RNA) to find each other has been enormously useful, because it has allowed molecular biologists to isolate particular DNA coding sequences from mixtures. For example, if you wanted to isolate the region of human DNA that codes for the protein in hemoglobin, you could start by isolating the corresponding mRNA from young red cells (which are full of it, because hemoglobin is about the only protein they are making); you would then chemically bind this mRNA onto some kind of filter; if melted human single-stranded DNA is passed through this filter at just the right temperature, the filter will pick out (bind) the DNA strands that are complementary to the mRNA for hemoglobin and let all the other sequences pass through. You would then take the filter and treat it with an enzyme that breaks down RNA; that leaves you with DNA strands that are complementary to the mRNA. DNA polymerase can then be used to convert the single-stranded DNA into double helices, and now you have achieved the separation of globin sequences from all the hundreds of thousands of other sequences present in a human cell. (The actual purification of globin sequences is rather more complicated than I have made out, but that should give you a rough idea of the possibilities of what is called nucleic acid hybridization.)

I must now introduce an important new actor. Although bacteria can benefit from picking up strange genes, this is obviously a dangerous game; if you are the beneficiary of billions of years of evolution, a bit of someone else's instruction manual is more likely to do more harm than good. So bacteria have developed ways of protecting themselves against invasion by the DNA of other species. It is done in the following way.

Each strain adds a specific marker to its DNA, and makes an enzyme that cuts any incoming DNA molecule that does not bear this marker. One example will serve to show how this is done.

A strain of *Escherichia coli*, called *R1*, marks its DNA by adding a methyl group (CH_3) to one of the adenines in the sequence GAATTC. So wherever that sequence occurs in the DNA of *E. coli R1* (and that, in the natural course of things, is about once every 4,000 bases), the bacterium has marked it with a methyl group. Actually it marks it with two methyl groups, because the sequence is, in a sense, a palindrome (i.e., the two complementary strands have the same sequence when read in the 5-to-3 direction) so both strands are modified at this *restriction site*. The marking occurs just after the DNA is replicated, when the marking enzyme is confronted with a

> 5..............GAATTC................3
> 3..............CTTAAG................5

sequence that is already methylated on one side (the old strand) and not yet on the other side (the new strand). *E. coli* R1 protects itself against foreign DNA by having an enzyme that cuts any DNA double helix that contains GAATTC sequences that are not methylated in either strand, and once cut in this way the foreign DNA can be broken down. (Here I cannot resist mentioning the similar use of the word Shibboleth, which served to distinguish the Ephraimites from the Gileadites.)[37]

The cut occurs in each strand between the G and the A. So when a big DNA molecule is cut into pieces by the *E. coli R1* enzyme, every piece will have the same sequence at each end, namely

> 5....................G
> 3....................C-T-T-A-A at the right end

and

> A-A-T-T-C.................3
> G.................5 at the left end

The existence of DNA-cutting enzymes with this type of specificity has created enormous opportunities for manipulative genetics. Suppose, for example, that you want to make large quantities of a protein such as human growth hormone. The cheapest way of producing the protein would be to move the gene into a bacterial resistance transfer factor (RTF) and then introduce this slightly enlarged RTF into a bacterium that is easy to grow. The first step might be to take human DNA and cut it into pieces with a restriction enzyme. At the same time, you would also cut up RTF DNA with the same enzyme; cleverly, you would choose a species of restriction enzyme for which there was only one restriction sequence in the RTF so that a single cut converted the circular DNA molecule into a linear molecule. All the DNA fragments will therefore now have the same ends (as shown above). If the chopped up human and RTF DNA are now mixed and put at just the right temperature, the single-stranded tails at each end of each molecule will anneal together, because they have the same sequence. At this point, the restriction sites will become re-united, although usually not with their original partners.

$$5...................G/A\text{-}A\text{-}T\text{-}T\text{-}C...................3$$
$$3...................C\text{-}T\text{-}T\text{-}A\text{-}A/G...................5$$

The phosphate chains will not actually be joined between each G and A, but these gaps (marked /) can now be joined up with an enzyme called ligase that is used by all cells for sealing any gaps in DNA that result from the excision and repair of damaged sequences. Finally, you introduce these joined up pieces of DNA into a large population of some convenient strain of bacterium.

At this point, you will have a population of bacteria containing many different kinds of joined-up molecules. Perhaps only one in a million contains an RTF bearing the gene for human growth hormone. Your task is to find that one bacterium. The first step is to pick out the bacteria that contain a working RTF, and that is easy because those are the only bacteria that will be able to form colonies in the presence of antibiotic. The remaining job is to test these colonies, one by one, for the presence of human growth hormone. Once you have done this (and there are quick ways of doing it), you have engineered the gene for human growth hormone into a bacterium, and you can move into commercial production.

I have made this description as simple as possible, by using the smallest number of steps and ingredients—the idea of melting and re-annealing, and the use of an RTF and one kind of restriction enzyme. By now, however, a huge array of procedures is available. DNA molecules can be marked and moved around in many ways. There are numerous different restriction enzymes, and there are many possible vectors that can play the role played here by the virus-like RTFs.

Restriction enzymes have other uses, apart from genetic engineering. For example, each of us is genetically unique (unless, of course, we have a twin), and therefore each of us will yield a unique spectrum of fragment sizes when our DNA is digested with restriction enzymes. Many parts of your DNA will be slightly different from the equivalent parts of my DNA, and if these differences involve a restriction site (or are fairly long sequences, present in one DNA but not in the other) then the length of one or more fragments produced by a restriction enzyme will be different. Such differences are called *restriction fragment length poly-morphisms* (RFLPs) and can be used in paternity cases and in criminology. They can also, indirectly, be used to determine whether or not someone is carrying some undesirable gene. For example, Huntington's chorea is a fatal neurological disease caused by a dominant gene; unfortunately, the disease is not manifest until middle age, which is after the usual time for producing children. Until recently, the children of an affected parent could not tell whether half of their own children would be similarly affected. Thanks to the existence of restriction enzymes, it is now possible to determine whether or not someone has inherited from an affected parent the region of the parent's DNA that contains the abnormal gene by looking in their DNA for whatever RFLPs are known to be closely linked, in that family, to the Huntington's chorea gene. It is, however, an exercise that raises many ethical problems. Over the next few years we may expect to have available an increasing number of tests for inherited susceptibility to various diseases, including cancer, and it is obviously going to be very important to have regulations that govern the way these tests are used by employers and insurance companies.[38]

Signal Transduction and the Regulation of Cell Behavior

The ability to move genes around from one creature to another and to alter them in any way we want has produced a vaste amount of information about the functions of the oncogenes and tumor-suppressor genes. As we might have expected, most of them turn out to be concerned with the sending and receiving of signals (i.e., the regulation of the "social" behavior of cells or the interaction between the different programs within individual cells).

In the previous chapter I described how bacteria regulate the transcription of their few thousand genes to match the changes in their environment. Much of the time each bacterium is living in a world of its own, apparently little influenced by what other bacteria are doing; actually this is an oversimplification because populations of bacteria can, on occasion, show intricate patterns of behavior, but broadly speaking each bacterium worries more about its diet than the opinions of its neighbors. For the cells in a multicellular creature, life is far more complicated. A plant or animal consists of a collection of many kinds of cell, each of which is programmed to respond in its own particular way to each kind of signal (an obvious analogy is the different response of each player on an American football team to a given signal from the quarterback). The fertilized egg has to carry enough genes to set up several hundred different kinds of cell, each with its own program and each capable of sending and receiving appropriate signals in response to every change in its circumstances. The possibilities for disaster are obviously much greater during the development and maintenance of such a system than during the life of solitary cells, and that may be why it apparently took a billion years or so to evolve bacteria (which have a few thousand genes) and then 3 billion years to evolve the complicated animals (with up to 100,000 genes) that populate the earth today.

Each cell has specific receptors for every kind of signal it is likely to receive. The smallest signals used by cells, such as calcium atoms, ammonia and nitrous oxide, can pass through the surface of the receiving cell, so the receptors for these atoms and small molecules can be kept inside the cell. The receptors for the larger signals are on the cell surface and communicate with the interior by alterations in their shape (allostery) because the receptor proteins stretch from the outside to the inside of the cell (as described in chapter 3). Commonly, the part of these proteins that lies within the cell can act as an enzyme when the signal substance is attached to the exterior portion of the molecule.

One typical reaction carried out by these enzymes is that of adding a phosphate group to certain amino acids in certain proteins, which slightly changes the structure of the proteins and therefore modulates their action. For example, the product of the *src* gene is an enzyme that can add phosphate to the amino acid *tyrosine* in certain proteins (thereby altering their properties and functions) and it is called a tyrosine kinase. The normal *Src* protein does not acquire its ability to act as an enzyme until it has been activated by interaction with a signal substance at the cell's surface. The abnormal (mutant) *src* gene, found in transforming RSV, is active the whole time and adds phosphates to other proteins whether the signals are there are not. So a cell containing such a mutant *src* gene will behave as if it is receiving signals (to divide) all the time. (The story is rather more complicated than this because some of the phosphorylatable proteins are themselves enzymes that phosphylate other proteins, so the arrival of a signal at the cell surface can inaugurate a cascade of changes in a multitude of different enzymes and structural proteins within the cell.)

Another group of receptor proteins act upon small molecules within the cell which then act as signals that affect the performance of other proteins. For example, *Ras* is that kind of receptor protein. Some receptor proteins sit at the cell surface. Others are located within the cell; for example, the *Myc* protein is in the nucleus and its function is to bind to specific sequences within DNA and increase the level of expression of nearby genes.

The function of the cancer-suppressor gene *p53* is to monitor the state of the DNA and prevent the cell from embarking on DNA synthesis and division if there is any unrepaired damage. Mutations in *p53* cause cancer presumably because they make the cell more likely to acquire defects in other genes. Similarly, mutations in genes that are directly involved in certain kinds of DNA repair have been found in a fair proportion of cancers and can be picked up because they result in easily detected sequence changes scattered throughout the DNA.[39] This fits with an old idea that an increase in mutation rate is a common early step in carcinogenesis.[40]

Each cell has many versions of genes such as *src* and *ras*. Part of the difference in behavior of the different types of cell in the body is determined by which of these genes are being expressed: each of the versions has its own specific list of targets. To return to the analogy with American football, at any moment each cell is like a player who is having to adjust continually to a flow of instructions from many different quarterbacks, and its response to these signals will be partly determined by its own preset program (which will depend, for example, on which of the many different types of *src* gene it is expressing).

To summarize, plants and animals have managed to evolve systems of control that generate many different kinds of cell and allow large groups of such cells to collaborate together in multicellular arrays. This is achieved by a system of communication that affects every kind of biochemical event occurring within each cell—the transcription of genes, the handling and rate of translation of mRNA, and finally (by protein phosphorylation) the specificity and level of activity of many of the enzymes in the cell.

I find it hard to believe that we will ever have a complete description of all this. A human cell contains genes for about 1,000 different protein-phosphorylating enzymes, and at any moment it will be expressing about 100 of them. So the combinatorial possibilities of just this one system of control defy the imagination. Furthermore, many proteins interact with each other to form complex structures containing several different proteins; for example, the machine that translates mRNA base sequence into amino acid sequence is known to contain roughly 100 different proteins, all locked together like a three-dimensional jigsaw puzzle. To understand the function of any one particular species of protein, you therefore have to understand all the possible interactions it can have and all the contexts in which it has to operate.

In many ways, the problem is like that of designing a computer program for translating one language into another. In every language, words (like proteins) have become extraordinarily versatile. The subtler meanings are dependent on context, and to determine the exact meaning of a word the computer may have to search through pages of text. Similarly, if you want to understand every one of the ramifications of the functioning of the *Src* protein, you will have to learn about the behavior of all the proteins that interact with each of the many, slightly different *Src* proteins and then go on to learn about their interactions with other proteins. In a way, we seem to have returned to the uncertainties of the 1920s and 1930s, when biology was thought, in the final analysis, not to be understandable. The switch from three dimensions to one dimension, which was the triumph of the early days of molecular biology, gave us forty years of increasing clarity. But now we are getting back to three dimensions, and uncertainty returns. There is of course a difference in that we now feel that at least we understand the principles and it is just the intricate details that defeat us.

Fortunately for us, the systems that regulate our cells' behavior seem to have excess capacity for accommodating defects. For example, you can introduce a mutation into *ras* that totally deregulates its stimulatory action on cell division, but this one change on its own is not enough to wreck the system. If a cell is to escape its network of controls it has to be damaged in several different ways. That is why the production of cancer requires the alteration of many genes. We should perhaps have expected that. Each of us is made up of about 10 million million cells and has to be able to survive for roughly half a century. To make this possible, our cells must be hedged around with many disciplinary layers that have been rigorously tested for millions of years in many hostile environments, and by now the system as a whole is conspicuously robust.

For a time there was the hope that all forms of cancer would show some feature in common that could be the target for some all-encompassing form of treatment. Unfortunately, this is clearly not the case. I have already mentioned that certain cancers tend to be associated with particular defects (for example, the overexpression of *myc* due to a chromosome rearrangement seen in one kind of leukemia). Similarly, the various inherited mutations that raise the risk of getting cancer each raise the risk for one or two particular types of cancer rather than for all kinds of cancer. For example, inherited defects in the retinoblastoma gene cause a limited spectrum of rather unusual cancers; inherited defects in the major pathway for excising damaged bases from DNA raise the rate of certain brain tumors and the sunlight-induced cancers of skin but not the rates of the common internal cancers; defects in another form of DNA repair raise the risk of colon cancer; mutation of *bcl2*, a gene required for programmed cell death, is associated with one particular kind of cancer; and so on. Even the example of *p53*, the gene found altered in about half of all human cancers, turns out to be more complicated than expected, because the alteration in *p53* typically occurs early in the development of some kinds of cancer and late in others. It seems therefore that each tissue has its own particular Achilles' heel.

Perhaps we should have expected this to be so. For if there were one weak point that was common to most tissues of the body, natural selection should have eradicated it. Instead, evolution has just left us with a lot of minor weaknesses in our defenses, and most of us are able to survive into great old age without having developed a single progressively growing cancer.

It is only in the last few years that techniques have been available to look directly for sequence changes, so people have only just started to make inventories of the changes found in the various kinds of cancer. A torrent of information is pouring forth, and it is not easy to guess what the future holds in store. But already we can see that a better understanding of the molecular biology of cancer could bring several benefits.

1. If we knew what signals each cancer was failing to detect or what genes were being expressed inappropriately, it is imagineable that some substitute signal or regulatory protein could be administered. This kind of treatment is already in use for certain cancers (e.g., the control of prostate and breast cancer by synthetic estrogens), but it might be much more effective if more were known about the defects characteristic of each kind of cancer. For example, the overexpression of certain genes that is associated with the chromosomal rearrangements charcteristic of certain leukemias could be blocked by infecting the cells with a virus bearing the gene for a strong repressor protein.[41]

2. By knowing the exact spectrum of changes in the DNA of a patient's cancer, it might be possible to derive a more precise estimate of the future course of the disease, and this in turn could be used to decide what would be the ideal treatment. For example, it is currently a problem to decide what is the best treatment for the earliest stage in breast cancer. Full-scale assault with radiation and chemotherapy is not without risk; about 1 percent of the patients die from the treatment (e.g., by developing leukemia) rather than from the disease itself. If untreated, only 10 percent of patients with Stage I breast cancer are going to die of their cancer, so only ten in every 100 such patients are in need of any additional treatment. Conceivably, molecular biology could identify those ten patients so that they would be the only ones who have to be given radiation and chemotherapy.

3. Some of the sequence changes that are common in certain cancers lead to some abnormal nucleic acid or protein that is circulated in the body or excreted and can be detected. People could be screened for such abnormal products, and this might lead to earlier treatment.

4. We can imagine a time coming when the nature of the sequence changes in each cancer is used to determine the likely cause. Skin cancers typically show the kind of sequence changes in *p53* that are absolutely characteristic of DNA damage by ultraviolet light; liver cancers

that occur in regions of the world where the diet contains aflatoxin (a fungal carcinogen) show the kind of sequence change that is characteristic of DNA damage by aflatoxin. So it is conceivable that information about sequence changes may eventually disclose causes that the epidemiologists have failed to identify, and that could be very important for the prevention of cancer. Prevention, when all is said and done, is the preferred solution for any disease.

5. Humans probably vary greatly in their susceptibility to the different kinds of cancer. For example, about 10 percent of all breast and ovarian cancers are associated with an inherited risk factor, and the genes involved have now been identified. If more were known about such factors it might be possible to concentrate efforts at prevention of many kinds of cancer onto just a subsection of the population.[42]

6. Last, and perhaps most important of all, it is already clear that the great expenditure on cancer research and the molecular biology of mammalian cells has generated a technology that is being applied to many diseases. For example, if good vaccines are ever developed against diseases such as malaria and trypanosomiasis, which still kill millions every year, they will have been made possible partly as a result of cancer research.

But this discussion is drifting from molecular biology into straightforward epidemiology, and that is the subject of the next chapter.

CHAPTER 5

The Epidemiology of Cancer

> If you can look into the seeds of time
> And say which grain will grow and which will not,
> Speak then to me
>
> —Shakespeare, *Macbeth*

Although research on the molecular biology of cancer has been spectacularly successful, our understanding of the causes of cancer and our attempts at prevention still derive almost entirely from what is known about the actual statistics of the different human cancers. Therefore, every description of the changes found in the genes of cancer cells should, ideally, be accompanied by an account of the epidemiology of the cancer.

I shall not attempt to give an inventory of what is known about the causes and management of human cancers, still less a guide to do-it-yourself prevention; the best piece of advice that can be given with absolute certainty is too well known to need repeating. Instead, this penultimate chapter contains a set of essays describing some of the problems that face the average reader when trying to understand the results of epidemiological surveys of human diseases such as cancer.

If we want to know what we should do to minimize our chances of dying of cancer, we have to ask the epidemiologists. They know who are most at risk of cancer and who are least at risk. Unfortunately, study of the epidemiology of diseases tends to be held in low regard by practicing physicians and laboratory scientists. The lack of interest of physicians is, I think, easily understood; if you are confronted every day by a stream of people coming to you for treatment, it must be hard to tear your mind away from the needs of each particular patient and to start worrying instead about the root causes of the various diseases. Similarly, scientists in their laboratories are always dealing with one particular version of causality and find it hard to imagine that their own view of the causation of disease might be incomplete. Yet the history of human public health, which I described in chapter 1, showed that the conquest of most diseases was mainly the indirect result of changes in the human condition brought about by technical advances during the Industrial Revolution, rather than a result of the direct application of science to the treatment of diseases.

One notable example of the neglect of epidemiology occurred at the outset of the war against cancer. In the late 1960s, the United States convened a panel, under Senator Yarborough, to plan an attack on cancer. As Yarborough said, "My personal desire was to press forward with a giant project similar to that under which the atomic bomb had been developed in World War II, or the man placed on the moon in the NASA project, to funnel money into a massive effort to find a cure for cancer and also be uncovering the cause at the same time."[1] The panel consisted of surgeons and physicians and a few experimentalists, but it did not contain a single epidemiologist. So it was hardly surprising that its final report, issued in 1970, concentrated on developing new treatments for cancer and tended to play down the opportunities for prevention that were already available. Since then there have been some notable advances in the treatment of cancer, and by 1983 these were saving on the order of 10,000 lives in the United States each year;[2] how many people die as the direct consequence of their treatment is not known. But it is clear that if a similar effort had gone into prevention, the saving of life over the past twenty-five years could have been at least ten times higher.

There are, I think, two features that make epidemiology seem an unattractive subject to the general public: it is relentlessly empirical, and it relies very heavily on statistical methods. Each of these aspects of epidemiology is worth further discussion.

꠸꠸꠸

The Empirical Nature of Our Understanding of Diseases and Their Treatments

Although molecular biology is essentially the same for all living creatures, the particular form of each species reflects chance events in its evolutionary history. We can be confident that any newly discovered animal will have the same kinds of informational macromolecules and roughly the same genetic code as other forms of life. But even if we were given a complete description of the animal's habitat, we could not predict exactly what the animal would look like because that would depend on the history of its ancestors. Still less could we predict the animal's diseases. Who could have guessed that *Homo sapiens* would share with the humble guinea pig the unenviable distinction of being incapable of synthesizing vitamin C, or share with armadillos a susceptibility to the bacterium that causes leprosy, or that intestinal cancer usually occurs in the large intestine of humans and the small intestine of sheep?

If we cannot predict the existence and characteristics of each disease, we certainly have no basis for deciding a priori how diseases should be treated. It would seem to be a short step, therefore, to conclude that the treatment of diseases ought to be based on the results of some rational system of trial and error. Yet this is a rather new idea in the annals of medicine.[3] For example, one nineteenth-century critic maintained that it was actually improper to compare the way different patients responded to treatment. "By invoking the inflexibility of arithmetic in order to escape the encroachments of the imagination, one commits an outrage upon good sense."[4]

Of course, there were exceptions. In the eighteenth century, a careful test, using six sailors, showed that lemon juice would cure scurvy whereas various other commonly employed treatments were useless, and from then on scurvy was regarded as a preventable disease (even though there was much argument over whether it was due to the absence of something good or the presence of something bad).[5] But it was not until the 1940s that new forms of treatment started to be subject to what are called *clinical trials*. Since then, trials have become common and, gradually, the inflexibility of arithmetic has come to be accepted as a necessary adjunct to the practice of medicine. However, the use of clinical trials does occasionally come under attack from the general public, who find it hard to imagine the extent to which medicine is empirical and therefore tend to believe that clinical trials consist simply in doctors amusing themselves by withholding from one group of patients a treatment that (somehow intuitively) is known to work.

I have introduced the subject of clinical trials because it is a nice demonstration of the empiricism that underlies all of biology. There is, I think, only one law in biology, which is that biological systems cannot break the laws of physics. Aside from that, there are no fundamental principles that say what can happen and what can not. Living systems exploit the laws of physics in various ways, but our understanding of the chemical mechanisms available for this exploitation derives from observation, not intuition. If life were to evolve again, we have no reason to think that it would necessarily follow the same path.

For most of biology, the absence of hard and fast principles presents no problem. You simply assume that every phenomenon is the result of the operation of previously observed mechanisms. This is usually adequate for the description of the normal behavior of any particular living system. When novel phenomena are observed in biology, they sometimes lead to the discovery of a new, unexpected mechanism. And, from that moment on, the new mechanism becomes accessible as an explanation for other phenomena in biology. It was through observation, not theory, that our understanding of the workings of biology was progressively enlarged and refined.

At the same time, every interpretation in biology is subject to certain overriding restraints, not least of all the laws of physics. For example, study of the development of embryos suggested that certain cells change their behavior in response to signals coming from their nearby neighbors; but this explanation depended on showing that the distances that had to be traveled by these signals were small enough to be compatible with the physics of diffusion. Interpretations in biology are also subject to other kinds of limitation. To take a very different example, it is known that *Homo sapiens* is the only creature susceptible to measles and that the disease produces lifelong immunity; knowing the incubation period and duration of infectivity, it was possible to work out the minimum size of the intermingling groups of humans in order to provide at all times enough new, susceptible infants to keep the virus going. If measles had been found to survive in the absence of such conurbations, the model for the natural history of measles would have had to have been wrong.

Similarly, the interpretation of the cause or causes of cancer is subject to many kinds of restraint. Some of these restraints operate at the level of sequence changes in DNA and the functional changes in certain proteins; for example, if we are right in thinking that skin cancer is due to the mutagenic action of ultraviolet light, the cells in these cancers should contain the kind of sequence changes that are known to be produced by ultraviolet light (luckily, they do). Some restraints lie at the level of tissue organization; for instance, if we are right in thinking that certain fairly common abnormalities that develop in the uterine cervix can be precursors of cervical cancer, excision of these early lesions should decrease the incidence of cervical cancer.

Last, there are some overall restraints imposed by what is known about the epidemiology of cancer. In some ways, these are perhaps the most important of all. If you want to blame much of your nation's cancer incidence on exposure to mutagens produced by the chemical industries (as many people do) you should, before going any further, check whether affluent, industrialized nations do indeed have higher cancer rates than affluent, nonindustrialized nations. In fact, a half-hour in a library is enough to show that no such difference exists. For example, women in Ireland, Iceland, and New Zealand have much the same rates of cancer as women in the United States, Great Britain, and Czechoslovakia;[6] (incidentally, I chose women rather than men for this comparison, because men started smoking long before women, so their rates of cancer have been dominated for many years by the late consequences of exposure to tobacco). So the hypothesis has failed to comply with an external restraint and therefore, in its simplest form, it has to be discarded.

The rest of this chapter is a brief review of the kind of information that comes from studying the epidemiology of cancer. At the moment the epidemiologists, not the molecular biologists, are our main source of information about the causes of cancer. By knowing something about these causes, it may eventually be possible to prevent most forms of cancer, just as in the past the richer nations conquered the infectious diseases. First, however, I should say something about statistics and probability. Epidemiology relies heavily on the science of statistics, and that is one of the reasons why it is treated with such suspicion.

By statistics, most people mean the kind of collection of half-truths that are used by politicians to achieve their ends. Yet there is another kind of statistics that we all use to determine what is likely and what is not. Like Molière's M. Jourdain, who had been speaking prose for forty years without knowing it, we are all statisticians at heart, even if we do not have a clear understanding of the rules.

Probability and Statistics

Each of us has a rough idea of what we mean when we say that something is likely or unlikely, probable or improbable. We would guess that it is not uncommon for one of the players in a game of bridge to have all four aces, and much less common that they should also have all four kings. But before we accused someone of cheating, we should first try to calculate exactly how unlikely it is that their run of good hands could be simply due to chance. Similar problems arise in epidemiology. For example, a small township may believe that it has recently had an excessive number of cases of leukemia, and it calls in an epidemiologist to determine whether there really have been far more cases than one would expect from the incidence of leukemia in the nation as a whole.

This is not the place to give a complete description of the mathematics involved in such calculations, which can become quite complicated. But I would like to describe the logic underlying our ideas about chance events and the methods used by statisticians to handle problems such as a possible cluster of cases of leukemia. I will start with a simple example, the tossing of a coin. If the coin is evenly weighted, most of us would agree that the two possible outcomes (heads or tails) should be equally likely. Actually that belief contains within it another less obvious belief. On any particular occasion the outcome will be either heads or tails, but we can only believe that on each occasion the two possible outcomes are equally likely if we believe that the result of each toss is not influenced by what happened on previous occasions or by what is going to happen in the future. In other words, although you may have just tossed three heads in succession, calm reason suggests that this will not affect the outcome of the next toss (amateur gamblers find this hard to accept, which is one of the reasons why they tend to lose when up against professionals).

The calculation of what is the exact probability of getting three heads in succession (or a run of any given length) illustrates how statisticians handle the notion of probability. If you toss a coin three times, there are eight possible outcomes—HHH, THH, HTH, HHT, TTH, THT, HTT, and TTT. If the result of each toss is independent of the results of the others, then each of these eight outcomes will be equally likely. It follows therefore that the probability of getting three heads is one in eight (or 0.125), and the probability of not getting three heads is 7 in 8 (or 0.875). If, instead, we want to know what is the chance of getting one head and two tails, we look at our list of eight possible answers and see that three of them (TTH, THT, and HTT) have one head and two tails, so we know that the chance is 3 in 8 (0.375).

We have here, incidentally, a demonstration of the rule that the probability of any particular combination of independent events is the product of the probabilities of the individual events; thus, the probability of getting a head is ½ and the probability of getting three heads in succession is ½ × ½ × ½. Put another way, there are two possible equally likely results for each toss of the coin and eight (2 × 2 × 2) possible results for three tosses, and only one of those eight is HHH.

Similarly, we can calculate what is the chance of a throw of four dice giving at least three sixes. Now we have six possible equally likely results for each throw, and the act of tossing four dice can produce 1,296 possible results (6 × 6 × 6 × 6). If we are to get at least three sixes, three of the dice have to give a six and one of the dice can give anything. There are six acceptable results for the "anything" dice and four possible ways of choosing which is the "anything" dice, so the probability of getting at least three sixes is (4 × 6)/1,296 or 1 in 54.

All this is perfectly straightforward. Let me now introduce another less obvious way of looking at these calculations of probability, which will prove to be very useful in other, more complicated cases. We can imagine that someone has tossed our evenly weighted coin a very large number of times and has written down the result of each toss on a separate card. Because the coin is equally weighted, the number of cards in the collection that have "head" written on them will roughly equal the number saying "tail." Our act of tossing a coin can be thought of as our picking one of these cards at random. If the collection of cards is virtually infinite in size, the ratio of head cards to tail cards will not be significantly altered by our withdrawing a few cards from the collection (the collection has to be very large in order to fit with our idea that the result of each toss is not influenced by previous results).

When we come to ask what are the chances of tossing three heads in succession, we imagine that we are withdrawing a card from a collection of cards that have written on them the results of three tosses; in this collection, therefore, there are eight kinds of card, which are present in equal numbers. The usefulness of this strange way of looking at such problems will become apparent in a moment.

We are now ready to return to the town that thinks it has too many cases of leukemia. In the country as a whole, the average incidence of childhood leukemia is 1 case per 50,000 children per year. Our town happens to have roughly 10,000 children and so might expect an average of two cases in any ten-year period. In fact, it had six cases in the last ten years, and that is why it has asked a statistician whether it is in the grip of an epidemic. The first test is to work out the probability that this is due to chance. In the nation as a whole, the chance that a child develops leukemia in any given year is one in 50,000, and the chance that it does not is therefore 49,999 in 50,000. Just as the chance of tossing three heads in succession was ½ multiplied by itself three times, so the chance that there is no case of leukemia in a given year in a town with 10,000 children will be (49,999/50,000) multiplied by itself 10,000 times. This may seem an appallingly difficult calculation, but if you have a pocket calculator and are confortable with logarithms, you can quickly work out that the answer is roughly 0.82. The chance that the town does not have a single case for ten years in succession is 0.82 multiplied by itself ten times, or roughly 0.13.

We are therefore treating the problem as if it were simply the act of tossing a dice that has 50,000 faces on one of which is written the word leukemia. Just as we could calculate the chance of having exactly one head in three tosses of a coin, we can now calculate the chance of there being exactly one case in ten years, and we can extend the calculation to two cases, three, four, five, six, and so on. We now imagine a very large collection of cards which, like the cards recording the results of tossing coins or dice, record the numbers of cases of leukemia that would be expected to occur by chance alone, in an imaginary collection of townships like the one we are investigating. We can therefore ask what is the probability that a single card drawn from this collection will bear a number as large as 6. The answer comes to about 0.016 (or 1.6 percent); the calculation, as I have given it here, would be extremely laborious, but there are mathematical shortcuts that make it much easier.

The statistician therefore tells the town that 1.6 percent of towns of this size would expect, *by chance alone*, to have at least six cases in any ten-year period. Since the country as a whole contains several hundred such townships, it should contain several towns with a record as bad or worse than that.

The town's inhabitants, however, are not satisfied with this answer. They point out that the statistician has calculated what is the probability of getting at least that number of cases just by chance; he cannot calculate the probability that the extra cases are actually due to some local cause. This is an important distinction. You can, for example, calculate the probability that, by chance alone, Mr. Smith will have all four aces on three successive deals, but that is different from deciding if he is cheating; if he is a known card-sharper he probably is cheating, but if he is a pillar of rectitude he probably isn't.

So the statistician tells the town that there are additional pieces of information that might markedly change the odds. Obviously, if the town suffers a similar excess of cases in the next ten years, the plausibility of an explanation based on chance will be that much lower. Again, if the town discovers within its boundaries something that is known to cause leukemia (which is the equivalent to finding that Mr. Smith is known to cheat at cards), the odds will change dramatically, though not in a quantifiable way. The statistician may also point out that it would be worth looking at the statistics for the nation's other towns; if the number of cases of leukemia varies much more than would be expected from chance alone, it might be possible to show that the towns with the highest rates had some factor in common. Last, if several of the six leukemia cases turn out to have a kind of leukemia that normally is extremely rare, then the probability that these cases should congregate in just one town is obviously very small indeed.

The last point is illustrated in the following example. A medical officer working for the Goodrich Rubber Company was surprised to see two cases of angiosarcoma of the liver in the company's work force. This is such a rare cancer that it is not mentioned in most textbooks of pathology and probably is responsible for less than one death in a million. To see one case could just be chance; to see two was most unlikely. He therefore searched through the company records and found a third case.

These three cases were enough to show that the workers were being exposed to an unusual carcinogen and led to the discovery that vinyl chloride can cause cancer.

The examples I have given have been of what are called discontinuous variables, where a coin is a head or a tail and a child does have or does not have leukemia and there is nothing in between. But the methods used for handling continuous variables (such as height and weight) operate on exactly the same principles. I have discussed the calculation of statistical probabilities at some length because these matters tend to be misunderstood even though they lie at the very heart of our ideas about causality. It is not that the calculations lead you to causes, but rather that they serve as restraints and lead you away from assigning causes for observations that are readily attributable to chance. Just as the results of epidemiology act as restraints on our hypotheses concerning the causes of diseases, so the statistics of chance events restrain epidemiological hypotheses.

Preventible Causes

It is all too easy to turn the whole idea of causality into an impenetrable thicket. It is generally agreed that the behavior of the universe is, in its finer details, unpredictable and chaotic. Yet we all manage to organize our lives on the basis of some simple ideas about cause and effect. For want of a nail the shoe was lost; for want of a shoe the horse was lost; for want of a horse the rider was lost. And, as Benjamin Franklin said, the simplest view of that chain of events is that it was due to neglect.

Luckily, for most practical purposes, we do not have to analyze causes very deeply in order to take evasive actions. This is just as true in epidemiology as it is in our everyday lives. The history of public health clearly shows that diseases can sometimes be eradicated before their causes are properly understood. As we have seen, various social reforms in the middle of the nineteenth century started the decline in mortality among the poor before the discovery of the bacteria that were causing this mortality.

The first and all-important fact about the statistics of cancer is that every common form of cancer numbers among its causes something that, if it were ever identified, could be the basis for evasive action. This strong statement rests on the following observations.

1. The pattern of cancer is very different in different countries. Whenever some particular kind of cancer is found to be common in one part of the world, some country can be found where it is rare (table 5.1).[7]

2. Of course, these differences between one nation and another do not necessarily mean that cancers are preventible. They could, for exam-

Table 5.1
Regions of High and Low Incidence of Cancer

Site/Type of Cancer	Annual Incidence per 100,000	
	High Region	Low Region
Liver (Males)	36 (The Gambia)	2 (United Kingdom)
Esophagus (Males)	17 (Parts of China)	3 (Norway)
Stomach (Males)	93 (Japan)	8 (U.S. whites)
Colon (Males)	31 (U.S. whites)	1 (The Gambia)
Prostate (Males)	62 (U.S. whites)	7 (Japan)
Breast (Females)	56 (United Kingdom)	18 (Japan)
Cervix (Females)	42 (Colombia)	4 (Kuwaitis)
Skin melanoma (Females)	25 (ACT, Australia)	0.2 (Kuwaitis)

Source: D. M. Parkin et al., Cancer Incidence in Five Continents. Volume VI. (Lyon: IARC, 1992).

ple, be the result of some of the genetic differences that characterize the different ethnic groups. To distinguish between genetics and environment, we would like to know what happens when people move from one country to another. Over the last 200 years, there have been several massive migrations, some forced and some voluntary. Furthermore, many of the migrant groups have preserved their genetic make-up by tending to marry among themselves rather than intermarry with other groups. These populations allow us to distinguish between the effects of nature and nurture. The results are clear-cut. Within one generation or thereabouts, each group acquires the pattern of cancer that is typical of its new home. This is true for the Africans transported to the United States in the slave trade; it is true for the Jews who moved from Europe and Russia to Israel; and it is true for the Japanese who migrated to the western United States (table 5.2).[8]

3. Although each part of the world imposes on its inhabitants its own particular pattern of cancers, this does not necessarily mean that the cancers are preventible. It is, I suppose, just imaginable that there are unavoidable consequences of living, say, in the United States. But obviously the next step in the pursuit of causes is to look for evidence that there are prevailing habits and features of the life-style in each country, such as diet for example, that influence the pattern of cancer. The first class of evidence consists of changes in time. In the Western world, there has been a marked change in the pattern of cancer.[9] In particular, the incidence of stomach cancer, the commonest lethal cancer when I was a medical student fifty years ago, has declined by almost tenfold and its place has been taken by lung cancer, which is now responsible for about one-third of all cancer deaths. Changes like these (figure 5.1) imply the

Table 5.2

The Effect of Migration on the Incidence of Cancer

	Incidence per million		
West Africa to the United States			
Cancer (Sex)	*West Africa*	*U.S. Blacks*	*U.S. Whites*
Colon (M)	34	349	294
Pancreas (M)	55	200	126
Prostate (M)	134	724	318
Breast (F)	337	1268	1828
Liver (M)	272	67	39
Cervix (F)	559	507	249
Japan to Hawaii			
		Hawaii	*Hawaii*
Cancer (Sex)	*Japan*	*Japanese*	*Caucasian*
Colon (M)	78	371	368
Prostate (M)	14	154	343
Breast (F)	335	1221	1869
Stomach (M)	1331	397	217
Cervix (F)	329	149	243

Source: R. Doll and R. Peto, *The Causes of Cancer*. (Oxford: Oxford University Press, 1981).

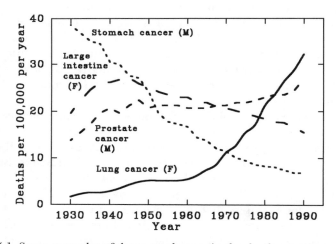

Figure 5.1. Some examples of the great changes in the death rates from some of the common cancers that have occurred in the United States during the past sixty years.

TABLE 5.3
Death Rates in Californian Mormon and non-Mormon Males

Total Death Rate (deaths per thousand)	Age				
	35–44	45–54	55–64	65–74	75–84
Californian whites	3	8	21	46	95
Never-smoked whites	2	6	17	36	95
Californian Mormons	1	3	8	23	62
Cancer Death Rate (deaths per thousand)		45–54	55–64	65–74	75–84
U.S. whites		1.7	5.0	10.0	15.9
Never-smoked whites		0.8	3.1	6.6	13.8
California Mormons		0.8	1.7	4.4	11.4

Source: J. E. Enstrom, "Cancer and Total Mortality Among Active Mormons." Cancer 42: 1943–51, 1978.

existence of environmental variables that, once identified, could presumably be avoided.

4. The second class of evidence comes from the study of different social groups. It turns out that almost every kind of cancer (and in fact most other major causes of death) are commoner among the poor, less well-educated members of society; just about the only exceptions are breast and prostate cancer, which are commoner in the rich.[10] In the United States, certain religious groups, such as Mormons, Seventh Day Adventists, and Protestant clergymen, have cancer rates that are about half the national average (table 5.3).[11] Although the rich are said to have difficulty in entering the kingdom of heaven, it is hard to believe that wealth per se (or religion, if it comes to that) has any direct effect on your chances of getting cancer. So we should be looking for more prosaic, down-to-earth differences in the environments of the rich and the poor. But before continuing this pursuit of the causes of cancer, I should describe what is known about the time course of development of human cancers.

Cancer in Relation to Age and the Duration of Exposure

For most forms of cancer, incidence rises very steeply with age, being at least 100 times higher in the old than the young. There appear to be two, somewhat interconnected reasons for this.

Although experimentalists had observed, early in the twentieth century, that it could take months or years for animals to develop cancers, it was not until the 1950s that people began to realize that human cancers might not arise until thirty or forty years after the start of exposure. For example, when smoking was first identified as a possible cause of lung cancer, the obvious test of the hypothesis was to show that each nation's incidence of lung cancer was related to its cigarette consumption. Unfortunately no such relationship could be detected (to the great delight of the tobacco companies). However, in the 1960s people started to realize that there is usually a long interval between the initial stimulus and the appearance of any cancer. When cancers arise as the result of a brief exposure to some known cause, such as irradiation resulting from the explosion of an atom bomb, they do not start to arise until some ten years later. So it seems that, in human beings, ten years or more must elapse between the first step in carcinogenesis and the formation of a detectable cancer; the exceptions to this rule are certain kinds of leukemia, which can appear within five years of irradiation, and of course the rare cancers that arise in very young children. Even when populations are exposed to such massive doses of a carcinogen that almost everyone gets cancer, the first cancers do not appear for about ten years (figure 5.2).[12]

If smoking causes lung cancer, we would expect each nation's incidence of lung cancer to be related to its consumption of cigarettes at some earlier time. And when looked at this way, the relationship became obvious (figure 5.3). This kind of delay between cause and effect must tend to push cancers into the older age groups.

Before anything was known about the molecular biology of cancer, it had seemed likely that the long time course of cancer was because the formation of a cancer cell requires multiple changes that have to accumulate over a period of months or years. In the case of human cancers, perhaps the most persuasive evidence has come from the study of lung cancer in smokers. Exposure to cigarette smoke is almost certainly the largest experiment in carcinogenesis that anyone is ever likely to do, having already involved several billion human beings, and the results of this massive experiment tell us a lot about the way cancers arise. Lifetime studies have been carried out of smokers who differed in the amount they smoked and who started (and stopped) smoking at different ages, and from these it is clear that smoking stimulates both the early and the late steps in the formation of lung cancer (figure 5.4).[13] Old smokers' risk is higher if they started smoking when young, showing that their first few years of smoking had to have been stimulating the early steps (figure 5.4a); smokers of many years' duration can, however, stop the inexorable increase in risk with age if they stop smoking, showing that the later years of smoking are stimulating the late steps (figure 5.4b).

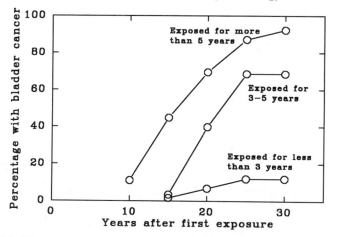

Figure 5.2. The great delay in the appearance of cancer that occurs even after very high doses of carcinogens. The figure shows the time of appearance of bladder cancer in a group of 78 men exposed to large amounts of 2-naphthylamine, early in the twentieth century before the dangers of this were discovered. The group with the greatest exposure (more than five years) did not start to develop their cancers until about ten years after first exposure.

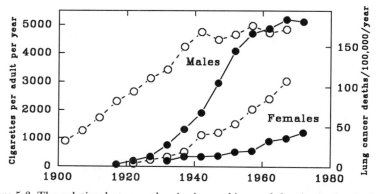

Figure 5.3. The relation between the rise in smoking and the rise in deaths from lung cancer. The figure shows the increase in cigarette consumption (open circles) and lung cancer death rates (filled circles) for males and for females observed in England and Wales during the twentieth century.

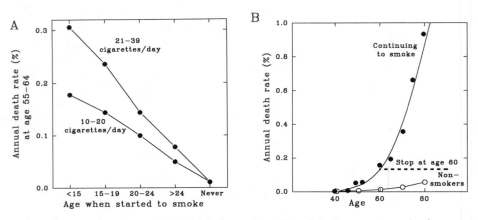

Figure 5.4. Smoking stimulates both the early steps and the late steps required to form a lung cancer (from Peto et al.; see note 13).

Left: The death rate from lung cancer for men aged 55–64 is much greater if they started smoking under the age of 15 than if they started after the age of 24. This shows that even in the days of our youth our behavior is determining our chance of getting cancer in old age.

Right: For men who stop smoking at the age of 60, the annual incidence of lung cancer remains roughly constant from then on, whereas for men who continue to smoke the incidence keeps climbing steeply. So even after the age of 60, smoking continues to contribute to the risk of lung cancer.

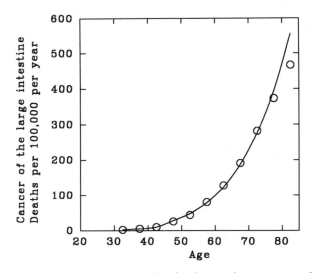

Figure 5.5. The increase with age in the death rate from cancer of the large intestine. The line drawn through the points is the curve that would be expected if death rate were proportional to roughly the fifth power of age.

This picture of cancer as the end result of multiple steps, some or all of which can be stimulated by external factors such as cigarette smoke, fits nicely with what is known about the relation of cancer incidence to age (figure 5.5). For, if the probability that a cell has suffered some particular change is proportional to how long the cell has been exposed to risk (i.e., the owner's age) and if, for example, five such changes are needed to make the cell into a cancer, then the probability that this cell will have undergone each of the five necessary changes will be proportional to the fifth power of time (the calculation is exactly analogous to our calculation of the probability, when throwing dice, of getting a certain number of sixes in succession).

The statistics of human cancer are therefore telling us two very important facts. (1) Cancer has external causes, and (2) these causes usually have to operate over a long period of time. If the causes could be identified, we could prevent cancer. Failing that, we might have more success with treatment if we could pick up cancers in their early stages. The problem of earlier diagnosis is the next topic in this chapter, after which I discuss certain particular causes of cancer that offer opportunities for prevention.

Screening and the Interrelation of Mortality, Incidence, and Prevalence

Each year, a certain number of people are diagnosed as having cancer and a certain number die of cancer; these are the statistics for *incidence* and *mortality*. You could, however, imagine inspecting the entire population to find out, at any moment in time, how many people have cancer, and this is what is called *prevalence*. The interrelationship between these three measures is more complicated than you might imagine.

MORTALITY

One easy set of numbers to get hold of are the statistics for mortality; in many countries there is, for every death, a death certificate giving primary and contributing causes of death, and these national records of mortality are compiled and published every year. If, for example, you want to know the extent to which the war against cancer has achieved its objective, the simplest thing to look at is present overall age-standardized mortality from all kinds of cancer. This will tell you what is the chance that someone of your age will die of cancer during the next year. Put in these terms, the war has not been conspicuously successful. Overall age-standardized mortality has hardly changed in the last thirty years.

You could argue, however, that this is not fair. In the last thirty years there has been an epidemic of lung cancer that now accounts for about

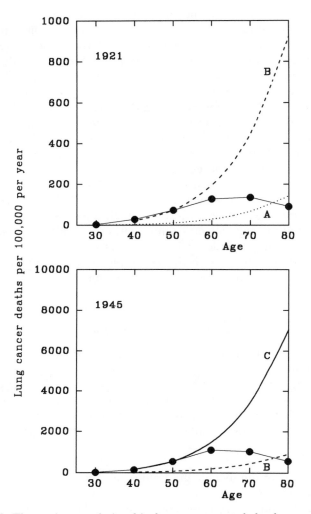

Figure 5.6. The ominous relationship between age and death rate from lung cancer in the first half of the twentieth century (from Korteweg; see note 14). Instead of the usual steep increase with age that is seen for most cancers, death rates from lung cancer were as high at age 50 as they were at age 75. Thus in 1921 (the upper graph), the observed death rate for people aged 75 would have predicted that the death rates in younger age groups would fall on curve A; but the observed death rate for people aged 50 was roughly tenfold higher, suggesting that, in future years, their death rate would follow curve B. Twenty-five years later (lower graph) it was clear that that cohort had indeed followed curve B. Unfortunately, in 1945 the observed death rate for the next crop of 50-year-olds was once again about tenfold higher than expected, and it was reasonable to suppose that they were going to follow curve C and be part of a further tenfold increase in death rate from lung cancer in the next 25 years.

one-third of all cancer deaths, and it is the fault of governments rather than of doctors, epidemiologists, or molecular biologists that this epidemic has been allowed to continue. If we exclude deaths from lung cancer, we see that mortality has slightly declined. A few kinds of cancer are causing more deaths, but most have stayed steady or declined.

The figures for mortality can be put to another use. When a nation is suddenly exposed to some novel cause of cancer, we would expect the effects of this to be detectable in the young sooner than in the old. For if risk is a function of the level of exposure and its duration, and the population is moving suddenly from a low to a high level of exposure, someone aged seventy may have had sixty years of risk R and ten years of risk $5R$ (giving a total of $110R$ instead of $70R$), whereas someone aged 30 has had 20 years of R and 10 of $5R$ (giving a total of $70R$ instead of $30R$); the old person's risk is up by 57 percent and the young person's by 133 percent. Similarly, when exposure to some risk factor is going down, the effects will first be seen in the younger age groups. So by watching cancer rates among the young we could get advance warning of what is likely to happen in the future. This is not a hypothetical argument. From the statistics for England and Wales, it was possible to deduce in 1950 that the population had recently become exposed to some potent cause of lung cancer and the future course of the epidemic was predicted with remarkable accuracy, even though this was before the role of cigarettes had been established (figure 5.6).[14]

INCIDENCE

As long as you do not already have cancer, what you most want to know is your overall chance of dying of cancer, and you have no special interest in any particular kind of cancer. But once you know you have cancer, your mind becomes concentrated on the statistics for your kind of cancer and you want to know the chance of survival for people like you. The best source of information is the statistics for countries like Norway, which have been keeping cancer registries for many years. Whenever a doctor makes the diagnosis, the patient's name is put into the registry and the patient's fate is followed until death (from cancer or some unrelated cause). If you want to know your chance of surviving for the next five or ten or twenty years, you can find out from the cancer registry what fraction of patients are still alive who, when they were your age, were found to have your kind of cancer five or ten or twenty years ago. And since treatments tend to improve, you can assume that your chances will be somewhat better than theirs.

There is, however, one complicating factor that has to do with the prevalence of cancer and changes in diagnostic practices.

The results of treatment would presumably be much improved if cancers could be detected earlier in their evolution, before they had spread beyond the reach of simple surgery. So various screening programs have been set up to search for small symptomless cancers.

Most cancers seem to arise as the result of a succession of changes that make the cells behave in an increasingly abnormal fashion. Cancer of the uterine cervix, for example, usually starts off as a small patch of cells of slightly abnormal shape and organization. This condition is called cervical dysplasia. Later, the cells may look even more abnormal and this stage is called carcinoma *in situ*. Finally, some of the cells may start to invade nearby tissues, and at this stage the abnormality is classified as cancer. We know a lot about this particular progression simply because it is so easy to monitor. Fortunately, progression from one stage to the next seems to be the exception rather than the rule. Usually dysplasia disappears of its own accord and nothing need be done. Any large-scale screening program to catch cervical cancer in its earliest stages will therefore pick up far more women with cervical dysplasia than are ever going to develop cervical cancer (figure 5.7).[15] In other words, the prevalence of cancer-like lesions of the cervix is far higher than you would have guessed from the figures for mortality. For this reason it has not been easy to determine the right advice to give to these women—have the abnormal cells removed (which is a minor operation but incurs some expense and is not totally devoid of risk) or wait and see.

Obviously, you would like to intercept each cancer before it had spread beyond the reach of surgery, but this is difficult if you cannot tell which grain will grow and which will not. If it is difficult to decide what to advise the patient, it is equally difficult to determine whether screening brings any benefit. Ideally, you would carry out an empirical trial, screening one group of women and leaving another comparable group to its own devices. Unfortunately, Pap smears were introduced before the days of clinical trials, and now the main evidence that Pap smears are worthwhile comes from comparisons of cervical cancer mortality in countries that have different levels of screening.[16] In the case of cervical cancer there is an added complication. This is one of the cancers that is conspicuously much more common in the poorer nations; and, in any given nation, it is commoner among the poor than the rich. Even when screening is free, the poor (for complicated reasons) seem less willing to be screened than the rich, and so any screening program will tend to miss the people most likely to benefit.

In some respects, breast cancer is like cervical cancer. It too has been the subject of screening programs, although it is less accessible and

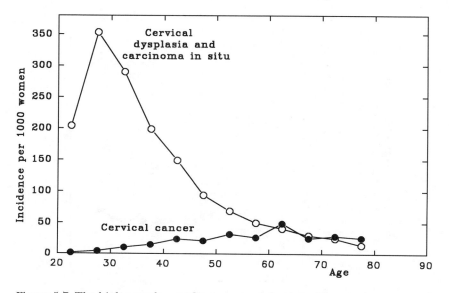

Figure 5.7. The high prevalence of precancerous lesions of the cervix, compared to the much lower rate of subsequent appearance of cervical cancer. These statistics come from British Columbia (see note 15), where the majority of all adult women had been checked at least once, and show that most precancerous lesions disappear spontaneously and do not progress to form cancers.

harder to monitor and happens to be commoner among the rich. Again, there appear to be many more abnormalities of the breast that, like cervical dysplasia, can be picked up in screening programs than are going to progress to cancer. But because these cannot be so easily monitored, much less is known about their natural history, so they tend to be treated as if they were actual cancers. As a result, screening programs have led to an apparent increase in the incidence of breast cancer. It seems clear that most of these extra cases do not represent proper cancers, because the actual mortality from breast cancer has scarcely changed (figure 5.8).[17] In the face of all this conflicting evidence, it is hard to judge what progress has been made in dealing with breast cancer. If you look at the statistics for countries like Norway, where screening is not sufficiently widespread to inflate the estimates of incidence, it does not look as if there has been much improvement. In the United States it could be argued that overall mortality is staying the same because modern treatments are roughly compensating for the increase in mortality that might be expected as the affluent become more affluent. Certainly, new treatments have been developed that do definitely reduce mortality when tested in clinical trials.

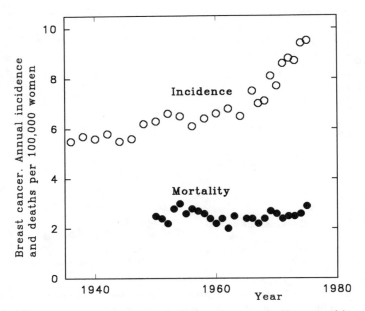

Figure 5.8. The war against cancer led to an increased effort to achieve early diagnosis and this resulted in an increase in the United States in the apparent incidence of breast cancer, but it did not lead to any detectable drop in mortality (from Fox; see note 17). Only in recent years have new treatments been introduced that, in clinical trials, prove to decrease mortality.

The problem of prevalence is not confined to cancers of the cervix and breast. For example, detailed microscopic examination of the prostates of men who have died from other causes has shown that small cancerous lesions are very common. Even though only about 3 percent of men in western nations die of prostate cancer, roughly 25 percent of men of my age have lesions that a pathologist would classify as small cancers.[18] Obviously, most of these little cancers, like many of the lesions in cervix and breast, are either not growing or are going to disappear. Until some way is found for determining which will grow and which will not, it would seem useless to embark on any kind of screening program. For, the act of removing the prostates of one-quarter of all old men would be the occasion of much misery and expense and might well cause more loss of life-span than doing nothing.

What is needed is some test that can distinguish the cancer that will grow from the one that will not. This may prove to be one of the major contributions of molecular biology. I could easily imagine that in the development of each major class of cancer there is one critical step that is accompanied by the appearance in the cells of some unusual, monitorable gene product. Already, several tests are in use for determining the likely response to treatment; for example, breast cancers that retain estrogen receptors on the surface of their cells tend to respond better to hormone therapy. And for the cancers that can be caused by viruses, the presence or absence of viral nucleic acids and proteins can be an important indicator of the likelihood of progression to a fully malignant cancer.

The Infective Origin of Certain Cancers

As I mentioned in the previous chapter, viruses have been known since the turn of the century to be a cause of cancer in domestic animals. So it has always seemed likely that the same would be true for humans, but proof has come only fairly recently. Two examples, cancer of the liver and the cervix, are particularly important because together they cause almost 1 million deaths a year.

LIVER CANCER

This is one of the commonest cancers in Africa and Asia, though it is fairly rare in Western nations. In the world as a whole, about 250,000 people die from liver cancer each year. For a long time, the cancer was thought to be caused simply by certain mutagens in food, in particular a toxic substance called aflatoxin which is produced by a fungus that infects peanuts. Indeed, this almost certainly is a risk factor because the liver cancers that arise in people exposed to aflatoxin have sequence changes in their oncogenes that are the kind of change known to be produced when aflatoxin interacts with DNA. But by the late 1970s, a more pervasive and powerful risk factor was discovered, namely infection with hepatitis B virus (HBV).

Unlike the ordinary kind of hepatitis which is usually caused by hepatitis A virus and is spread by mouth, HBV is passed from mother to child shortly after the child is born. Infection of adults usually requires the direct transfer of blood or semen. The virus multiplies only in liver cells, but these liberate huge numbers of virus particles into the bloodstream. Infection can run one of two courses. It is either controlled by the immune system so that you end up with circulating antibodies and little or no virus, or it leads to chronic infection so that you become a "carrier" and circulate infective virus for the rest of your life. The world today contains an estimated 200 million carriers, and these carriers have almost a hundredfold higher risk of getting liver cancer than noncarriers. Of course, it could have been argued that the association of liver cancer with HBV infection did not per se indicate a direct causal connection, but similar viruses have been found in certain animals that can be shown to give rise to a carrier state and to be the direct cause of liver cancer.

Once someone is infected with a virus, there is little you can do to influence the course of infection. So we may not be able to help the 200 million people who are already carriers. But the genes of HBV that code for the virus's surface proteins have been moved into yeast cells which then make the proteins, and these proteins can be used to immunize people at risk of being infected. Such immunization is now being employed in developing nations to protect newborn children, and in developed nations to protect certain groups at special risk (surgeons and dentists, people such as hemophiliacs who need frequent blood transfusions, and drug addicts who share needles). Already, it has been shown to protect children from becoming HBV carriers and no doubt will in time be shown to protect these children against liver cancer.[19]

We have here, therefore, a very straightforward strategy for preventing one of the major cancers. Immunization is not expensive and, if widely used, should eventually diminish the prevalence of carriers and in turn diminish the need for immunization. It also demonstrates an important principle in the prevention of any disease. Here we have a disease with several causes—diet, habits, a virus, and no doubt other factors we have not yet discovered. But in order to intervene, you do not need to understand the entire causal chain. It is sufficient to block one step in the chain. In this instance, one of the causes is accessible. Diet is not easily modified especially in populations that have barely enough to eat, and pleasurable habits are hard to change when there is nothing better on offer. But an infectious agent such as HBV is an ideal target because it is of no value to anyone. No one will mourn its disappearance.

CERVICAL CANCER

Breast cancer kills almost 700,000 women a year, and cancer of the uterine cervix is second with almost 500,000 a year. In several respects these two cancers behave in opposite ways. Since early in the nineteenth century breast cancer has been known to be commoner in nuns, whereas cervical cancer is commoner in married women and virtually unknown in nuns. Again, breast cancer is much commoner in rich nations than in the developing world, whereas the reverse is true for cervical cancer. For years, the conventional explanation has been that breast cancer is due to some reproductive or dietary factor associated with affluence, and that cervical cancer is due to an infectious agent transmitted sexually, like any other venereal disease. But it has been very difficult to pin down which, of all the agents that are transmitted sexually, is the one that causes cancer, because they tend to go hand in hand. Since cervical cancer tends to be associated with having many sexual partners, we would expect any sexually transmitted agent to be more prevalent in women with cervical cancer. So here, as is so often the case, simple association is not proof of causality. The two main candidates have been the herpes viruses and the papilloma viruses, but it now seems clear that the papilloma viruses are the more important.

Many, perhaps most, animal species are host to a very large number of interrelated papilloma viruses. More than sixty different types of human papilloma virus (HPV) have been identified, and these include the types that cause the transient warts that are common in children. In animals, papilloma viruses certainly can cause cancer when in conjunction with other factors; for example, one of the bovine papilloma viruses can be shown to cause esophageal cancer in cattle that eat bracken, and this is a major cause of death of cattle in Scotland.

The life cycle of these viruses is closely linked to the program of cell division that renews the layers of cells in our surface epithelia. In our skin, for example, the deeper cells divide and, as a result, push up the overlying cells toward the surface. As these superficial cells move outward they change their shape, and before they are shed from the surface they start making specialized gene products such as the insoluble protein called keratin, which serve as protection for the underlying cells. In an epithelium infected with a papilloma virus, the virus persists in the deepest cells and does not indulge in extensive replication of its DNA until the cells start to move outwards and embark on their own final program of development (which, incidentally, is a form of programmed cell death). By the time the cell is shed, it is full of virus particles and these are then free to be transferred to a new host, but the cell itself is dead.

This interaction between virus and host would be perfectly benign, were it not for the operation of two forms of natural selection. As I have described it, the total amount of virus produced by an epithelium is limited by programmed cell death and by the restraints the cells put on their own multiplication within the basal layer of the epithelium. So there has been intense selection in favor of any virus that contains genes that can override programmed cell death, and this is presumably why papilloma viruses contain genes that immortalize the cell they infect. At the same time, there is selection for cells that can escape the restraints on cell multiplication; very occasionally, papilloma virus DNA becomes integrated into the host cell's DNA, and its strong promoters for transcription start controlling the expression of genes nearby; if these genes are important in the regulation of cell division this virus-carrying cell, by multiplying without restraint, may become able to supplant its normal neighbors and give rise to a cancer. For example, the most widely used cultured line of human cells (called HeLa cells, because the patient's name was Henrietta Lacks) came from a cervical cancer. The cells of this patient have been able to keep growing for almost fifty years because they had been immortalized by a papilloma virus, and they were forming a cancer because a piece of virus DNA with its powerful promoters of gene expression had become integrated near to the cell's *myc* gene which, as I explained on page 153, is known to regulate cell division and to be involved in several kinds of cancer.

Although the molecular biology of carcinogenesis by HPVs is fairly well understood, the demonstration of a true causal connection has been greatly complicated by existence of many varieties of HPV that do not cause cancer. But for the techniques of modern molecular biology, it would have been impossible to disentangle the role of the few kinds of HPV that are important. Thanks, however, to DNA-DNA hybridization (see page 98) it has been possible to link the development of cervical cancer to infection with just a few types of virus, in particular HPV types 16 and 18. And when Pap smears are backed up by DNA hybridization tests, it is now possible to predict more accurately which group of cells will grow and which will not.[20]

At the moment there is no immediate prospect for an effective and safe vaccine, so the exercise of reducing the mortality from cervical cancer rests on screening programs and on trying to engineer a change in sexual habits. This raises an interesting and not immediately obvious point about the spread of sexually transmitted diseases. Plainly, your chance of becoming infected is determined by the chance that your partner is already infected, which in turn was determined by the chance that some partner of theirs was infected, and so on. It is therefore not so much the general level of promiscuity that matters (i.e., the average number of sexual partners) but rather the characteristics of the sexual network. If a very few members of a population have very many partners, then each of those partners will be only one link away from many partners and so will be at high risk. It is not what might be called primary connectivity but secondary connectivity that is important. For example, sexually transmitted diseases will be most prevalent when recourse to prostitutes is a common practice, and they will tend to be less common when a general acceptance of a low level of promiscuity makes prostitution less acceptable. Certainly, this seems to be the factor that determines the widely different rates of cervical cancer in countries that have the same average number of sexual partners. Whether prevention can be achieved by changing the form of the sexual network remains to be determined.

The study of viruses as a cause of cancer may seem straightforward. Two examples show that this is not always true.

Hodgkin's disease is a cancer involving several kinds of cell in the immune system. Because of its microscopic similarity to certain chronic diseases such as tuberculosis and leprosy, it was officially classified as an infectious disease until well into the twentieth century. It is one of the few cancers that can occur in children and young adults, as well as in older people. Hodgkin's disease and certain kinds of childhood leukemia are known to be commoner in first-born children. This suggests that they are caused by viruses that normally produce a harmless infection in young children and are dangerous only when infection is postponed until later in life. The argument goes as follows. As every parent knows, when your children start going to school they bring back a seemingly endless succession of colds and other upsets that tend to affect you more than them. The idea is therefore that the first child in a family is infected when it meets other children at school and it brings the infection home to its siblings who are therefore infected when they are younger and less likely to develop Hodgkin's disease or leukemia, as the case may be. This kind of increase in susceptibility with age is well known for viruses such as poliomyelitis and certain viruses of mice. So the hypothesis is not unreasonable.

In 1971, a report appeared describing a cluster of twelve cases of Hodgkin's disease in upstate New York among a group of children who had graduated from high school between 1953 and 1955.[21] The twelve cases were all friends or relatives of each other, or friends of friends, and the suggestion was made that they had passed some virus from one to another that would fairly quickly cause Hodgkin's disease in most (but not all) of the children who became infected. Because the numbers were rather small and it was not clear how probable it was that such a cluster could have arisen by chance alone, the study was extended to cover the records of a group of schools in Long Island for the period 1960–1969.[22] From these records it appeared that the schools that had cases of Hodgkin's disease in the years 1960–1964 were far more likely to have cases in the next five years than schools with no cases in 1960–1964. This seemed to confirm the conclusion reached in upstate New York that Hodgkin's disease is due to some infectious agent.

Studies like this are fraught with difficulties. If you have Hodgkin's disease you will almost certainly end up in a clinic that specializes in its treatment, so you meet other patients; in other words, each patient will help the investigator hear about other cases. If there had been any failure to pick up cases in the Long Island study, this would have been most likely for the schools that had no cases in the first five-year period. Indeed, on standing back from the whole study it became clear that the difference between the two groups of schools was that those without cases in the first period had about half as many cases in the second period as you might have expected from the overall national incidence of Hodgkin's disease.[23] So though Hodgkin's disease may well be caused by a virus, these studies certainly did not constitute proof.

I have described this episode partly to show how difficult it is to investigate the clustering of cases. But I am also using it to illustrate another important aspect of epidemiology. The papers describing these studies in New York State were widely publicized and generated a lot of excitement. (I myself was not very worried even though my own children were in high school in Long Island at the time, because I knew that the incidence of Hodgkin's disease is only about four cases per 100,000 people per year, so it is not one of the major hazards in the life of a teenager.) However, the publicity was so great that a number of the children with Hodgkin's disease committed suicide in order to ensure that they would not infect their friends.[24] The moral of this story is obvious. All public pronouncements about risks and benefits, whether experimental or epidemiological in origin, have to be cautious and great efforts have to be made to put the conclusions in their proper context.

My other example is also of an apparent cluster of cases, and it too has ramifications that go beyond the science itself. Clusters of leukemia have been reported among children who live near nuclear reprocessing plants. Since these plants are very expensive, are usually managed by governments, and tend to be shrouded in secrecy, the suggestion that something dangerous is leaking out is as much a political as an epidemiological statement. I have already described the steps taken to determine how likely it is that some rare event could be due simply to chance. Here we have the added complication that while one political group very much wants the cluster to exist and to indicate leakage, another group very much wants it to be due to chance. Until recently, it seemed that these were the two possible answers. Now, however, a third hypothesis has emerged, and it is as follows.

Nuclear reprocessing plants are set up in the remote countryside to minimize the damage that might come from any accident, and they are run by a sophisticated group of technocrats. So around each plant there is a population who have recently migrated from town to country. So their children (who, when quite young, have mingled with all the cities' viruses) now mingle with country children (who have not). If the kind of model of viral carcinogenesis that I described for Hodgkin's disease were true for childhood leukemia, we would expect these country children to face an increased risk of leukemia. So this hypothesis makes two predictions: (a) whenever a large group of city folk move into the country this should lead to a local outbreak of leukemia, and (b) the extra cases of leukemia should be among the indigenous children and not among the incoming children. The test, therefore, was to look at regions where, for some other reason, there had been a sudden migration from town to country.[25] Two such regions were found, and in each case the local children had suffered an increase in leukemia. Indeed, it turns out that the evacuation of roughly 1 million children from London into the country at the start of World War II had a similar effect.[26] Over the next ten years, the regions that received most of the children showed an increased rate of childhood leukemia in the local population.

I am sure that, in the years to come, a clear causal connection will be established between other viruses and other cancers. And I would, until recently, have said that infectious agents are satisfactory causes for diseases because they offer so many opportunities for prevention, in particular prevention by immunization. However, the extreme difficulty in devising protection against the AIDS virus shows that infectious agents can be very hard to control, even in affluent populations.

The Inheritance of Increased Risk of Cancer

If you live in an industrialized nation and want to have a long life, the statistics of mortality say that you should not smoke, you should not be overweight, you should be well educated, and you should have long-lived parents. These four ingredients are of roughly equal importance. The fact that we cannot choose our parents does not, however, mean that there should be no research into the inheritance of susceptibility to diseases. It may be politically correct to hold that "all men are created equal," but we know that humans vary in countless ways and we would guess that the upper limit to the risk posed by each of the hazardous variables in our environment will often be set by the sensitivity of the most susceptible members of the population. A minority of the population become sensitized to metals such as beryllium and nickel, and the regulations governing industrial exposure are based on their sensitivity. It is in part because some children seem to have an inherited susceptibility to a form of asthma caused by something in the air of modern cities that we have to try to control urban air pollution. Disregard of the possible existence of sensitive minorities on the grounds of political correctness is hardly in the best interests of humankind.

Any property of humans that you can measure will, to some extent, be determined by which particular versions of genes they inherit from their parents. Among other things, these genes will determine your susceptibility to cancer. Some of the effects operate at a fairly crude level. For example, your degree of pigmentation is determined by several genes, and if you have not inherited the high-pigmentation versions of any of these genes and are exposed to high levels of sunlight, you will have a high risk of developing skin cancer. Your chance of developing nasopharyngeal cancer (which is associated with air pollution and exposure to a virus called EBV) seems to be much greater if you are of mongoloid origin, perhaps because of some slight difference in the anatomy of the nasal bones in these ethnic groups.

Since cancer cells are known to contain mutations in certain genes (oncogenes) that regulate cell division, we might expect to find occasionally that one or another of these mutations has been inherited from one of the patient's parents rather than acquired during the patient's lifetime. This would raise the incidence by cutting out one of the steps in the formation of cancer. Several examples of this are now known.

In the previous chapter I mentioned mutations in a gene called *Rb* which lead to tumors of the retina in children. The *Rb* gene is one of the genes involved in the control of the division of all cells, but its proper functioning is apparently particularly important during development of the retina; inheriting a defective *Rb* raises the risk of retinoblastoma from roughly 1 in 100,000 to about 90,000 in 100,000.[27] Equally spectacular in their effects are mutations in a gene called *APC* which causes multiple adenomatous polyps of the colon followed by multiple colon cancers; this is one of the causes of the condition called polyposis coli.[28] Fortunately each of these mutations is rare and these two forms of inherited susceptibility do not cause many deaths. More important in terms of total deaths are certain inherited mutations that raise susceptibility to breast cancer. It has been known for almost fifty years that breast cancer sometimes runs in families, but only recently has modern molecular biology made it possible to identify the genes involved. Mutations in one gene have been shown to raise the risk of breast cancer about fiftyfold and be responsible for about 5 percent of all breast cancers and therefore, in the United States, for several thousand deaths each year.

The exercise of identifying the different forms of inherited susceptibility to cancer (and other diseases) has only just begun and we must prepare ourselves for what is certain to emerge. Obviously, if you are born into a family with a history of high risk for some kind of cancer and can afford to pay for the test, you would like to know whether or not you have inherited the mutant gene that is causing the cancers; if you have, you could save your life by undergoing regular testing. It is imaginable, for example, that a program of early screening and selective abortion could greatly decrease the frequency of desperately severe diseases like inherited polyposis coli. In this way a rich family (such as the hemophilic descendants of Queen Victoria) might free itself from a mutant gene that had dogged its past.

The worrying aspect of all measures of genetic variability is the effect that these may have on people's prospects for support and employment. It is easily imaginable that molecular biology will eventually make it possible for the richer members of the human race to check their genes to see which of their tissues are most at risk, and this would allow them to adjust their life-styles accordingly. For the poor, who cannot adjust their life-styles, the prospects are more alarming. Even quite a small advance in techniques for predicting risks could perturb the delicate balance between the business of life insurance and the people who are insured. This is already an area that has required government intervention and takes us into the whole area of the economics of health.

Certain Problems of Economics in the Treatment and Prevention of Cancer

The explosion in the world's population has occurred because, in almost every country, mortality declined before there had been any compensating decline in the birthrate. The process began in the industrialized nations. Initially, it did not create any problems because the technologies that decreased mortality also created more jobs. Somewhat later, the rise of technology spread into medical practice and ways were found for preventing some diseases (e.g., by immunization) and for treating others (e.g., by antibiotics). This too did not create any economic problems. It is much cheaper to immunize a population against an infectious disease than to treat all those cases that would arise in the absence of immunization; it is much cheaper to add iodine to salt and vitamin D to milk than to look after people with goiter and rickets. Apart from their effectiveness, the most impressive feature of the early antibiotics, such as the sulfonamides and penicillin, was that they could be used without any accompanying technical backup. It is vastly cheaper to cure pneumonia by giving patients penicillin than by nursing them until they recover.

The same can be said for some of the recent advances in medicine; for example, it is probably less expensive for society if a patient is given a pacemaker than not given one. But the same cannot be said for some of the more exciting recent advances in the treatment of cancer. For example, childhood leukemia was once invariably fatal but it can now be cured by intensive chemotherapy. This requires most sophisticated and expensive supervision. Ten years ago, the cost of the cure was over $100,000 and it must be much more than that now.[29] The reason that nations can afford to pay for the treatment is because childhood leukemia is not common; in the United States, for example, there are only about 1,000 cases a year, so the total bill is $100–200 million a year.

Similarly intensive forms of radiotherapy plus chemotherapy have been used to treat the common kinds of cancer, but so far they have not proved sufficiently effective to be pursued with much enthusiasm. It may be only a matter of time, however, before ways are found for raising the intensity or specificity of the treatments and making cancer a curable disease. At that point, societies will have to make a difficult choice. The United States has about 700,000 new cases of cancer each year. If $200,000 is to be spent on each of these patients, the total bill will be $140 billion a year, or roughly 5 percent of the gross national product.

Faced with that prospect, the obvious answer is to devote more resources to the much cheaper exercise of prevention. If all forms of cancer could be prevented and all other causes of death kept at their present level, this would add an average of twelve years to the lives of those who would otherwise have died of cancer. Because only about one-sixth of all deaths are due to cancer, life expectancy would increase by about two years, and that would not greatly increase the proportion of the population who are retired and have ceased to generate wealth.

The most important single step in the prevention of cancer would be the abolition of cigarettes. Roughly one-third of all deaths from cancer in countries like the United States are caused by smoking. And now, with the spread of cigarettes into developing nations, lung cancer has just moved to the top of the list for the world as a whole. The English epidemiologist Richard Peto has predicted that if there is no reduction in the sales of tobacco, more people who are alive today are going to die from smoking than the total number who have died in all the wars and revolutions of the twentieth century.

Unfortunately, it has proved difficult to persuade certain governments to accept the economic consequences of such a step, because the cigarette plays such a large part in each nation's economy. The problem can be expressed in the following way.[30] The expense of rearing a child from the moment of its conception until it starts earning is met partly by the family and partly by the nation; once the child is earning it starts contributing to the various forms of taxation and paying back its debt to nation and family; after a few years, the debt is wiped out, and from then on the taxes can be thought of as payment into a pension scheme; eventually the moment of retirement arrives, and the capital in the pension scheme starts to be withdrawn. In other words, we are debtors for the first 15–25 years of life, we then have a positive bank balance, and finally if we live long enough we can get back into debt.

Figure 5.9 shows the trajectory followed by the average inhabitant of the British Isles, where the calculation is fairly straightforward because most of the social services are run by the government. Under steady-state

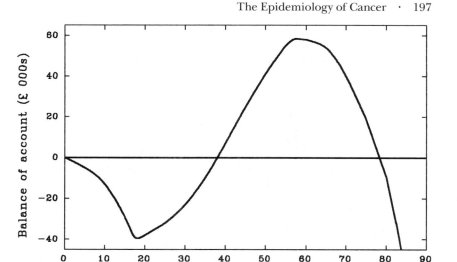

Figure 5.9. A nation's investment in each member of its population reaches its greatest value just before the person starts to earn a living; the person's investment in their own future security reaches its greatest value just before they retire and then declines as they draw upon this saving (from West; see note 30). The general form of the curve is shown in this figure, but the exact values depend on exactly how the calculation is carried and what assumptions are made about how the assets and liabilities of a nation should be divided among its populace. Any increase in life expectancy beyond the average age of retirement moves the population down the righthand end of the curve, decreasing the average worth of the population and increasing government expenditure.

conditions, where the size and age distribution of a population is not changing, a government could balance its books by shaping the trajectory in such a way that the average area under the curve is zero (i.e., the area above the line equals the area below the line). This is difficult to arrange when populations are growing, unless the direct and indirect payments on retirement are being continually reduced by inflation.

Smokers follow a trajectory that is more favorable from the government's point view. Although they are more likely to require treatment for nonfatal illnesses, the big difference is that when they start earning they contribute extra taxes (because of the high tax on cigarettes) and finally when they retire they are less expensive because they die, on average, some seven years sooner than nonsmokers. They are therefore making two contributions to the state. In Britain these are roughly equal in size and together amount to about half of the cost of The National Health Service. Presumably it was for reasons such as this that the British government recently vetoed a proposal that would have banned all cigarette advertising in Europe.

Actually, I think the issue of smoking is even more complicated than that. In most developed nations, the rich are now much less likely to smoke than the poor. I imagine that this is because the rich have better access to other forms of gratification and are more likely to consider the long-term consequences of their actions; at the two extremes, the rich man worries about preserving his wealth for his children while the poorest peasant has no choice but to live from day to day. And, perhaps correctly, the poor seem to have decided that their life in old age is not going to be very enjoyable and that it is not worth making sacrifices in their youth in order to gain a few extra years at the far end.

My view, for what it is worth, is that this is a choice all adults should feel free to make for themselves, unless they live in the company of small children whose health will be damaged by passive smoking. Advertising of tobacco should certainly be banned because its purpose is to make people smoke, but I think that tobacco products should not be subject to a special tax because that is putting an extra burden on the people least able to pay.

The Cancers of Affluent Societies

In the poorer nations of the world, the main cancers seem to be caused by viruses and by substances in the diet that affect the upper end of the alimentary tract and the liver (which, at least in experimental animals, is the main target of dietary mutagens). Because wealth brings freedom of action, the rich nations have learned how to avoid many infectious agents and have organized the distribution of food so that most of their citizens can enjoy a fresh and highly varied diet. As a result, the frequency of cancers of the mouth, esophagus, stomach, liver, and cervix have gone down by roughly a factor of ten. Unfortunately, as these have declined, others have risen to take their place. Cancers of the breast, colon, rectum, and prostate are fairly uncommon in poor nations, but they account for about one-third of the nonlung cancer deaths in rich nations.

To me the most surprising feature of these cancers of affluence is that we still do not have any direct evidence as to their cause. Their incidence can be related to various features of each nation's diet. For example, colon cancer is commonest in the nations that have the highest consumption of meat (figure 5.10).[31] Any hypothesis about the cause of colon cancer has to account for this correlation. But it is important to remember that correlation need not imply causality. Meat is one of the more expensive components of our diet, and in this case meat consump-

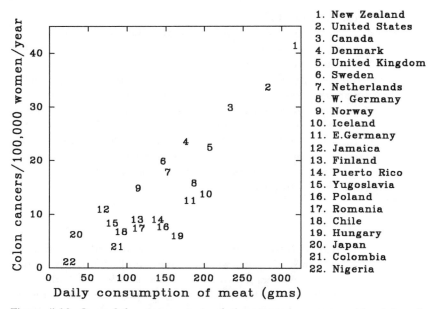

Figure 5.10. One of the strongest correlations seen in cancer epidemiology is between meat consumption and colon cancer rates (from Doll and Peto; see note 31). Different countries vary over roughly a tenfold range for each of these two measures. What remains to be determined is whether colon cancer is really caused by eating meat or is caused by some factor that is itself correlated with meat eating.

tion may be no more than a convenient way of measuring affluence and may be a reflection of some other unidentified variable, associated with affluence, that is the directly acting cause (in the sense that it is the thing that stimulates cells in the colon to undergo changes that make them form cancers). The correlation may, however, be not so much with each nation's present level of affluence but rather with its lifestyle thirty or forty years ago. For example, Japan has the colon cancer rate of a poor nation (which it certainly is not), but this may be because it had a singularly ascetic lifestyle when the older members of its population were young children.

Similar effects are seen in experimental animals. Mice that are allowed limitless food and become overweight suffer an increased incidence of many kinds of "spontaneous" cancer; conversely, if they are slightly underfed so that they are smaller and lighter, they live longer and have a lower rate of cancer. The important factor, for these animals, appears to be total calories rather than the exact source of the calories.[32]

Conceivably the same may be true in humans.[33] For nonsmokers in the United States, the risk of dying from cancer is roughly proportional to the extent to which you are overweight for your height;[34] (this relationship is not seen for smokers, because smoking decreases your appetite and weight but increases your risk).

Perhaps the most plausible explanation for the cancers of affluence is that they not are due to viruses or mutagens but to excessive cell multiplication caused directly or indirectly by excessive nutrition.[35] I can easily imagine that this excessive proliferation and turnover of cells may allow far greater opportunity for the selection of fitter cell variants.[36] If this view is correct, we may find it almost impossible to prevent the cancers of affluence unless we are prepared to change our idea of what are the desirable rewards of affluence.

❧

It is, I think, proper that this chapter ends in obscurity. Obviously, in time we will understand what really are the major risk factors for the cancers of affluence and we will perhaps adjust our life-styles to minimize the incidence of most forms of cancer. Eventually, methods may be developed for treating cancer that are as effortless and inexpensive as the treatment of certain infections by antibiotics. For the biological sciences are moving forward at such a breakneck pace that everything seems almost within our grasp.

Yet there is a certain inexorable order to the process of discovery. If you could go back in time to the beginning of the century, bearing with you the knowledge of some crucial discovery, such as penicillin for example, you would find that this knowledge could not be put to use because not enough was known then about chemical technology. Even if I knew which grain would grow and which would not, I suspect that I could not put this knowledge to use, ahead of its proper time.

Nevertheless, coming as I am to the end of my life, I do wish I knew what discoveries are going to be made in biology and in cancer research. But most of all I would like to know what is going to happen to the tenuous hold of *Homo sapiens* on the surface of this unstable planet. And that is the subject of the final chapter.

CHAPTER 6

Population

> And I myself have lost two or three children, even while they were still being nursed; it was with regret but I did not make a fuss about it.
>
> —Montaigne, *Essay on the Taste of Goods or Evils*, 1572

Sooner or later every nation will have gone through the demographic transition and have adjusted to its new, reduced death rate by lowering its birthrate. Judging from the past, these two parts of the process tend to occur in the wrong order. Deaths go down a few generations before births go down. As a result, the change in pattern of mortality is almost invariably accompanied by a huge increase in population. Having written about the history of mortality, I felt therefore that I really ought to learn something about the history of the population explosion.

In fact, it is the vision of the prospects for the future that makes demography such an important subject. The recent explosion in human population is something that could have been viewed with equanimity if we were still in the pre-industrial age: eventually the population would have to stabilize or decline, for one reason or another, and we could reorganize society or start the build-up all over again. Unfortunately, as a result of the Industrial Revolution, humankind has acquired a heightened ability to consume resources, and this great proliferation of one of the world's mammals will bequeath to the earth as a whole a legacy from which it may never recover. In the past, over-exploitation of resources sometimes caused irreversible changes in the earth's surface, but the disasters were quite local in their effects. This time, however, the loss will not be like the collapse of the Mayan civilization, just the destruction of one fertile area of farmland, but could be a change affecting the whole surface of the earth. This time, the disaster promises to be on a global scale.

Much is being written about our need to control the way we despoil the world. Endless plans are produced for restoring the forests, saving the ozone layer, and clearing the atmosphere and the seas of all pollutants. These plans, perhaps rightly, concentrate on altering human behavior. But the problem is the product of two factors, two independent variables. One factor is indeed human behavior, but the other is simply the number of humans whose behavior has to be modified. Yes, the average inhabitant of the Western world consumes too much; but that is bad for the earth because there are already too many of these consumers and soon there are going to be many more.

It is hard to tell how far human behavior is capable of modification. North America produces about twenty times as much carbon dioxide per capita as does Africa[1] and must, at the moment, accept an appropriate share of the responsibility for the greenhouse effect. Perhaps its inhabitants could be persuaded to reduce their demand for energy by, say, a factor of two. But that is not enough. Asia already contains almost ten times as many people as North America and is growing fast. Africa is much larger in area than North America (and much, much richer in natural resources than Asia), and its population already exceeds that of North America even though its growth phase has barely begun.

If the 1 billion inhabitants of Europe and North America are enough to produce measurable global warming in less than 150 years, how can Planet Earth be expected to tolerate a population of several billion in Africa and several billion in Asia, all of whom must long to live the life of rich Americans? The solution (if there is to be one) must depend on politics and economics. Obviously, technology will play its part by developing renewable sources of energy and better forms of birth control, but even the most sophisticated technology will be of no avail in the absence of political and economic incentives.

As soon as I started reading about population (after retiring from the Harvard School of Public Health), I discovered that I was caught up in a kind of research that I had never previously encountered. The actual words used by scientists are seldom very important. You will find few quotations in the average scientific textbook; what matters is the thing, the discovery, the change in point of view, not the telling phrase (though there are some scientists who write most beautifully). The history of population is different. For it is in large measure the story of human expectations. Like many animals (see page 215), humans tend to adjust their rate of reproduction to match what they believe will be the opportunities for the next generation. So the opinions of the average citizen become of prime importance. Also, even more than in the case of the force of mortality, the rate of change of birthrates reflects political judgments: and most people's political opinions are imposed on them by others.

So I found myself having to learn just as much about people's opinions (which are often obscure or devious) as about demography itself (which seems a fairly straightforward subject). Finally, I discovered that demography was taking me back to history again, though this time it was the history of the earth's climate—a subject that is likely to become more and more important in the years ahead.

The following chapter is therefore divided into three sections. The first is an account of certain people's opinions. Not being a historian by trade I cannot claim to understand the forces that gave rise to those opinions, so I have to accept what people wrote as truly representing what they thought. The second section describes the actual change in the population of various countries up to the end of the twentieth century. The third describes the recently emerged picture of the changes that have taken place in our climate and of the physical factors that are likely to determine what the future holds in store.

❧❦❧

THE MALTHUSIAN VIEW OF THE WORLD

"Population Malthus"

If, like Darwin, Marx, or Wagner, you find that your name has been turned into an everyday adjective, you can be certain that some people will be using it as a term of abuse. This curious phenomenon is not very common in the sciences but it seems almost the rule in politics and economics, perhaps because these are essentially adversarial systems: hypotheses can seldom be put to the test, so the survival of an idea depends, more than anything else, on the strength of someone's advocacy.

I doubt, for example, if you can find many scientists who would use the words Euclidean, Newtonian, or Cartesian as an insult. Malthus, however, has suffered almost 200 years of attack, and to political economists the word "Malthusian" is taken to mean a model or view of population growth that is politically incorrect and has been shown to be unsound. It seems to me, however, that his analysis of the problem of overpopulation describes perfectly the state of the world's population at the end of the twentieth century.

Malthus wrote two essays on "The Principle of Population," one in 1798 and the other in 1803. Like much of the writing of that period, they strike a twentieth-century reader as unnecessarily verbose. Few of us have time to read any long treatise from beginning to end; nowadays, information comes to us in soundbites and the message has got to be short. So we are left not with what Malthus wrote (which is too long for most of us) but with the vague recollection of what others wrote about him. In particular, Marx and Engels chose to single him out for criticism and had no hesitation in putting his arguments into untenable forms so that they could refute them. Their version of Malthus is, I suspect, now more widely known than anything that Malthus actually wrote. Certainly, my understanding was that Malthus had announced a simple proposition about the growth and limits of population which subsequent events have shown to be incorrect. It therefore came as something of a revelation to discover what Malthus actually said.

"The following *Essay* owes its origin to a conversation with a friend, on the subject of Mr. Godwin's essay on 'Avarice and Profusion' in his *Enquirer.* The discussion started the general question of the future improvement of society. . . ."[2] So begins the preface to Malthus's first book. The "friend" was his father, Daniel Malthus, an independently wealthy country gentleman who was a friend of Hume and admirer of Rousseau. The son, Thomas Robert Malthus, had trained in mathematics and classics at Cambridge and at the time of this conversation was curate of a small church near the village of Albury in Surrey, nine miles from where his father lived. The full title of the book is *An Essay on the Principle of Population as it affects the future Improvement of Society, with Remarks on the Speculations of Mr. Godwin, M. Condorcet, and other Writers.* Before discussing the essence of Malthus's first essay, we should look at what these other authors had written.

The Forerunners of Malthus

Compared to the nations of Europe at the end of the eighteenth century, we live today in a relatively stable world. By eighteenth-century standards, most governments of the industrialized world are reasonably democratic, and there is little sign that this will change in the near future. It was not so in the time of Malthus. After more than a century of political upheavals, which had started with the English Revolution and just ended with the American and French Revolutions, no one could see what the future held in store. Between 1543 and 1686, in a period of just 150 years, Copernicus, Galileo, and Newton had removed man from the center of the universe and had undermined the authority of church and state. And in the next 100 years, the Enlightenment had extended this scientific revolution into political philosophy, so that by the end of the eighteenth century it must have seemed that society could be reorganized in any way you wished. The possibilities appeared to be limitless.

Perhaps the most extreme revision of the order of things was proposed by William Godwin, whom many consider to have been the founder of anarchism. Godwin was a Calvinist minister who came to see religion as "an accommodation to the prejudices and weaknesses of mankind"[3] and to believe that all forms of property and accumulated wealth were evil. Neither the state nor any individual should have power over anyone. Marriage was bondage and ought to be abolished. Justice demanded that property should go to him that needs it most: "What magic is there in the pronoun 'my,' to overturn the decisions of everlasting truth? . . . If land were perpetually open to him who was willing to cultivate it, it is not to be believed but that it would be cultivated in proportion to the wants of the community, nor by the same reason would there be any effectual check on the increase of population."[4] It was a grand vision, which saw no limits.

Godwin's mixture of anarchy and what came to be called communism appeared in 1793 in a book entitled *An Enquiry concerning Political Justice and Its Influence on Morals and Happiness.* The thesis did not endear the author to the political establishment, but the book escaped being banned because it was thought to be too expensive for its intended audience.[5] In fact, it sold very well and Godwin, almost overnight, became a celebrity and found himself temporarily fairly well off.

Four years later, he extended his argument in a second book, *The Enquirer. Reflections on Education, Manners and Literature, in a series of essays,* and one of its chapters, an essay on "Avarice and Profusion," supposedly provoked the argument between Malthus and his father. In this essay, Godwin argues that there is more virtue in the avaricious miser than in the rich man who profusely spends his wealth. Money is of no intrinsic value and so the miser, who "sees the folly of profusion," deprives the world of nothing; in contrast, the rich man who spends his money destroys society. "It is a gross and ridiculous error to suppose that the rich pay for anything. There is no wealth in the world except this, the labour of man. . . . What is misnamed wealth is merely a power vested in certain individuals by the institutions of society, to compel others to labour for their benefit."[6]

The essay tempers anarchy with a little socialism. "The principles of virtue require . . . that the inequalities which inevitably arise, should be repressed, and kept down within as narrow limits as possible."[7] Perhaps that was the idea Malthus felt was impractical, but it seems likely that the argument with his father was more about Godwin's views on population, which had been laid out in *Political Justice.* Godwin felt that

> It would be truly absurd for us to shrink from a scheme of effectual benefit to mankind, lest they should be too happy, and by necessary consequence at some distant period too populous. . . . Three fourths of the habitable globe is now uncultivated. The parts already cultivated are capable of immeasurable improvement. Myriads of centuries of still increasing population may probably pass away, and the earth still be found sufficient for the subsistence of its inhabitants.[8]

As for the distant future, Godwin offered the following unusual solution. "The men . . . who exist when the earth shall refuse itself to a more extended population, will cease to propagate, for they will no longer have any motive, either of error or duty, to induce them. In addition to this they will perhaps be immortal."[9] In this, Godwin said he was following the opinion of Benjamin Franklin, who apparently had often been heard to say that "mind will one day become omnipotent over matter," though it seems doubtful whether sexual abstinence was what Franklin had in mind.

A little more should be said about Godwin, the man. He was, as Virginia Woolf put it, "a mixture of meanness and magnanimity, of coldness and deep feeling."[10] Having argued against the institution of matrimony, he nevertheless was willing to forsake his principles and married twice. Later, he again forgot his principles and was furious when Shelley ran off with both his daughter and his stepdaughter and the stepdaughter became Byron's mistress. Finally, he compounded his inconsistency by forgiving Shelley so that he could continue to receive financial support from Shelley's father. Apart from this failure to live up to his own ideals, he suffers from the contrast with his first wife, Mary Wollstonecraft, who always stuck by her principles and was in every respect a formidable character. Having written the radical feminist *Vindication of the Rights of Woman* (which was dedicated to Talleyrand), she went to Paris and stayed throughout the Reign of Terror so that she could observe the Revolution at first hand. Any woman, who when deserted by her common law husband stands in the rain until her clothes are soaking wet in order to ensure that she will sink when she jumps into the river, must have been a force to be reckoned with. But alas, she died giving birth to Mary Godwin (who later was to be Shelley's wife) and this tragedy left Godwin without the anchor that might have kept him true to his principles.

The other person mentioned in the title of Malthus's book was the Marquis de Condorcet, author of *Sketch for a Historical Picture of the Progress of the Human Mind* (*L'Esquisse d'un tableau historique des progrès de l'esprit humain*).[11] Like Godwin, Condorcet believed in the perfectibility of humankind, but his argument was based on history, in particular the history of science, rather than simply his desire for radical political reform.

Condorcet was an accomplished mathematician and for many years had been Secretary of the French Academy of Sciences. In 1791, following the attempted escape of Louis XVI, Condorcet was one of the first to propose that France should become a republic, but like many of the early revolutionaries he fell out of favor and had to go into hiding in the house of a courageous friend who is reported to have said, "The Convention has the right to declare you an outlaw, outside the law, but they cannot put you outside the human race. You shall stay!" To occupy his mind he was prevailed upon by friends to start upon his long-projected *History of the Development of the Human Mind*. Nine months later, in early April 1794, he was captured, imprisoned and, the next morning, was found dead in his cell (probably having taken poison).

The first nine chapters of his book trace the history of humankind, from primitive beginnings, through the invention of tools, agriculture, and writing, to the elaboration of complex societies and the development of the arts and of wonderful discoveries in the sciences. Looking at this progression, Condorcet concludes that, barring some cosmic disaster, advance in the human condition will continue indefinitely.

In its final chapter the book offers, I think, an astonishingly accurate forecast of the intellectual and political developments of the next 100 years. For example, Condorcet considers some of the possible applications of probability theory (what we would now call statistics). "The knowledge of physical man, medicine and public economy is bound to benefit from the researches about the duration of human life and the way it is influenced by differences in sex, temperature, climate, profession, government and ordinary habits; about the dependence of the death-rate on various illnesses; about changes in population, and the extent to which they depend on the action of various causes; about the distribution of population in the various countries according to age, sex and occupation."

He sees statistics being applied to economics to minimize the inequitable distribution of wealth, status, and education. A proper understanding of statistics will allow the invention of a system of National Insurance

> guaranteeing people in old age a means of livelihood produced partly by their own savings and partly by the savings of others who make the same outlay but who die before they need to reap the reward. . . . No one can doubt that, as preventitive medicine improves and food and housing become healthier, as a way of life is established that develops our physical powers by exercise without ruining them by excess, as the two most virulent causes of deterioriation, misery and excessive wealth, are eliminated, the average length of human life will be increased. . . . The improvement of medical practice, which will become more efficacious with the progress of reason and of social order, will mean the end of infectious and hereditary diseases and illness brought on by climate, food, or working conditions. It is reasonable to hope that all other diseases may likewise disappear as their distant causes are discovered.

He admits, however, that he does not know whether the increase in lifespan will truly be indefinite in the sense of limitless, or will merely approach nearer and nearer (asymptotically) to some limiting value (the other sense of indefinite). Indeed, he makes the point, several times in the book, that the reader should always be aware of these two meanings of the word indefinite when considering the author's predictions for the future progress of humankind.

Thus man's intellectual development should be able to continue indefinitely. ". . . as more relations between various objects become known, man is able to reduce them to more general relations, to express them more simply . . . so truths that were discovered only by great effort, that could at first only be understood by men capable of profound thought, are soon developed and proved by methods that are not beyond the reach of common intelligence." With this increasing wisdom and technical sophistication will come increased productivity. Food production will increase and in consequence the population will go up. "Might there not come a time . . . when, the number of people in the world finally exceeding the means of subsistence, there will in consequence ensue a continual diminution of happiness and population, a true regression, or at best an oscillation between good and bad?" He admits that this may come to pass, "but by then men will know that, if they have a duty towards those who are not yet born, that duty is not to give them existence but to give them happiness; their aim should be to promote the general welfare of the human race . . . rather than foolishly to encumber the world with useless and wretched beings."

Condorcet was described by a colleague as a volcano covered with snow. I find him more friendly, more optimistic, less political than Godwin. He too looks forward to the time when there will be a "complete annihilation of the prejudices that have brought about an inequality of the rights between the sexes, an inequality fatal even to the party in whose favour it works." He sees the salvation of the world coming not from ideology but from reason. For example, "Nations will learn that they cannot conquer other nations without losing their own liberty; that permanent confederations are their only means of preserving their independence; that they should seek not power but security."

His treatment of the French Revolution is more accommodating than mine would have been if I had been in his shoes. Nowhere does he voice any criticism of The Convention. His patriotism remains unshaken. "Already in Great Britain, friends of humanity have set us an example; and if the Machiavellian government of that country has been restrained by public opinion from offering any opposition, what may we not expect of this same spirit, once the reform of a servile and venal constitution has led [in France] to a government worthy of a humane and generous nation." Perhaps he might have written rather differently if he had known that, a few months later, the Convention were going to send Lavoisier to the guillotine with the words "The Republic has no need for scholars."

Finally, right at the end of the book the volcano breaks through the snow.

> How consoling for the philosopher who laments the errors, the crimes, the injustices which still pollute the earth and of which he is often the victim is this view of the human race. . . . Such contemplation is for him an asylum, in which the memory of his persecutors cannot pursue him; there he lives in thought with man restored to his natural rights and dignity, forgets man tormented and corrupted by greed, fear or envy; there he lives with his peers in an Elysium created by reason and graced by the purest pleasures known to the love of mankind.

Who could wish for a more moving epitaph?

Malthus and the First Essay on Population

Godwin and Condorcet are the two people specifically mentioned by Malthus in the title of his first *Essay on the Principle of Population*. It may have been their general optimism (embraced by his father, Daniel Malthus) rather than their specific opinions that initially goaded Malthus into taking a pessimistic view of the future, and his argument was so persuasive that his father urged him to put it down on paper. And that was the origin of the first essay, published in 1798. In fact, he had already written, two years earlier, an unpublished article on the problem of deciding what was the most effective form of poor relief.[12]

His life as a country parson had shown Malthus the results of extreme poverty.

> The sons and daughters of peasants will not be found such rosy cherubs in real life as they are described to be in romance. It cannot fail to be remarked by those who live much in the country that the sons of labourers are very apt to be stunted in growth, and are a long while arriving at maturity. Boys that you would guess to be fourteen or fifteen are, upon inquiry, frequently found to be eighteen or nineteen. And the lads who drive plough, which must certainly be a healthy exercise, are very rarely seen with any appearance of calves to their legs: a circumstance which can only be attributed to a want either of proper or of sufficient nourishment.[13]

Much of the *Essay*, therefore, is taken up with the practical consequences of the existing laws for relief of the poor, but the part that concerns us here is his discussion of the factors that control the size of human populations. Malthus's argument in his first Essay runs roughly as follows:

1. Within any given territory, the ability of a human population to produce food will, at best, be proportional to the number of people employed in producing food; thus, when land is plentiful, the absolute amount of food will increase as the population increases. But once all the cultivable land has come under cultivation, the amount of food will be determined simply by the productivity of the land. In other words, the amount of food available for human consumption may transiently depend on the number of people but eventually will reach some maximum value that is determined by technology.

2. In contrast, the ability of a human population to grow (i.e., produce more people) will always be proportional to the size of the population. When land is plentiful (as in the American colonies), the population can double as often as every twenty-five years; once resources become limited, growth in numbers will necessarily be limited.

From these two premises it follows that every long-established human population will, most of the time, be pressing up against the limits of subsistence; indeed, the same can be said for all natural populations of animals and plants. Our capacity for increase in numbers must sooner or later exceed our capacity for increasing our resources.

Now, one could imagine a nation where the size of the population so precisely matched the available resources that everyone had enough of everything. But Malthus saw that the existence of the poor and the destitute shows that nations had not, so far, achieved the right balance. In his view, the persistence of poverty meant that the growth of human populations was being restrained in ways that are unjust and immoral. He therefore asked what are the existing restraints and what would be an equitable way of limiting population.

He defined two kinds of checks to population—the positive checks and the preventive checks. (Sometimes, rather obscurely, he felt compelled to refer to these checks as "misery" and "vice," which allows him to add a third "moral check", but this is a confusing terminology and not up to his usual standard of clarity.)

The positive checks are the forces that actively dispose of excess population by untimely death—infant mortality, malnutrition, occupational diseases, wars, epidemics. All these, he pointed out, are to some extent inequitable because they prey more heavily upon the poor. In this he was following Adam Smith who had written, twenty years earlier, that "poverty, though it does not prevent the generation, is extremely unfavourable to the rearing of children."[14]

The preventive checks are the various ways for controlling population size by limiting birthrate—postponement of marriage, the provision of a means of livelihood for unmarried women, abstinence and, of course, contraception and abortion (which he hints at only with the utmost delicacy). Unlike the positive checks, the preventive checks are under human control, and it was the relaxation of these preventive checks that had allowed populations to recover their numbers after epidemics and, at the end of the eighteenth century, was allowing the American population to expand into the vast spaces of the New World. (I would have found his whole discussion easier to understand if he had called the positive checks negative and the preventive checks positive, but nothing can be done about that now.)

Surely none of this could have been objectionable to Godwin or Condorcet. But the difficulty arises when Malthus comes to consider the future. What can be done to eradicate "misery" and "vice"? What forms of help should be given to the poor? Adam Smith had written that "a person who can acquire no property, can acquire no other interest but to eat as much, and to labour as little as possible."[15] Property is everything. It is useless, Malthus said, simply to hand out money to the poor because then they would assume that their children will similarly be rescued, which would inhibit their use of the preventive checks and ensure that, when finally the money runs out, the problem will have been magnified. It would be far better to give them land so that they can provide for themselves because, he felt, this would put them in the same position as other people of property, who have to assess the carrying capacity of their territory in order to judge when to marry and how many children to produce. But that is not an option, because land and resources are limited (except in the New World). So he concluded that every society in the Old World must inevitably contain a large number of people who are trapped in extreme poverty, because every established society has expanded in size until it has exceeded its capacity to feed itself. "The lower classes of people in Europe may at some future period be much better instructed than they are at present ... they may live under better and more equal laws than they have ever hitherto done, perhaps, in any country ... but it is not in the nature of things that they can be awarded such a quantity of money or subsistence as will allow them all to marry early, in the full confidence that they shall be able to provide with ease for a numerous family."[16]

In retrospect, it seems that Godwin, Condorcet, and Malthus were really taking rather similar positions. Only the gloss was different. Godwin, coming from a puritanical religious background, believed that the world's population would expand until all land was being cultivated and, at that point, growth would cease because people would start to despise "the commerce of the sexes" (in other words, the world would be saved by asceticism). Condorcet, as a follower of Descartes, believed that in time people would become more rational and choose one or other of the preventive checks in order to ensure that all children could be properly provided for; (in other words, the problem would be solved by the power of reason). Malthus, reared in the tradition of Bacon and Newton, simply believed the evidence of his eyes. "I expect that great discoveries are yet to take place in all the branches of human science, particularly in physics; but the moment we leave past experience as the foundation for our conjectures concerning the future ... we are thrown upon a wide field of uncertainty, and any supposition is then just as good as another."[17] And he chose to be pessimistic about the future because he disapproved of all forms of contraception and held out little hope for the other preventive checks such as abstinence and delayed marriage; in other words, the world would not be saved.

The Antecedents to the Second Essay on the Principle of Population

Pessimism was not fashionable at the end of the eighteenth century; as Wordsworth had written, "Bliss was it in that dawn to be alive, But to be young was very heaven." Malthus immediately came under attack from several quarters. As he said in the preface to his second essay,[18] the first essay had been written "on the spur of the occasion, and from the few materials which were within reach in a country situation." But he quickly discovered that much more had been written about population than he had imagined.

In the eighteenth century, it was a commonly held belief that God had ordained the rates of birth and death for all living creatures so that their numbers should match the carrying capacity of their surroundings. In a widely distributed set of sermons about the creation of the physical and biological worlds, published in 1711, William Derham had written that "the whole surface of the globe can afford room and support only to such a number of all sorts of creatures; and if by their doubling, trebling, or any other multiplication of their kind, they should increase or double or treble that number, they must starve, or devour [one] another. The keeping of the balance even, is manifestly a work of divine wisdom or providence."[19] In 1741, Johann Süssmilch had produced a book entitled *Proof for a God-given Order to the Changes in Male and Female Births and Deaths and the Reproduction of Human Populations,*[20] which was full of statistics about age distributions, birth rates and life expectancy in various parts of Europe. Malthus frequently referred to Süssmilch (though his German was very weak and there was no English translation available), and he probably knew of Derham's work, which had gone through many editions.

Two earlier authors, Wallace and Franklin, are specifically mentioned by Malthus at the beginning of the *Second Essay,* and they are worth discussing in greater detail because they show the range of opinions about population that were current in the eighteenth century.

Robert Wallace, a minister of the Scottish church, had produced two books on population. Like most clerics of the day (including Malthus) he accepted Bishop Ussher's calculation (on biblical evidence) that the world had been created about 6,000 years ago. In his first book,[21] published anonymously in 1753 and mentioned by Malthus, Wallace calculates what the population of the world must have been in the time of Alexander the Great, assuming that it had been reduced to Noah's three sons around 2150 B.C and that the number of inhabitants would have doubled every thirty years between then and the reign of Alexander; it followed therefore that there must have been more people in the fourth century B.C. than in the eighteenth century A.D. This conclusion was in perfect accord with the idea that the golden age of humankind was around 300–400 B.C. and that everything had been downhill since then. In a second book,[22] Wallace extended the argument and considered the relationship between population size and the fertility of the earth. This led him to the grim conclusion that the better and more liberal the form of government, the sooner would the world's population outstrip its food supply and be plunged into misery. "Limits are set to the fertility of the earth . . . [and when there is no more room] the tranquility and numerous blessings of the Utopian Governments would come to an end."[23] The only solutions he could come up with were infanticide, and making it the custom to castrate males and cloister women in nunneries. (Curiously, Malthus did not refer to this second book, and for that reason some people accused him of plagiarism.)

Far more modern in outlook was the article by Benjamin Franklin entitled "Observations concerning the Increase of Mankind, Peopling of

Countries, &c." which was published in 1755.[24] (The pamphlet was re-printed on several occasions, but apparently Malthus had not seen it when he wrote the first Essay although he did refer to Richard Price's "Observations on Reversionary Payments . . ." which was published in 1771 and mentions Franklin's pamphlet.) In 1750, Britain had passed a law prohibiting any further development of iron and steel mills in the American colonies, in the hope that this would encourage its own iron industry. Franklin argued that there was no need for such a law, because the pressures in the two countries were totally different. America would not become a manufacturing country for at least another 100 years and, in the meantime, was in no position to compete with Britain. In America, where there is limitless land, a young man works for someone else only long enough to make sufficient money to buy land, build a house, and raise a family; therefore labor is expensive, the average age at marriage is quite low, the average family size is about eight, and the population doubles every twenty years or so. In Europe, however, "all Lands being occupied and improved to the Heighth, those who cannot get Land must Labour for others that have it; when Labourers are plenty, their Wages will be low; by low Wages a Family is supported with Difficulty; this Difficulty deters many from Marriage, who therefore continue Servants and single."

Franklin's article is only about 2,500 words long, but it manages to cover much of what Malthus was to say about population and economics, as well as much else. The difference is that Malthus looks at his proposi-tions from every possible angle, whereas Franklin throws his on the table as if they were self-evidently true. Malthus sifts through the evidence and tends to avoid bold predictions. Franklin leaps from subject to subject— the cost of slaves, the balance of trade, the consequences of migration and, almost in passing, an astonishingly accurate forecast of the growth of the U.S. population over the next 100 years. It is a dazzling display. In a few pages, Franklin anticipates Adam Smith's *Wealth of Nations* and Malthus's *Essays*. His essay also played an important part in the idea of natural selection, and this deserves further mention (somewhat out of chronological order) because Franklin's and Malthus's essays gave rise to one of the most dramatic episodes in the history of science.

Franklin, Malthus, and the Struggle for Existence

Near the end of Franklin's pamphlet on the Increase of Mankind, he produces the following magnificent generalization. "There is in short, no Bound to the prolific Nature of Plants or Animals, but what is made by their crowding and interfering with each others Means of Subsistence. Was the Face of the Earth vacant of other Plants, it might be gradually sowed and overspread with one Kind only; as, for Instance, with Fennel; and were it empty of other Inhabitants, it might in a few Ages be replenish'd from one Nation only." (He then goes on to discuss which nation would be the best choice, and the less said about that the better.)

Malthus had independently reached the same conclusion.

> Through the animal and vegetable kingdoms, nature has scattered the seeds of life abroad with the most profuse and liberal hand. She has been comparatively sparing in the room and the nourishment necessary to rear them. The germs of existence contained in this spot of earth, with ample food, and ample room to expand in, would fill millions of worlds in the course of a few thousand years. Necessity, that imperious all pervading law of nature, restrains them within the prescribed bounds. The race of plants and the race of animals shrink under this great restrictive law. . . . Among plants and animals its effects are waste of seed, sickness, and premature death.[25]

In the second essay he would embellish this idea. "The preventive check is peculiar to man. . . . Plants and animals have apparently no doubts about the future support of their offspring. The checks to their indefinite increase, therefore, are all positive."[26]

This last point, as it turns out, was incorrect. As Darwin frequently pointed out a few years later, many examples have been found where animals and plants have evolved patterns of behavior that adjust their reproduction rate to match their circumstances. The number of eggs laid by a bird, or the size of territory annexed by the male, can change in response to changes in the richness of its environment; tropical fish in a fish tank adjust their growth rates specifically according to the concentration of their own species; the amount of seed set by a plant can reflect its level of crowding; and so on. Such preventive checks to reproduction are sensible strategies for responding to limited resources and it is not difficult to see how they could have evolved. It would be surprising if humans had not evolved a similar set of unconscious responses to environmental pressure. We have an elaborate and largely subconscious set of rules governing our interaction with others; some are easily observed, as for example when strangers are temporarily forced into proximity in a confined space such as an elevator and instinctively try to maximize their distance apart; other rules are less obvious. It is not clear whether we have similar instinctive rules that adjust reproductive behavior to match resources, but we are certainly subject to physiological mechanisms that diminish fertility when food is short (see chapter 1).

As it happened, the two inventors of the theory of Evolution by Variation and Natural Selection, Charles Darwin and Alfred Russel Wallace, each came to see the evolutionary implications of the struggle for survival as the result of re-reading Malthus's second essay. Darwin, who had read Franklin's essay,[27] wrote that "In October 1838 . . . I happened to read for amusement Malthus on Population, and being well prepared to appreciate the struggle for existence which everywhere goes on from long-continued observation of the habits of animals and plants, it at once struck me that under these circumstances favourable variations would tend to be preserved and unfavourable ones to be destroyed."[28] Wallace later described how the idea suddenly came to him, in 1858; "The most interesting coincidence in the matter, I think, is, that I, *as well as Darwin*, was led to the theory itself through Malthus—in my case it was his elaborate account of the action of 'preventive checks' in keeping down the population of savage races to a tolerably fixed but scanty number. . . . I was lying on my bed in the hot fit of intermittent fever, when the idea suddenly came to me. I thought it almost all out before the fit was over."[29]

Strangely enough, Malthus himself did not, at any time, suggest that the struggle for existence will reward the strong and penalize the weak, although he apparently recognized that "no two grains of wheat are exactly alike" and that this was also true for humans, as witness the fact that children varied in their inherited level of susceptibility to diseases.[30] He did occasionally mention competition among plants and animals for space and resources, but his central concern was with the human condition. The idea that humans may also have been subject to a Darwinian struggle for survival is not an obvious thought, particularly for someone whose profession called on him to do no more than distinguish the Just from the Unjust. Indeed, his essay sprang from his concern for the Poor because he considered them no less just than the Rich.

Malthus's Second Essay

Because of "the degree of public attention which the essay excited" (preface to the second essay), Malthus decided to back up his argument with some hard numbers. So he set about ferreting out statistics from all over the world, using everything he could lay his hands on—the ancient history of Greece and Rome, the journals of explorers and missionaries, the surveys of colonial administrators, and the reports of the many political statisticians who were springing up all over Europe. He did not have much money of his own, but luckily an acquaintance of his had just come into a fortune and wanted to see the world, and as a result Malthus was able to join a party touring Scandinavia. Over the next two or three years he traveled extensively through Europe and Russia, checking and cross-checking, all the time with a skepticism that is twentieth century in style. Finally, after five years' work, he published his second *Essay on the Principle of Population*, this time with the subtitle *A View of its past and present*

Effects on Human Happiness; With an Inquiry into our Prospects respecting the future Removal or Mitigation of the Evils which it occasions.

More than half of the *Essay* is taken up with a lengthy survey of the pattern of life and death, both in ancient times and among various contemporary societies, ranging from the most primitive to the most sophisticated in Europe, Asia, North America, Africa, and Russia. Then, having established a base of solid facts, Malthus gives a brief rebuttal to the utopian visions of Godwin and Condorcet, following which he moves into a discussion of the Poor Laws and his ideas about the nature of wealth and the distribution of resources. Finally, he gives his own vision of the future.

In many ways the second *Essay* seems less harsh than the first, perhaps because more of it is based on actual statistics than on grim foreboding. In the opening chapter he mentions the special case of North America where no checks were operating and, as Franklin had pointed out, the population was doubling every 20–25 years. For the rest of the world, he found that almost everywhere populations were pressing up against the limits of resources, although different factors turned out to be controlling population size in different societies. The wretched inhabitants of Tierra del Fuego lived permanently on the edge of famine (the ultimate check). In New Zealand, the population was held back by continual intertribal warfare. In Europe, populations tended to be controlled more by preventive checks than by the positive checks of warfare, famine, and disease. One extreme case was the parish of Leyzin in Switzerland, where the statistics showed a remarkably healthy population with a life expectancy of more than sixty, and where the birthrate had somehow been kept almost exactly equal to the death rate for at least the previous thirty years. The local minister thought this was because "God has wisely ordered things in such a manner as that the force of life, in each country, should be in inverse ratio of its fecundity" (Malthus's translation), but Malthus believed it was simply because the pasture for cattle could not be expanded further, and the inhabitants observed the custom that no man should marry until he had acquired a herd of cattle, plus grazing rights, from someone who had died. For most of Switzerland, however, and for many other countries in Europe, population was not being held back by preventive checks. (Malthus reports meeting a Swiss peasant, who was alarmed at the increase in the population of the Jura and believed that the country would be much happier and healthier if men were not allowed to marry until they were over forty and then only with older women; "he appeared to understand the principle of population almost as well as any man I met with.")[31]

Throughout the second *Essay*, Malthus treads a fine line between condemnation of certain forms of population control and a wish to do the best for the poor (who he firmly believed are made poor by the pressures of population). Feeling that the first *Essay* had been misunderstood, he is at pains to make his position absolutely clear: "To those who shall still think that any check to population whatever would be worse than the evils which it would relieve, the conclusions of the [first] essay will remain in full force; and if we adopt this opinion, we shall be compelled to acknowledge that the poverty and misery, which prevail among the lower classes of society are absolutely irremediable."[32] But they would be remediable if we learned how to control population in the right way. He turns to the analogy of the farm. "A farmer could not be considered as an enemy to a large quantity of stock, who should insist upon the folly and impropriety of attempting to breed [the greatest quantity of cattle], before the land was put into a condition to bear it." The exercise, in short, should always be to match population to resources, and this should be done in the most benign way possible. For example, when discussing innoculation against smallpox, he says "In many parts of this Essay I have dwelt much on the advantage of rearing the requisite population of any country from the smallest number of births . . . a decrease of mortality at all ages is what we ought chiefly to aim at."[33]

The second *Essay* went through several major revisions over the following twenty-three years, because Malthus found that some of his less cautious remarks continued to give offense and were being picked on by his enemies. Also, his opinions were changing slightly with time. What gave most offense were his thoughts about the interaction between poverty, unemployment, the cost of labor, and the wealth of nations (most of which subjects are beyond the scope of my chapter). He is in favor of preventive checks (although he is against contraception and abortion), but he worries that they could be carried too far. "I have never adverted to the check suggested by Condorcet without the most marked disapprobation. Indeed I should always particularly reprobate any artificial and unnatural modes of checking population, both on account of their immorality and their tendency to remove a necessary stimulus to industry."[34]

This idea—that people are industrious solely so that they can provide for themselves and their children—may have been partly what turned Marx and Engels against Malthus. They may also have been reacting against his rather sour remarks about the kind of "speculative philosopher [who] . . . allows himself to indulge in the most bitter invectives against every present establishment, without applying his talents to consider the best and safest means of removing abuses. . . ." Unfortunately, it was their custom, once they had identified an enemy, to reject that person totally and in every possible way. In Marx's *Capital,* Malthus is subjected to a stream of corrosive footnotes. The *First Essay* "is nothing more than a schoolboyish plagiary of De Foe, Sir James Stuart, Townsend, Franklin, Wallace &c., and does not contain a single sentence thought out by himself";[35] "It was, of course, far more convenient, and much more in conformity with the interest of the ruling classes, whom Malthus adored like a true priest, to explain this 'over-population' by eternal laws of Nature, rather than by the historical laws of capitalist production."[36] Malthus, "the fat holder of benefices,"[37] was "greeted with jubilance by the English oligarchy as the great destroyer of all hankerings after human development."[38] Finally, Marx accused Malthus of corruption; "The [English working class] were right here in sensing instinctively that they were confronted not with a man of science but with a bought advocate, with a pleader on behalf of their enemies, a shameless sycophant of the ruling classes."[39]

This, of course, was grossly unfair. Malthus had never argued that the ruling classes should be cherished or that a section of society should be kept in extreme poverty. Quite the contrary. He was against forcing an increase in population to keep down wages; any attempt to do this "should be carefully watched and strenuously resisted by the friends of the poor." His prime interest was in trying to work out what is the best way of relieving poverty. "If all [the poor] could be completely relieved, and poverty banished from the country, even at the expense of three-fourths of the fortunes of the rich, I would be the last person to say a single syllable against relieving all, and making the degree of distress alone the measure of our bounty."[40]

Furthermore, none of Marx's criticisms are to the point. What now matters most (and mattered then) is whether Malthus was right or wrong, not his originality or his sources of income. Like Marx and Engels, Malthus got many of his ideas and statistics from others, and like them he often acknowledged as much. Malthus had a cleft palate and gave indistinct sermons; Marx was antisemitic and did not pay his tradesmen's bills; Engels recorded the sufferings of factory workers but showed little concern for the workers in his own cotton firm in Manchester, whose labors assured him his place in society. As for their income, Malthus was a relatively wealthy curate, but he probably had less unearned income than Marx and was certainly not as rich as Engels. What was important about these three men, however, was the impact of their ideas and the relevance of these ideas to the problems of the world today.

Unfortunately, it seems to have been Marx's modus operandi to make enemies whenever possible. So, Malthus was anathematized. This had dire consequences. Marx and Engels found themselves having to imply that communism would obviate the need for any check on population, positive or preventive. (Actually, Engels hedged his bets slightly. "Even if Malthus were altogether right," he wrote "it would still be necessary to carry out this socialist reorganization immediately, since only this reorganization, only the enlightenment of the masses which it can bring with it, can make possible that moral restraint upon the instinct for reproduction which Malthus himself puts forward as the easiest and most effective countermeasure against overpopulation.")[41] And so it became the party line in the twentieth century that no form of population control would prove necessary in a Communist world. "In the conditions of the capitalistic mode of production a certain part of the population systematically becomes relatively superfluous. . . . In a socialistic society . . . the problem of excessive population no longer arises" (A Soviet spokesman at the UN Conference on Population, held in Rome in 1954).[42] This apparently was why the Communists joined forces with the Catholics, at the end of World War II, to force the newly formed World Health Organization to pass a resolution that it would never discuss what effect its actions might have on the growth of population in the developing nations or what steps could be taken to accommodate any increase.

Before considering whether Malthus's predictions were more nearly correct than his contemporaries', we should look a little more closely at historical changes in population and the operation of Malthus's positive and preventive checks in the centuries before the first and second *Essays*. Much more is known about this subject now than was known in Malthus's time.

THE EXPLOSION IN THE POPULATIONS OF *HOMO SAPIENS*

Population Changes in the 250 Years before Malthus

Although accurate censuses did not become available until the nineteenth century, it has been possible to construct a running tally of the population of certain European countries using the church records of marriages, baptisms, and deaths. This was discussed briefly in the first chapter in connection with the change in life expectancy that occurred in the nineteenth century. Here we are concerned not with the influence of public health and medical practice on mortality, but with the influence of economic environment on births and deaths. What follows has been taken, almost entirely, from Wrigley and Schofield's book, *The Population History of England, 1540–1871*.[43]

In his first essay, Malthus suggested that the natural tendency of populations to increase was opposed by two forces. When populations go up, food becomes scarce and labour becomes plentiful, so prices will tend to go up and wages go down, and the buying power of wages (real wages) will necessarily go down; and this, he believed, would lead to increased mortality for at least the poorer sections of society. This is the positive

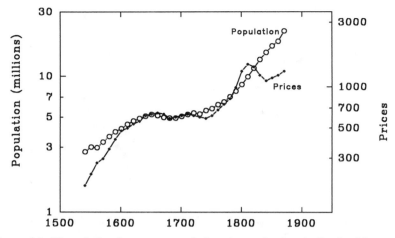

Figure 6.1. The relation between population size and prices in England between 1540 and 1840 (from table 3.1 and figure 10.1 in Wrigley and Schofield; see note 43). Prices are the cost of a basket of consumables (food, drink, fuel, and clothing).

check. At the same time, in the face of an increasing population, people will see that it has become harder to support a large family, and this will lead to more people choosing not to marry, or to marry late and produce fewer children. These are the preventive checks.

The first question to ask is whether growth of population does tend to raise prices. The answer, at least in the case of England up to the start of the nineteenth century, appears to have been "Yes." Figure 6.1 shows the changes in population and prices in England from 1540 onward; both are plotted on logarithmic scales, because the important thing is not the absolute increase in, say, the price of a loaf of bread (in pennies per pound) but in the relative increase (for example, percentage increase in a year). For the 250 years before Malthus's time, prices had moved hand-in-hand with population. Between 1550 and 1650, Europe was recovering from the Little Ice Age and from the famines and plagues of the fourteenth and fifteenth centuries; population was steadily increasing, and prices were going up even more steeply. From 1650 to 1750, English population and prices hardly changed at all. But then, in the middle of the eighteenth century, population started to increase again, and prices began to go up even more steeply than population. Up to the end of the eighteenth century, therefore, population and prices did go hand in hand, exactly as Malthus had supposed. It is obvious from figure 6.1, however, that the relationship breaks down, just after the time he wrote

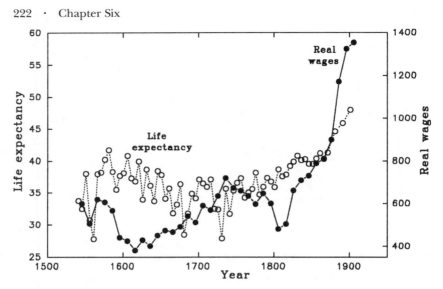

Figure 6.2. The relation between real wages and life expectancy in England between 1540 and 1840 (from tables A3.1 and A9.2 in Wrigley and Schofield; see note 43).

his *Essays*, at the beginning of the nineteenth century; suddenly, for reasons that will be discussed later, population behaves as if it were no longer limited by resources. It seems that Malthus was right about the previous 250 years but wrong about the immediate future.

The next question is whether the growth of population was being limited by positive checks—that is, whether changes in real wages were producing changes in life expectancy. Figure 6.2 shows how these two measures were changing in England from 1540 onward. Obviously, real wages were responding to population changes in the way he expected. During the period of population increase, between 1550 and 1650, the real wages for craftsmen and laborers were falling; during the next 100 years, when population was steady, real wages crept steadily upward; and then, when population started to go up again, wages temporarily dropped; finally, at the beginning of the nineteenth century, everything changed and both population and wages rocketed upward. Life expectancy, however, was not behaving in the way Malthus had postulated in his first *Essay*. Until the nineteenth century, life expectancy fluctuated between thirty-five and forty, with occasional precipitous drops down into the twenties. There was no obvious trend, and even the occasional sudden declines in life expectancy did not bear any obvious relation to wages. If, therefore, there were positive checks to population that were killing off the less privileged members of society when resources become

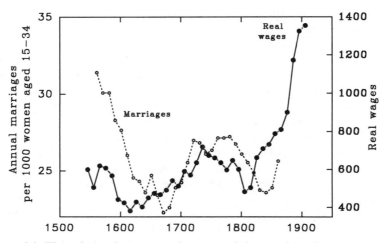

Figure 6.3. The relation between real wages and the number of marriages each year in England between 1540 and 1840 (from table A9.2 and figure 10.9 in Wrigley and Schofield; see note 43).

scarce, these checks were not affecting a sufficient fraction of the population of England to be detectable in the statistics for mortality. (Malthus had pointed out in the first *Essay* that very little was known about the poorest sections of society. "Many reasons occur why . . . oscillation [in the fortunes of the poor] has been less obvious, and less decidedly confirmed by experience. . . . One principal reason is that the histories of mankind that we possess are histories only of the higher classes."[44] The objection does not apply to the statistics shown in the figure because these were derived from church records and include all strata of society.)

Malthus did, however, consider that populations might, instead, adjust their growth rate to match their circumstances by operating various preventive checks to reproduction, such as postponement of marriage and reduction in birthrate. Figure 6.3 shows that there was indeed a relationship between real wages and marriage; before the nineteenth century, the proportion of women aged 15–34 who married in any given year was highest when the real wages were high. Interestingly, there seems to have been a lag of about 30 years in the response to falling wages, suggesting perhaps that parental support may have been important in determining when a couple chose to be married. By comparison, the records of births in England and elsewhere showed a very quick response to shortages; for example, the poor harvest of 1693 led to a halving of birthrates in the affected regions of France in the following year.[45]

That is a brief summary and does not do justice to all the elegant detail of Wrigley and Schofield's reconstruction of the demographic history of

England. But it is sufficient to show that, for the 250 years before Malthus, England and other European nations were constantly adjusting the rate of growth of their populations to match their circumstances, using what Malthus called the preventive checks. Perhaps for this reason, the positive checks to population, which Malthus felt must inevitably prey upon the poor, seem to have been largely avoided. There were occasional crises of mortality but these were probably due to epidemics rather than to famine brought on by low wages.

Malthus's insistence, in the first *Essay*, that famine is necessarily the prime check to population may be explained by the peculiar circumstances of the times. In 1797, when he was writing the *Essay*, population and prices were soaring upward (figure 6.1). Real wages had steadily fallen by some 30 percent over the previous fifty years, but there had been only a slight decline in marriages (figure 6.3). The United States had triumphantly established its independence, and the nations of Europe were having to assimilate the lessons of the French Revolution. Meanwhile France itself was desperately trying to recover from the disorder created by the revolution and from the effects of a very severe winter. Although everywhere there were signs of an impending technological revolution, it was hard to tell what the future held in store—expanded markets and plenty for all, or a slide into political chaos. "It was the best of times, it was the worst of times, it was the age of wisdom, it was the age of foolishness, it was the epoch of belief, it was the epoch of incredulity, it was the season of Light, it was the season of Darkness, it was the spring of hope, it was the winter of despair, we had everything before us, we had nothing before us. . . ." And there, in the opening of Dickens's novel about the French Revolution, you have the essence of the argument between Malthus father and son.

Up to the end of the eighteenth century, therefore, Malthus seems to have been right. Population was indeed being controlled by resources. His first *Essay* overestimated the importance of the positive check of mortality due to shortage of food. But the statistics, assembled in his second *Essay*, led him to conclude (correctly) that most European communities were adjusting their growth rates to match the growth in their resources and opportunities for employment. About the future he was, unlike Benjamin Franklin, very cautious. And this was just as well, because in the next century the populations of Europe were to behave in a totally unexpected way. As he himself had said at the very start of the first *Essay*,

> The great and unlooked for discoveries that have taken place of late years in natural philosophy, the increasing diffusion of general knowledge from extension of the art of printing, . . . the new and extraordinary lights that have been thrown on political subjects which dazzle and astonish the understanding, and

particularly that tremendous phenomenon in the political horizon, the French Revolution, which, like a blazing comet, seems destined either to inspire with fresh life and vigour, or to scorch up and destroy the shrinking inhabitants of the earth, have all concurred to lead many able men into the opinion that we were touching on a period big with the most important changes, changes that would in some measure be decisive of the future face of mankind.

The Nineteenth Century

The inhabitants of Europe early in the nineteenth century would surely have been astonished to hear that the technological developments going on at that time were of more lasting importance for the fate of humankind than the Napoleonic wars; (no doubt we too will be judged to have been, in some way, equally obtuse when our time comes). But, perhaps even more than Malthus expected, the end of the eighteenth century marked a turning point in the millions of years of human history, because it was the beginning of the demographic transition. In the next century and a half, the population of Europe was going to double and then double again, and the rest of the world would follow suit. This was the moment in human history when the first few nations made the transition from what is called a high-pressure system with a high birthrate and death rate to a low-pressure system where almost everyone lives to a ripe old age and birthrates and death rates are low.

It is commonly believed that the Industrial Revolution removed all Malthusian restraints. This is the conventional wisdom in the social sciences and can perhaps be traced to Marx's decision to turn Malthus into An Enemy of the People. But the actual behavior of the different countries of Europe in the nineteenth and twentieth centuries show that growth never became a free-for-all. Each country managed its balance of the various positive checks in its own particular way.

Leaving aside the effects of immigration and emigration, changes in population size are simply a function of gross reproduction rate and life expectancy—that is to say, the number of female children born each year and the probability of female children surviving to become the breeding females for the next generation. If these two variables are kept in balance, the population will not change; if either of them suddenly increases, the population will start growing. Figure 6.4 shows how the two variables changed in England, France, and Sweden at the start of the nineteenth century. The method of presenting the data is a little complicated and needs some explanation. For any value of life expectancy there is a reproduction rate that will exactly maintain the population at

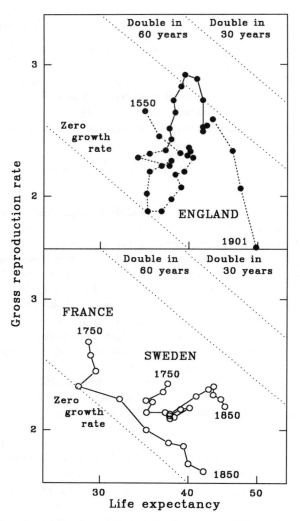

Figure 6.4. The changing values of reproduction rate and life expectancy in England, France, and Sweden (from figures 7.12 and 7.13 in Wrigley and Schofield; see note 43). Gross reproduction rate is the number of female children produced by the average breeding woman; life expectancy is the average number of years lived by newborn infants. Because the figure shows reproduction rate and life expectancy on logarithmic scales, the possible values for a population with zero growth rate lie roughly on a straight diagonal line; similarly the values for a population that doubles every 60 years or 30 years lie on parallel diagonal lines. (This is an approximation that is not precisely true for higher values of life expectancy or for societies where postponement of marriage significantly raises the interval between one generation and the next.)

The upper figure shows the values for England between 1550 and 1740 (interrupted line), between 1740 and 1840 (solid line), and between 1840 and 1901 (interrupted line).

The lower figure shows the values for France and Sweden between 1750 and 1850.

a constant level; the lower the expectancy, the higher must be the reproduction rate. In a plot of reproduction rate against life expectancy, the possible values for zero growth rate will fall on a line running across the graph, from top left to bottom right; as long as a country can stay on that line, it will have zero growth. Similarly, the possible values leading to a doubling every sixty years will form a different diagonal line, and every thirty years another diagonal. Plotting the changing values of reproduction rate and life expectancy for any particular country will show how fast the country's population is growing and also whether the changes in growth rate are due to a decrease in mortality or an increase in reproduction rate.

Between 1750 and 1850, the three countries—England, Sweden, and France—behaved in completely different ways. The population in England grew because the birthrate climbed steadily until 1810 without, initially, any accompanying change in life expectancy (indeed, life expectancy had hardly changed for 200 years). In Sweden, however, the main change was not in the birthrate but in life expectancy, which started to increase at the end of the eighteenth century. France differed from both Sweden and England in matching birthrate almost perfectly to the steady increase in life expectancy; throughout this period, France never strayed far from zero growth rate.

The obvious conclusion is that each country was adjusting its growth rate to match its changing circumstances. In Sweden the change in life expectancy did not apparently pose sufficient threat to the standard of living to demand any strengthening of the preventive checks. In England, life expectancy was not changing very much, but the increased opportunities for employment were leading to a relaxation of the preventive checks. France, an agrarian nation where the law required that each family's landholding had to be divided equally between the sons, had the strongest possible inducement to tread the diagonal line of zero growth, and that may have been why France was one of the few European countries that did not have a population explosion in the nineteenth century.

The Twentieth Century

Once beyond this period the industrialized nations all headed off far beyond the bottom righthand corner of figure 6.4, into the region where almost everyone survives into middle age and where zero growth rate is achieved by having a very low birthrate.

A hundred years later, at the end of the twentieth century, it is the turn of the developing nations to embark on the demographic transition. But now the rate of change is far greater (figure 6.5). In Africa as a

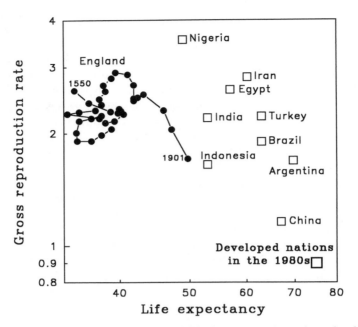

Figure 6.5. Gross reproduction rate and life Expectancy in various developing nations in the 1980s (see note 46), compared to the changes that occurred in England since 1550.

England was chosen as representative of the developed nations because it had a singularly dramatic explosion of population (see figure 6.4), but all the developed nations have now reached very similar values for reproduction rate and life expectancy to the current rates in England.

The developing nations shown here were chosen to represent the Far East, the Middle East, Africa, and South America. The figure shows that most of these nations have gross reproduction rates that are as high or higher than England's rate in the eighteenth century, combined with the life expectancy of England in the early twentieth century. For that reason, most of these nations are growing at a faster rate than ever achieved in Europe. Furthermore, their populations are mostly much larger. In the mid-1980s, Argentina, Egypt, Iran, and Turkey are roughly as populous as France, Germany, Italy, or the United Kingdom; Brazil and Nigeria each already has twice as many people; Indonesia has three times as many; and India and China have respectively fifteen and twenty times as many.

whole, life expectancy is now about fifty and the population of some of the African nations is doubling every twenty-five years. In Latin America and many Asian countries, life expectancy is in the sixties and their populations are doubling roughly every thirty-five years.

Fortunately, signs are beginning to appear in all developing countries that this sudden, extreme rate of growth is starting to decline. Thus the United Nations reported in 1991 that average family size over the previous ten years had dropped by about 0.3 children per family in Africa, Asia, Latin America, and the USSR.[46] Apparently, preventive checks are beginning to operate.[47]

The positive checks have certainly not been eradicated. Tropical diseases such as malaria, tuberculosis, and the various dysenteries still kill millions every year; there are going to be totally more than 20 million deaths from AIDS; and, of course, we must expect epidemics of other new diseases in the future. Finally, warfare still takes its toll; in the twentieth century, some 200 million people have died as the result of wars and revolutions. And with warfare comes starvation. Today, "the single most important obstacle to ending famine is the continued use of hunger as a weapon of war."[48]

Perhaps more important than wars and diseases, however, are two new and unexpected forms of positive check that have just become visible on the horizon.

CLIMATE AND THE LONG-TERM PROSPECTS FOR THE HUMAN RACE

Positive Checks in the Twenty-first Century

During the whole period when the populations of Europe and North America were undergoing their sharp increase, agricultural technology was becoming more and more sophisticated. Thanks to what has been called the "green revolution," food production could comfortably keep pace with demand. This has continued up to the present time; for example, grain yield per hectare in the United States has doubled even in the last thirty years. Furthermore, the green revolution has been successfully exported to certain developing nations; just in the last ten years India has managed to become self-sufficient in food, despite its huge increase in population.

Opponents of Malthus have therefore been quick to point out that continual advances in technology have apparently resolved the conflict between growth and supply. So far, the population size of the developed nations has not been limited by food; so far, science has always been able to come to the rescue; and it is natural to argue that what has happened in the past will continue to happen in the future. In most cases, I think it is not unreasonable to assume that the recent past is a good basis for predicting the future. In this case, however, there are grounds for thinking that the past 100 years are not part of a trend that can continue into the future.

First, we should remember that the history of civilizations tells us to beware of success.[49] The Fertile Crescent which supported the Mesopotamian civilization was eventually destroyed either by over-irrigation[50] or as the result of a change in climate;[51] Libya and Algeria were once the granary for the Roman Empire, but now they find themselves having to import grain from North America; the Mayan civilization vanished when the topsoil washed away.[52] And it is not beyond belief that exactly the same sort of disaster could happen to the agriculture of today.

The prospect of failure is made more probable by one other factor. Unlike earlier forms of agriculture, today's farming cannot be sustained indefinitely in its present form, because it relies on artificial fertilizers. In the wheat growing areas of North America, almost ten calories' worth of fossil fuel are used to mine and transport the fertilizer, cultivate the land, sow and harvest the crop, and then package and deliver to the consumer's kitchen one calorie's worth of food. In a sense, therefore, the revolution in agriculture may only have postponed the day of reckoning. After all, food is still the ultimate resource and, when all the fossil fuel and reserves of fertilizers have gone, famine may yet prove to be the ultimate check to human population.

But before that moment comes we are almost certain to run into another, insurmountable barrier, which could not have been anticipated in the eighteenth century. As we use more and more of the world's store of fossil fuels, it turns out that we are producing major changes in the chemical and physical composition of the earth's surface. Like the world's population, the rate of use of fossil fuels is doubling roughly every thirty years. What was bound up by plants and gradually converted into coal over hundreds of millions of years is, as it were, being consumed in the blink of an eye. Carbon makes up most of the weight of coal, and the burning (oxidation) of coal necessarily turns all that carbon into carbon dioxide (plus a few incomplete combustion products), which inevitably is released into the atmosphere. (The Industrial Revolution is having many other dire effects, such as acid rain, dispersal of radioactive waste, and depletion of the ozone layer, but the increase in carbon dioxide may prove to have the most far-reaching consequences.)

As a result of the Industrial Revolution, the carbon dioxide content of the atmosphere has been rising steadily. If nothing is done to curtail emissions, the level of carbon dioxide in the atmosphere will have doubled by about the year 2040. As a result, the earth will reflect back into space a smaller fraction of the infrared sunlight that falls on it and will therefore tend to become warmer.[53]

How much warmer is not clear. There are too many uncertainties in the calculation. The oceans and forests could conceivably be able to take up some of the excess carbon dioxide; other, unsuspected forces might also help to decrease the degree of warming; or the consequences could prove to be worse than expected. But irrespective of the magnitude of the change it is important that we do not underestimate the impact of climatic changes.

Climate has dominated the history of life on earth. The age of the dinosaurs is thought to have ended in the cretaceous extinction brought about by a temporary decrease in sunlight due to the dust kicked up by the impact of a meteor. Human civilization began with the invention of agriculture, which became possible 10,000 years ago at the end of the Ice Age. The increase, in the seventeenth century, in the population of countries as far apart as western Europe and China has been attributed to a slight change in climate. The massive exodus from the farmlands of New England into the western United States was due to the poor summer of 1816, caused by the atmospheric dust arising from the eruption of the Indonesian volcano Tomboro the previous year. These examples, large and small, suggest that all the technology in the world may be hard pressed to protect us from the effects of a really massive change in climate.

What Malthus might have called the ultimate danger is that the earth's climate may, for all we know, be delicately poised and easily pushed in one direction or the other. It seems to me that there is, at the moment, no certain way of knowing how rare it is for a planet to maintain a surface that is congenial for life. The database is, as it were, too small. Our sun has three planets that are neither too close nor too far off; one has lost its water and atmosphere; one is too hot; and only one is reasonably temperate. If there were no carbon dioxide in the atmosphere of that one hospitable planet, it would be too cold for most forms of life, and plant life would be impossible (depending as it does on the fixation of carbon dioxide by photosynthesis); if, alternatively, our atmosphere had as much carbon dioxide as on Venus, it would be far too hot.

Even if the average temperature of the earth is set to stay nicely poised between that of Mars and Venus, there is one other feature we require of our environment, and that is predictability. We may think of the weather as being rather unpredictable, from one year to the next. The occasional two or three years of drought can cause millions of deaths in Africa, and it took Europe 100 years or so to recover from the Little Ice Age. But overall, from one century to the next, there have not been any massive

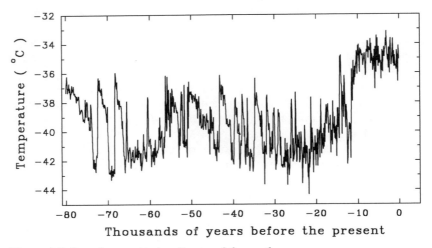

Figure 6.6. Past changes in the climate of the earth.

The proportion of the rare stable isotope of oxygen, ^{18}O, that is present in water when it freezes is linearly related to the ambient temperature when the water is freezing. So the history of the temperature in the northern Atlantic can be obtained by measuring the [18]O content of the successive layers of ice in Greenland. The record has been followed back for 200,000 years. The figure shows the temperature changes for the last 80,000 years (courtesy of J. White; see note 54).

changes in climate over the last five or six thousand years. This stability, it now turns out,[54] is quite exceptional (figure 6.6). For most of the last 250,000 years the climate of the earth has been wildly unstable, both during glacial periods and during the interglacial period 100,000 years ago. Sudden changes in climate and circulation of the oceans, far more dramatic than the Little Ice Age, could occur over periods as short as ten years and could last for 100–1,000 years. It was only in the last 10,000 years (the Holocene period), when the various periodicities in the earth's orbit around the sun were temporarily tending to cancel each other out,[55] that the climate of the earth gave up this instability. And it seems to me to be more than a coincidence that this unusual constancy came just when *Homo sapiens* was inventing agriculture and embarking on the journey toward civilization. The worry, therefore, is that the changes we are causing in the earth's atmosphere may unlock the earth from its present accommodating pattern of climate.

This issue may prove to be far more important than any of the other problems facing humankind. Wars may devastate nations, terrorists may take to using atomic weapons, the Middle East may run out of water, the AIDS virus (HIV) may acquire the ability to spread as a respiratory disease—none of these particular scenarios of human folly or misadventure match up in horror to the prospects of a man-made change in climate. For some time, we have known that it takes a sizeable measure of luck for a planet to be what might be called "life-friendly." But it has been only in the last few years that we have come to realize that it took an even greater measure of luck for our planet to enter a phase where it was civilization-friendly at exactly the time when *Homo sapiens* was ready to take advantage of the change.

Ours may therefore be a transient paradise. In this 10,000-year window of opportunity, we have had to invent civilization and then advance to the point where, if necessary, we have both the technology and the will to cope with the earth's return to its normal, inhospitable behavior. And now, after about 10,000 years, we have discovered that our use of fossil fuels which give us intensive agriculture and plentiful food may be helping to bring our paradise to an end.

Poverty: The Haves and the Have-nots in the Twenty-first Century

Malthus framed much of his argument in terms of the effect of population pressure on the poor, and about a quarter of the *Second Essay* was concerned with the various forms of poor relief. It is obvious that the problem has not been solved—either by capitalism or by communism. Newspapers, even in the richest nations, are still full of correspondence about the best ways of mitigating the effects of poverty. How should the state support single mothers without, at the same time, actively encouraging desertion by the father? What compensation can be given for unemployment that will not actively discourage the unemployed from seeking work? Those were two of the questions posed by Malthus, and it seems to me that they have still not been resolved. Almost 200 years ago he wrote that "It is a subject often started in conversation, and mentioned always as a matter of great surprise, that, notwithstanding the immense sum which is annually collected for the poor in this country, there is still so much distress among them." The same can be said today. Nothing much has changed—except, of course, our standards of what constitutes poverty. In this chapter, I have skirted round the subject of poor relief; economics is far outside my area of competence. But I feel I should venture some comments on the problem of poverty in the new and more menacing form that it has assumed at the end of the twentieth century.

In the time of Malthus, a rather large minority of the population of each European country lived in what we would now call abject poverty, and their existence was seen as both a reproof and a threat. In 1843, a contemporary of Malthus wrote that "the late war . . . was owing, in a very considerable degree, to the apprehension entertained by the aristocracy of the contagion of the French Revolution," but he added that the aristocracy "would have had less ground for apprehension, had the bulk of the people been easy in their condition. Few will deny that an easy command of subsistence is almost a panacea for discontent among the lower classes."[56]

Gradually the Industrial Revolution created a level of wealth that has now reached the point where, at the end of the twentieth century, the poorest members of the industrialized nations live lives that are, on average, far healthier than even the lives of the eighteenth-century rich. Among the least skilled manual workers, life expectancy is higher and infant mortality is lower than it was for the aristocrats of the eighteenth century (see figure 1.4). And, with a few exceptions, the improvement has continued at an ever-increasing pace in the second half of the twentieth century. For example, the poorest ethnic group in the United States are underprivileged in countless ways, but the decline in their level of infant mortality has been running only twenty-five years behind that of the rest of the nation, which is much less than the 100-year interval between the decline in mortality for the aristocrats in Europe and for the population as a whole. (The one recent exception to this steady improvement in the health of all developed nations has been in Eastern Europe and the USSR, where life expectancy has been declining slightly in the last twenty years or so.)[57]

Were the world to consist solely of the industrialized nations, we could reasonably look forward to a steady improvement in the human condition, even for the poorest members of society. After all, these nations have settled down close to zero growth and certainly have more than adequate resources to provide for all their inhabitants and to do so in a way that need not damage the environment. So even if governments adopted the most lackadaisical policies and the gulf within the rich nations between the rich and the poor remained as large as ever, the absolute condition of the poor would probably go on improving.

But the world is not just composed of the industrialized nations. Most people live in poor, undeveloped areas and this is where the population explosion is now taking place. And it is occurring on a scale that dwarfs what happened in Europe in the nineteenth century. During the 150 years when the developed nations were going through the demographic transition, the world's population rose from 1 billion to slightly more than 2 billion. But that is a tiny increase compared to what is going to happen. In the next 150 years, the developing nations seem set to move the total to somewhere between 10 and 20 billion.[58] Furthermore, the change is occurring much more quickly. Figure 6.4 showed how three European countries went through the demographic transition. Figure 6.5 shows where a sample of developing nations are currently placed in that kind of graph. For this, I chose the three most populous nations of Asia, and the two most populous in Africa, the Middle East, and South America. Most of them, as we can see, are now experiencing a combination of reproduction rate and life expectancy that produces a much faster growth rate than even that of England at the height of its population explosion.

A few of the developing nations are managing the transition with as much skill as was shown by Europe in the nineteenth century; in particular, China (which contains over 20 percent of the world's population) has instituted a strict program for controlling the birthrate, and as a result its populations should stabilize early in the twenty-first century. But many poor nations, especially in Africa, seem already trapped in poverty, even before their exploding population has outstripped the carrying capacity of the land.

To make matters worse, the help that has come from outside has often done more harm than good. Western nations have made massive loans to many developing nations. This has generated an endless debt, and the interest on the debt has to be paid by the export of primary produce into a buyer's market. To make matters worse still, it often turns out that most of these loans have been spent on armaments bought from the lending nations (who usually make more armaments than they themselves can put to use). In their interactions with the developing world, the rich nations have therefore acquired, in one step, a continuous source of income plus a stream of cheap primary produce plus a market for surplus armaments.

This should not, I believe, be interpreted as necessarily yet another example of lingering colonialism. It may just reflect the general rapaciousness of big business. After all, the same kind of thing has happened in many rich nations; when a country like the United States builds up an enormous national debt, what that means is that rich corporations have lent the government money and thereby ensured that a large part of the government's tax revenue has to be spent, each year, repaying the interest on the debt; in other words, government revenue ends up being used to provide income for the rich. Such a continuous transfer of wealth from poor to rich is somewhat damaging in an affluent country like the United States, but it is a devastating burden for a poor country.

The industrialized nations are now powerless spectators as they watch the population explosion in Asia, Africa, and South America. For example, across the southern border of the United States lies Mexico—one-fifth the size of the United States and with one-seventh of the wealth, but with a population that seems set to match that of the United States within fifty years or so. What is to come of that imbalance? A little apprehension would not seem inappropriate.

There have been occasions in the past when nations have outstripped their capacity to produce food, and this has led to mass migration; for example, the population explosion in Ireland, followed by failure of the potato crop in 1846, resulted in emigration of roughly one-third of its population to the United States in a period of fifty years. In most cases, including the Irish emigration to the United States, the receiving countries were easily able to accommodate the migrants. But now, with a few exceptions, the nations of the world are full and they do not want their populations to increase any further, still less by the immigration of outsiders.

Perhaps the best and most instructive analogy to the population pressures of today can be found in the recent history of the United States. In the late 1930s, the southern states contained about 20 million unskilled workers whose livelihood came from picking cotton. It seemed probable, however, that their jobs were about to be taken over by machines. A committee, meeting in Washington to discuss the likely developments in technology over the next fifteen years,[59] suggested that the invention of a machine to pick cotton would lead to a massive migration of unskilled cotton pickers into the cities of the north in search of work and various forms of social support. And that of course was exactly what happened. Little was done to accommodate the influx from the south, and the result has been damaging to migrant and nonmigrant alike. In retrospect, the country should have listened to the experts and, in advance of the migration, diverted some of the nation's resources to providing education and creating alternative employment for the unskilled cotton pickers who were being displaced by machines—that is to say, to providing the "easy command of subsistence" that is a "panacea for discontent."

I have mentioned this episode of the invention of a machine for picking cotton for an additional reason. It seems to me that the nonscientific public does not realize how accurate scientists can be when making predictions about future technological developments and about the consequences of such developments. These days, the most widely reported predictions tend to come from committees that have been, from the outset, designed to reach some politically convenient conclusion. But when freed from that constraint, the average group of scientists will usually prove to be fairly accurate in its predictions, even though it will often underestimate the speed of events. The 1937 report of the committee I have just referred to was called "Technological Trends and National Policy, including the social implications of new inventions," and it gave an astonishingly accurate forecast of the inventions and applications of the next fifteen years, and of their social consequences. Of course they missed a few things—the atom bomb, antibiotics, radar, the jet engine, the stimulating effect of World War II on American industry, and so on—but by and large they got it right: air pollution ("smoke always hurts the community more than it hurts the owner of the chimney"[60] and "the sulphur dioxide in coal smoke . . . eats impartially clothes and paper, throats, buildings, and vegetation"),[61] plastics, user-friendly computers, the revolution in all forms of communication including facsimile transmission and television, the mounting cost of medical care, the accelerating pace of invention and the resulting problem of capital obsolescence, the effects of increasing automation on levels of employment, and the development of international conglomerates. They were notably prescient on the subject of television, which they saw would be "placing theaters into millions of homes and increasing even more the already astounding possibilities of propaganda to be imposed on a none too critical human race,"[62] and they realized that television would allow advertisers to reach an audience of millions: "Whatever body wields such power might conceivably be able in time to undermine all opposition to its power. The question is evidently raised whether the control should be in the hands of private capital, presumably under Government supervision, or under direct Government management and control."[63] Aside from their far-sighted wisdom, the committee displayed an unusually elegant style. "The environment of modern men is to a surprising degree made up of machines, much as the environment of wild animals is made up of fauna, flora, wind, rain, and temperature. Even those men and women who do not work on a machine for a living are only once removed from it or its products. Modern man's problem of adaptation to his machine-made environment is different from the problem of primitive man in adapting to nature because the machine made environment is rapidly changing, and this is not the case with nature."[64]

If that committee could now return, after fifty years, and look at what has happened, I am sure that many things would horrify them. But perhaps worst of all would be the increasing unwillingness of governments and the general public to listen to what the scientists are saying. The committee had warned that the loss of livelihood for much of the rural population of the south would be catastrophic. "Will the governments plan and act in time, once the spread of this invention is certain?"[65] they asked, and the answer was "No." Yet the problem posed by the machine for picking cotton was tiny by comparison with the problems of today. It amounted to a local migration of a mere 10 percent of the inhabitants of the richest and most versatile country in the world. Now we face much more alarming predictions—exploding populations and diminishing resources, coupled with a reasonably firm prediction of a major change in the world's climate. Are the governments showing any signs of being willing to try to plan and act in time? Once again the answer appears to be "No."

In fact, it is worse than that because the many groups with a vested interest in the status quo have become more skilled in their delaying tactics. In a capitalist society every new ecological niche is quickly exploited. And, in response to a lot of expert testimony, obscurantism has become a marketable art. Nowadays, "the none too critical human race" is being continually worked upon by teams of skilled obfuscators. If you doubt that, just consider the ingenuity with which the tobacco industry has countered all the evidence for the hazards of smoking. By comparison, the give-and-take between Malthus and his contemporaries has a kind of open clarity that is missing from the public controversies of today.

So far, there have been several international discussions of the rules that governments should adopt to prevent global warming. Little has been achieved. Most heads of state must find it almost impossible to imagine how the economy of their country could survive the necessary revolution in its management of energy, so they turn to the professional obfuscators for evidence that more information is needed before drastic steps have to be taken.

Yet even if the industrialized nations of the world could somehow manage to take the appropriate action, I do not see that this would solve the problem. For these nations make up only about 15 percent of the world's population. The remaining 85 percent naturally want to follow in the footsteps of the West and become modernized consumers of energy, as quickly as possible. Who is to deny them that right? But when they do become industrialized, the world may quickly acquire such a hostile and unstable climate that it becomes unsuitable for most forms of human existence. Such a sudden, positive check to human population could far exceed Malthus's worst imaginings.

❧

My first chapter, on mortality, was really no more than a history of events. It was not primarily concerned with ideas and did not try to predict what changes in the force of mortality might happen in the future. If you are lucky enough to live in an affluent, industrialized nation, you can feel confident that there is not going to be a significant increase in life expectancy in the foreseeable future, or at least nothing to compare with what has already happened. In the last 150 years, life expectancy has risen from about thirty-five to about seventy-five, and it is unlikely to go up very much further (for example, if a cure for cancer were discovered, average life expectancy would increase by only about two years). Most of us can count on achieving a decrepit senescence. So any chapter on public health and the history of mortality is an account of a project that is nearing completion.

Not so, an account of population. The main increase in human numbers will have occurred in the 300 years between 1750 and 2050. We are now nearly at the end of this experiment and our primary concern is with what will be the final result. Over the last ten thousand years or so, the number of humans increased steadily at an average rate of about 0.1% a year, reaching one billion by 1800 AD. Since then it has been growing at almost 1% a year, reaching two billion in 1930, three billion by 1960, four billion in 1975, and probably over 6 billion by the end of the century.[66]

Until recently, anyone could take whatever position they chose on the subject of population. You could be an optimist (like Condorcet) and believe that the human race by virtue of its power of reasoning was inevitably moving toward a world of stability and happiness for all. You could be a pessimist (like Malthus) and believe that some suffering is needed to force populations to adopt the various "preventive" checks to continued growth. Or you could (like Wallace, Godwin, Marx, and Engels) say that any problems caused by overpopulation would come only in the far distant future.

In the last few years, however, two new ingredients have emerged. We have learned that there are now so many *Homines sapientes* and they are so industrious and inventive that they are affecting the climate of the earth. The human race may be about to destroy itself not by anything preventable such as nuclear war but by a virtually unpreventable consequence of the Industrial Revolution and the population explosion.

If that were not enough, we have discovered that the earth's climate is much less stable than we had imagined and that, in the not too distant past, it was subject to wild oscillations which could hardly have been survived by the most technologically advanced nations even in the absence of population pressure from their neighbors.

So the arguments about population have suddenly acquired a new dimension. Global changes in climate promise to dwarf the other calamities of human history. And the time scale may be very short. This is not just idle speculation about the fate of the human race in some far distant future. What I have been discussing here could be the fate of our grandchildren.

Notes

CHAPTER 1
A HISTORY OF MORTALITY

1. See the article on Census in *The Encyclopædia Britannica*, 1911.

2. See the article on Insurance in *The Encyclopædia Britannica*, 1911.

3. J. Graunt, *Natural and Political Observations Mentioned in a Following Index, and Made Upon the Bills of Mortality. With Reference to the Government, Religion, Trade, Growth, Ayre, Diseases, and the Several Changes of the Said City* (1662) (New York: Arno Press, 1975).

4. E. Halley, "An Estimate of the Degrees of the Mortality of Mankind, Drawn from Curious Tables of the Births and Funerals at the City of Breslau; With an Attempt to Ascertain the Price of Annuities upon Lives." *Phil. Trans. Roy. Soc. Lond.* 17: 596–610, 1693.

5. G. Y. Acsadi and J. Nemeskeri. *History of Human Life Span and Mortality.* (Budapest: Akadémiai Kiadó, 1971).

6. N. Howell. *Demography of the Dobe !Kung.* (New York: Academic Press, 1979).

7. D. E. Dumond. "The Limitation of Human Population: A Natural History." *Science* 187, 713–721, 1975.

8. E. Boserup. *Population and Technological Change. A Study of Long-Term Trends.* (Chicago: University of Chicago Press, 1981).

9. E. Boserup. *The Conditions of Agricultural Growth. The Economics of Agrarian Change Under Population Pressure.* (Chicago: Aldine Publishing, 1965).

10. W. H. McNeill. *Plagues and Peoples.* (Oxford: Blackwell, 1976).

11. F. L. Black. "Measles Endemicity in Insular Populations: Critical Community Size and Its Evolutionary Implication." *J. Theoret. Biol.* 11, 207–11, 1966.

12. W. R. MacDonell. "On the Expectation of Life in Ancient Rome, and in the Provinces of Hispania and Lusitania, and Africa." *Biometrika* 9, 366–80, 1913.

13. E. Gibbon. *The History of the Decline and Fall of the Roman Empire* (1779). J. M. Dent & Sons (London: Everyman Library, 1910), p. 78.

14. See note 3.

15. G. Rosen. "An Eighteenth Century Plan for a National Health Service." *Bull. Hist. Med.* 16, 429–36, 1944.

16. R. Price. *Supplement to the 2nd Edition of the Treatise on Reversionary Payments &c.* (London: T. Cadell, 1777).

17. T. H. Hollingsworth. "The Demography of the British Peerage." *Population Studies,* 18 (Suppl.), 1965; S. Peller. "Births and Deaths Among Europe's Ruling Families Since 1500." In *Population in History,* edited by D. V. Glass and D.E.C. Eversley. (Chicago: Aldine Publishing, 1965).

18. E. A. Wrigley and R. S. Schofield. *The Population History of England, 1541–1871. A Reconstruction.* (Cambridge, Mass.: Harvard University Press, 1981).

19. P. Townsend and N. Davidson. *Inequalities in Health: The Black Report.* (London: Penguin Books, 1982); G. D. Smith, M. Bartley, and D. Blane. "The Black Report on Socio-economic Inequalities in Health 10 years on." *Brit. Med. J.* 301, 373–77, 1990; A. Antonovsky. "Social Class, Life Expectancy and Overall Mortality." *Milbank. Memorial Fund Quarterly* 45(2): 31–73, 1967. M. G. Marmot, M. J. Shipley, and G. Rose. "Inequalities in Death—Specific Explanations of a General Pattern?" *Lancet* i: 1003–1006, 1984; M. G. Marmot, G. D. Smith, S. Stansfeld, C. Patel, F. North, J. Head, I. White, E. Brunner, and A. Feeney. "Health Inequalities Among British Civil Servants: The Whitehall II Study." *Lancet* 337: 1387–93, 1991.

20. E. M. Kitagawa and P. M. Hauser. *Differential Mortality in the United States: A Study in Socioeconomic Epidemiology.* (Cambridge, Mass.: Harvard University Press, 1973).

21. P. E. Razell. "Edward Jenner: The History of a Medical Myth." *Med. Hist.* 9: 216–29, 1965.

22. J. Haygarth. "A Sketch of a Plan to Exterminate the Casual Small-pox," 1793. See P. Razell. *The Conquest of Smallpox: The Impact of Inoculation on Smallpox Mortality in Eighteenth Century Britain.* (Sussex, UK: Caliban Books, 1977).

23. A. J. Coale and S. C. Watkins. *The Decline in Fertility in Europe.* (Princeton, N.J.: Princeton University Press, 1986).

24. T. McKeown, R. G. Brown, and R. G. Record. "An Interpretation of the Modern Rise of Population in Europe." *Population Studies* 26: 345–82, 1972.

25. P. E. Razell. "An Interpretation of the Modern Rise of Population in Europe—A Critique." *Population Studies* 28: 5–17, 1974.

26. S. Wing, M. Casper, W. Riggan, C. Hayes, and H. A. Tyroler. "Socioenvironmental Characteristics Associated with the Onset of Decline of Ischemic Heart Disease Mortality in the United States." *Amer. J. Publ. Health* 78: 923–26, 1988.

27. J. P. Frank. "Academic Address on the People's Misery: Mother of Diseases." *Bull. Hist. Med.* 9: 81–100, 1941.

28. J. C. Russell. Chapter 1, "Population in Europe, 500–1500." In *The Fontana Economic History of Europe. The Middle Ages,* edited by C. M. Cipolla. Fontana, 1972; F. A. Hassan. "Resources and Population: An Archeological Perspective." In *How Humans Adapt. A Biocultural Odyssey,* edited by D. J. Ortner. Smithsonian International Symposia Series, 1983.

29. W. H. McNeill. *Plagues and Peoples.* (Oxford: Blackwell, 1976).

30. W. Farr. *Vital Statistics: A Memorial Volume of Selections from the Reports and Writings of William Farr.* The History of Medicine Series, no. 46. (Metuchen, NJ.: Scarecrow Press, 1975).

31. W. Coleman. *Death Is a Social Disease: Public Health and Political Economy in Early Industrial France.* (Madison: University of Wisconsin Press, 1982).

32. E. Chadwick. *Report on the Sanitary Condition of the Labouring Population of Great Britain, Presented to the House of Lords on July 9, 1842.* (Edinburgh: Edinburgh University Press, 1965).

33. F. Engels. *The Condition of the Working Class in England.* 1845. Translated by W. O. Henderson and W. H. Chaloner. (Stanford, Calif.: Stanford University Press, 1968).

34. G. W. Roberts. "A Life Table for a West Indian Slave Population." *Population Studies* 5: 238–43, 1952.

35. See note 30.

36. N. Longmate. *King Cholera: The Biography of a Disease.* (London: Hamish Hamilton, 1966); W. E. van Heyningen and J. R. Seal. *Cholera: The American Scientific Experience 1947–1980.* (Boulder, Colo.: Westview Press, 1983).

37. T. McKeown. *The Role of Medicine: Dream, Mirage, or Nemesis.* (London: The Nuffield Provincial Hospital Trust, 1976).

38. S. Tesh. "Political Ideology and Public Health in the Nineteenth Century." *Int. J. Health Services* 12: 321–42, 1982.

39. G. F. Shrady. "The Health Board and Compulsory Reports." *Med. Rec.* 51: 305–6, 1897.

40. E. H. Ackerknecht. "Anticontagionism between 1821 and 1867." *Bull. Hist. Med.* 22: 562–93, 1948.

41. G. Rosen. *A History of Public Health.* (New York: MD Publications, 1958).

42. J. Henle. "On Miasmata and Contagia." 1840. Translated by G. Rosen. *Bull. Hist. Med.* 6: 907–83, 1938.

43. J. Snow. *Snow on Cholera.* (New York: Hafner Publishing, 1965).

44. W. E. van Heyningen and J. R. Seal. *Cholera: The American Scientific Experience, 1947–1980.* (Boulder, Colo: Westview Press, 1983).

45. J. P. Vandenbroucke, H.M.E. Rooda, and H. Beukers. "Who Made John Snow a Hero?" *Amer. J. Epidem.* 133: 967–73, 1991.

46. L. G. Wilson. "The Historical Decline of Tuberculosis in Europe and America: Its Causes and Significance." *J. Hist. Med. Allied Sci.* 45: 366–96, 1990.

47. G. F. Shrady. "The Health Board and Compulsory Reports." *Med. Rec.* 51: 305–6, 1987.

48. A. M. Lowell. *Tuberculosis. 1. Tuberculosis Morbidity and Mortality and Its Control.* (Cambridge, Mass.: Harvard University Press, 1969).

49. J. Vallin. *La Mortalité par Génération en France, depuis 1899.* (Paris: Presses Universitaires de France, 1973).

50. J. Duffy. *A History of Public Health in New York City, 1866–1966.* (New York: Russell Sage Foundation, 1974).

51. National Resources Committee. "Technological Trends and National Policy, Including the Social Implications of New Inventions." (Washington, D.C.: U.S. Government Printing Office, 1937).

52. National Program for the Conquest of Cancer. 1970. "Report of the National Panel of Consultants on the Conquest of Cancer." (Washington, D.C.: U.S. Government Printing Office, 1970).

53. J. B. McKinlay and S. M. McKinlay. "The Questionable Contribution of Medical Measures to the Decline of Mortality in the United States in the Twentieth Century." *Millbank Memorial Fund Quarterly* 55: 405–28, 1977; K. Poikolainen and J. Eskola. "The Effect of Health Services on Mortality: Decline in Death Rates from Amenable and Non-amenable Causes in Finland 1969–81." *Lancet* i: 199–202, 1986.

54. C. T. Stewart. "Allocation of Resources to Health." *J. Human Resources,* 6: 103–22, 1971.

55. P.C.A. Louis. "Researches on the Effects of Blood-letting in Some Inflam-

matory Diseases and on the Influence of Tontarized Antimony and Vesication in Pneumonitis." 1836. Translated by J. Jackson (Boston: C. G. Putnam); M. Bariéty. "Louis et la Méthode numérique." *Clio. Medica* 7: 177–183, 1972.

56. J. T. Hart. "A New Type of General Practitioner." *Lancet* ii: 27–29, 1983.

57. A. L. Cochrane, A. S. St. Leger and F. Moore. "Health Service 'Input' and Mortality 'Output' in Developed Countries." *J. Epidemiol. Commun. Health.* 32: 200–205, 1978.

CHAPTER 2
A HISTORY OF MOLECULAR BIOLOGY: THE STORAGE OF
BIOLOGICAL INFORMATION

1. M. J. Nye. *Molecular Reality. A Perspective on the Scientific Work of Jean Perrin.* (New York: Elsevier, 1972).

2. C. Darwin. *The Origin of Species by Means of Natural Selection, or the Preservation of Favoured Races in the Struggle for Life,* 1859. (London: Penguin Books, 1968); C. Darwin. *The Autobiography of Charles Darwin and Selected Letters,* edited by F. Darwin. (New York: Dover Publications, 1958); A. Desmond and J. Moore. *Darwin.* (London: Michael Joseph, 1991); J. Marchant. *Alfred Russel Wallace: Letters and Reminiscences.* (London: Cassell, 1916).

3. C. Darwin. *Charles Darwin's Natural Selection, Being the Second Part of His Big Species Book Written from 1856 to 1858,* edited by R. C. Stauffer. (Cambridge: Cambridge University Press, 1987).

4. W. Bateson. *Mendel's Principles of Heredity: A Defence.* (Cambridge: Cambridge University Press, 1902).

5. Ibid.

6. L. A. Callender. "Gregor Mendel": An Opponent of Descent with Modification." *Hist. Sci.* 26: 41–75, 1988; F. di Trocchio. "Mendel's Experiments: A Reinterpretation." *J. Hist. Biol.* 24: 485–519, 1991; B. Bishop, personal communication.

7. P. J. Vorzimmer. "Darwin and Mendel: The Historical Connection.". *Isis* 59: 77–82, 1968.

8. E. A. Carlson. *The Gene: A Critical History.* (Philadelphia: W. B. Saunders, 1966).

9. W. S. Sutton. "On the Morphology of the Chromosome Group in *Brachystola magna.*" *Biol. Bull.* 4: 24–39, 1902.

10. L. Cuénot. "L'Hérédité de la Pigmentation chez les Souris." *Arch. Zool. Exp. Gen.* 4° serie 1: xxii–xli, 1903.

11. A. E. Garrod. *Inborn Errors of Metabolism.* (London: Frowde & Hodder, 1909).

12. W. Bateson. "Problems of Heredity as a Subject for Horticultural Investigation." *Roy. Hortic. Soc.* 25: 54–61, 1900.

13. A. H. Sturtevant. *A History of Genetics.* (New York: Harper & Row, 1965).

14. G. W. Beadle and B. Ephrussi. "The Differentiation of Eye Pigments in *Drosophila* as Studied by Transplantation." *Genetics* 21: 225–47, 1936.

15. G. W. Beadle. "Biochemical Genetics. Some Recollections." In *Phage and the Origins of Molecular Biology,* Cold Spring Harbor, 1966.

16. G. W. Beadle and E. L. Tatum. "Genetic Control of Biochemical Reactions in Neurospora." *Proc. Natl. Acad. Sci.* 27: 499–506, 1941.

17. J. S. Huxley. *Evolution: The Modern Synthesis.* (London: Allen & Unwin, 1942).

18. F. Griffith. "The Significance of Pneumococcal Types." *J. Hyg. Camb.* 27: 113–59, 1928.

19. R. J. Dubos. *The Professor, the Institute, and DNA.* (New York: Rockefeller University Press, 1976).

20. O. T. Avery, C. M. MacLeod, and M. McCarty. "Studies on the Chemical Nature of the Substance Inducing Transformation of Pneumococcal Types." *J. Exp. Med.* 79: 137–58, 1944).

21. T. Dobzhansky. *Genetics and the Origin of Species,* 2d ed. (New York: Columbia University Press, 1947).

22. A. D. Hershey and M. Chase. "Independent Functions of Viral Protein and Nucleic Acid in Growth of Bacteriophage." *J. Gen. Physiol.* 36: 39–56, 1952.

23. E. Schrödinger. *What Is Life? The Physical Aspect of the Living Cell.* (Cambridge: Cambridge University Press, 1944).

24. E. Chargaff. "Chemical Specificity of Nucleic Acids and the Mechanism of Their Enzymatic Degradation." *Experientia* 6: 201–9, 1950.

25. J. D. Watson and F.H.C. Crick. "A Structure for Deoxyribosenucleic Acid." *Nature* 171: 737–38, 1953; M.H.F. Wilkins, A. R. Stokes, and H. R. Wilson. "Molecular Structure of Deoxypentose Nucleic Acids." *Nature* 171: 738–40; 1953; R. E. Franklin and R. G. Gosling. "Molecular Configuration in Sodium Thymonucleate." *Nature* 171: 740–41, 1953.

26. I. R. Lehman, M. J. Bessman, E. S. Simms, and A. Kornberg. "Enzymatic Synthesis of Deoxyribonucleic Acid. 1. Preparation of Substrates and Partial Purification of an Enzyme from *Escherichia coli.*" *J. Biol. Chem.* 233: 163–77, 1958.

27. M. Meselson and F. W. Stahl. "The Replication of DNA in *Escherichia coli.*" *Proc. Natl. Acad. Sci.* 44: 671–82, 1958.

28. W. Bateson. "Problems of Heredity as a Subject for Horticultural Investigation." *J. Roy. Hortic. Soc.* 25: 54–61, 1900.

CHAPTER 4
CANCER AND THE MOLECULAR BIOLOGY OF MULTICELLULAR SYSTEMS

1. P. Stragier, B. Kunkel, L. Kroos, and R. Losick. "Chromosomal Rearrangement Generating a Composite Gene for a Developmental Transcription Factor." *Science* 243: 507–12, 1989.

2. M. A. Di Bernadino and N. H. Orr. "Genomic Potential of Erythroid and Leukocytic Cells of *Rana pipiens* Analyzed by Nuclear Transfer into Diplotene and Maturing Oocytes." *Differentiation* 50: 1–13, 1992.

3. K. Yamagiwa and K. Ichikawa. "Experimental Study of the Pathogenesis of Carcinoma." *J. Cancer Res. Clin. Oncol.* 3(1): 1–29, 1918.

4. J. Clunet. "Recherches Expérimentales sur les Tumeurs Malignes." Thèse de Paris, quoted by L. Gross in *Oncogenic Viruses,* 2d ed. (Oxford: Pergamon Press, 1970).

5. L. Gross. *"Oncogenic Viruses."* (Oxford: Pergamon Press, 1970).

6. E. E. Tyzzer. "Tumor Immunology." *J. Cancer Res.* 1: 125–55, 1916.

7. H. J. Muller. "Artificial Transmutation of the Gene." *Science* 46: 84–87, 1927.

8. E. L. Kennaway and I. Hieger. "Carcinogenic Substances and Their Fluorescence Spectra." *Brit. Med. J.* i: 1044–46, 1930.

9. C. Auerbach and J. M. Robson. "Production of Mutations by Allyl Isothiocyanate." *Nature* 154: 81, 1944.

10. M. Demerec. "Mutations in *Drosophila* Induced by a Carcinogen." *Nature* 159: 604, 1947; L. C. Strong. "The Induction of Mutations by a Carcinogen." *Brit. J. Cancer* 3: 97–108, 1949.

11. E. Boyland and A. A. Levi. "Metabolism of Polycyclic Compounds. 1. Production of Dihrydroxyhydroanthracene from Anthracene." *Biochem. J.* 29: 2679–83, 1935; E. Boyland and F. Weigert. "Metabolism of Carcinogenic Compounds." *Br. Med. Bull.* 4: 354–359, 1947; E. Boyland. "The Biological Significance of Metabolism of Polycyclic Hydrocarbons." *Biochem. J.* 46: ii–iii, 1950.

12. E. C. Miller, J. A. Miller, and E. Enomoto. "The Comparative Carcinogenicities of 2-acetylaminofluorene and Its N-hydroxy Metabolite in Mice, Hamsters, and Guinea Pigs." *Cancer Res.* 24: 2018–32, 1964.

13. H. Weil-Malherbe. "The Solubilization of Polycyclic Aromatic Hydrocarbons by Purines." *Bioch. J.* 40: 351–63, 1946; E. Boyland. "Different Types of Carcinogens and Their Possible Modes of Action: A Review." *Cancer. Res.* 12: 77–84, 1952.

14. E. C. Miller and J. A. Miller. "*In vivo* Combinations Between Carcinogens and Tissue Constituents and Their Possible Role in Carcinogenesis." *Cancer Res.* 12: 547–56, 1952; W. G. Weist and C. Heidelberger. "The Interaction of Carcinogenic Hydrocarbons with Tissue Constituents. (2) 1,2,5,6-dibenzanthracene-9,10-C^{14} in Skin." *Cancer Res.* 13: 250–54, 1953; P. Rous. "Surmise and Fact on the Nature of Cancer." *Nature* 183: 1357–61, 1959.

15. H. C. Pitot and C. Heidelberger. "Metabolic Regulatory Circuits and Carcinogenesis." *Cancer Res.* 23: 1694–1700, 1963.

16. B. N. Ames, F. D. Lee, and W. E. Durston. "An Improved Bacterial Test System for the Detection and Classification of Mutagens and Carcinogens." *Proc. Natl. Acad. Sci. Wash.* 70: 782–86, 1973; M. Meselson and K. Russell. "Comparisons of Carcinogenic Potency and Mutagenic Potency." In *Origins of Human Cancer*, pp 1473–1481. Edited by H. H. Hiatt, J. D. Watson, and J. A. Winsten. Cold Spring Harbor, 1977; T. Sugimura. "Tumor Initiators and Promoters in Association with Ordinary Foods." In *The Molecular Interrelations of Nutrition and Cancer*, edited by M. S. Arnott, J. vanEys, and Y-N. Wang. (New York: Raven Press, 1982).

17. D. R. Charles and E. M. Luce-Clausen. "The Kinetics of Papilloma Formation in Benz-Pyrene Treated Mice." *Cancer Res.* 2: 261–63, 1942.

18. See note 15.

19. L. G. Koss, F. W. Stewart, F. W. Foote, M. J. Jordan, G. M. Bader, and E. Day. "Some Histological Aspects of Behavior of Epidermoid Carcinoma in situ and Related Lesions of the Uterine Cervix. A Long-term Prospective Study." *Cancer* 16: 1160–1211, 1963; Canadian Study. "Cervical Cancer Screening Programs." *Canad. Med. Assoc. J.* 114: 1003–1033, 1976.

20. J. M. Twort and C. C. Twort. "Comparative Activity of Some Carcinogenic

Hydrocarbons." *Amer. J. Cancer* 35: 80–85, 1939; W. F. Friedewald and P. Rous. "The Initiating and Promoting Elements in Tumor Production." *J. Exp. Med.* 80: 101–126, 1944; I. Berenblum and P. Shubik. "A New, Quantitative Approach to the Study of the Stages of Chemical Carcinogenesis in the Mouse's Skin." *Brit. J. Cancer* 1: 383–91, 1947.

21. Y. Berwald and L. Sachs. "In vitro Transformation of Normal Cells to Tumor Cells by Carcinogenic Hydrocarbons." *J. Natl. Cancer Inst.* 35: 641–62, 1965.

22. M. Abercrombie and J.E.M. Heaysman. "Observations on the Social Behavior of Cells in Tissue Culture. 2. 'Monolayering' of Fibroblasts." *Exp. Cell. Res.* 6: 293–306, 1954.

23. W. R. Loewenstein and Y. Kanno. "Intercellular Communication and the Control of Tissue Growth: Lack of Communication Between Cancer Cells." *Nature* 209: 1248–49, 1966.

24. P. C. Nowell and D. A. Hungerford. "A Minute Chromosome in Human Chronic Granulocytic Leukemia." *Science* 132: 1497, 1960.

25. P. Rous. "A Transmissible Avian Neoplasm. (Sarcoma of the Common Fowl)." *J. Exp. Med.* 12: 696–706, 1910; Rous. "A Sarcoma of the Fowl Transmissible by an Agent Separable from the Tumor Cells." *J. Exp. Med.* 13: 397–411, 1911.

26. H. M. Temin. "Mechanism of Cell Transformation by RNA Tumor Viruses." *Ann. Rev. Microbiol.* 25: 609–48, 1971; Temin. "On the Origin of RNA Tumor Viruses." *Ann. Rev. Genet.* 8: 155–77, 1974.

27. N. D. Zinder and J. Lederberg. *"Genetic Exchange in Salmonella." J. Bacteriol.* 64: 679–99, 1952.

28. M. Hill and J. Hillova. "Recombinational Events Between Exogenous Mouse DNA and Newly Synthesized DNA Strands of Chicken Cells in Culture." *Nature New Biology* 231: 261–65, 1971.

29. C. Shih, L. L. Padhy, M. Murray, and R. A. Weinberg. "Transforming Genes of Carcinomas and Neuroblastomas Introduced into Mouse Fibroblasts." *Nature* 290: 261–64, 1981; G. M. Cooper. "Cellular Transforming Genes." *Science* 217: 801–806, 1982.

30. C. J. Tabin, S. M. Bradley, C. I. Bargmann, R. A. Weinberg, A. G. Papageorge, E. M. Scolnick, R. Dhar, R. R. Lowy, and E. H. Chang. "Mechanism of Activation of a Human Oncogene." *Nature* 300: 143–49, 1982. E. P. Reddy, R. K. Reynolds, E. Santos, and M. Barbacid. "A Point Mutation Is Responsible for the Acquisition of Transforming Properties by the T24 Human Bladder Carcinoma Oncogene." *Nature* 300: 149–52, 1982.

31. J. D. Rowley. "Chromosome Abnormalities in Cancer." *Cancer Genet. Cytogenet.* 2: 175–98, 1980.

32. R. Taub, I. Kirsch, C. Morton, G. Lenoir, D. Swan, S. Tronick, S. Aaronson, and P. Leder. "Translocation of the c-*myc* Gene into the Immunoglobulin Heavy Chain Locus in Burkitt Lymphoma and Murine Plasmacytoma Cells." *Proc. Natl. Acad. Sci. Wash.* 79: 7837–41, 1982.

33. H. Land, L. F. Parada, and R. A. Weinberg. "Tumorigenic Conversion of Primary Embryo Fibroblasts Requires at Least Two Cooperating Oncogenes." *Nature* 304: 596–602, 1983.

34. H. E. Ruley. "Adenovirus Early Region 1A Enables Viral and Cellular Transforming Genes to Transform Primary Cells in Culture." *Nature* 304: 602–6, 1983.

35. R. de Mars, "Genetic Concepts of Neoplasia." 23rd Symposium of Fundamental Cancer Research, M. D. Anderson Hospital, 1970. p. 105.

36. A. G. Knudson. "Mutation and Cancer: A Statistical Study of Retinoblastoma." *Proc. Natl. Acad. Sci.* 68: 820–23, 1971.

37. Judges xii.

38. R. J. Podorski. "Genetic Information and Life Insurance." *Nature* 376: 13–14, 1995.

39. L. A. Loeb. "Microsatellite Instability: Marker of a Mutator Phenotype in Cancer." *Cancer Res.* 54: 5059–63, 1994.

40. L. A. Loeb. "Mutator Phenotype May Be Required for Multistage Carcinogenesis." *Cancer. Res.* 51: 3075–79, 1991.

41. Y. Choo, I. Sánchez-Garcia, and A. Klug. "*In vivo* Repression by a Site-Specific DNA-binding Protein Designed against an Oncogenic Sequence." *Nature* 372: 642–45, 1994.

42. M-C. King, S. Rowell, and S. M. Love. "Inherited Breast and Ovarian Cancer. What Are the Risks? What Are the Choices?" *J. Amer. Med. Assoc.* 269: 1975–80, 1993.

CHAPTER 5
THE EPIDEMIOLOGY OF CANCER

1. L. Breslow, L. Agran, D. M. Breslow, M. Morganstern, and L. Ellwein. "Cancer Control: Implications from Its History." *J. Natl. Cancer Inst.* 59: 671–86, 1977.

2. J. Cairns and P. Boyle. "Cancer Chemotherapy." *Science* 220: 252–54, 1983.

3. U. Tröhler. "To Improve the Evidence of Medicine: Arithmetic Observation in Clinical Medicine in the Eighteenth and Early Nineteenth century." *Hist. Phil. Life Sci.* 10 (Suppl.): 31–40, 1988.

4. M. Bariéty. "Louis et la Méthode Numérique." *Clio Medica* 7: 177–183, 1972.

5. A. M. Lilienfeld. "*Ceteris paribus*: The Evolution of the Clinical Trial." *Bull. Hist. Med.* 56: 1–18, 1982.

6. D. M. Parkin, C. S. Muir, S. L. Whelan, Y. T. Gao, J. Ferlay, and J. Powell. *Cancer Incidence in Five Continents. Volume VI.* (Lyon: IARC, 1992).

7. Ibid.

8. R. Doll and R. Peto. *The Causes of Cancer.* (Oxford: Oxford University Press, 1981).

9. Annual Statistics published by The American Cancer Society.

10. G. D. Smith, D. Leon, M. J. Shipley, and G. Rose. "Socioeconomic Differentials in Cancer Among Men." *Int. J. Epidem.* 20: 339–45, 1991.

11. J. E. Enstrom. "Cancer and Total Mortality Among Active Mormons." *Cancer* 42: 1943–51, 1978.

12. Data from M.H.C. Williams. "Occupational Tumors of the Bladder." In *Cancer*, vol. 3, edited by R. W. Raven. (London: Butterworth, 1958).

13. R. Peto, A. D. Lopez, J. Boreham, M. Thun, and C. Heath. *Mortality from

Smoking in Developed Countries 1950–2000. (Oxford: Oxford Medical Publications, Oxford University Press, 1994).

14. R. Korteweg. "The Age Curve in Lung Cancer." *Brit. J. Cancer* 5: 21–27, 1951.

15. The Canadian Cancer Study. "Cervical Cancer Screening Programs. 1. Epidemiology and Natural History of Carcinoma of the Cervix." *Canad. Med. Assoc. J.* 114: 1003–1033, 1976; A. B. Miller, J. Lindsay, and G. B. Hill. "Mortality from Cancer of the Uterus in Canada and Its Relationship to Screening for Cancer of the Cervix." *Int. J. Cancer* 17: 602–12, 1976.

16. E. Laara, N. E. Day, and M. Hakama. "Trends in Mortality from Cervical Cancer in the Nordic Countries: Association with Organised Screening Programmes." *Lancet* i: 1247–49, 1987.

17. M. S. Fox. "On the Diagnosis and Treatment of Breast Cancer." *J. Amer. Med. Assoc.* 241, 489–94, 1979.

18. N. Breslow, C. W. Chan, G. Dhom, R.A.B. Drury, L. M. Franks, B. Gellei, Y. S. Lee, S. Lundberg, B. Sparke, N. H. Sternby, and H. Tulinius. "Latent Carcinoma of Prostate at Autopsy in Seven Areas." *Int. J. Cancer* 20: 680–88, 1977.

19. M. Fortuin, J. Chotard, A. D. Jack, N. P. Maine, M. Mendy, A. J. Hall, H. M. Inskip, M. O. George, and H. C. Whittle. "Efficacy of Hepatitis B Vaccine in the Gambian Expanded Programme on Immunisation." *Lancet* 341: 1129–31, 1993.

20. For a general review see "Human Pathogenic Papillomaviruses," edited by H. zur Hausen. *Current Topics in Microbiology and Immunology* 186, 1994.

21. N. J. Vianna, P. Greenwald, and J.N.P. Davies. "Extended Epidemic of Hodgkin's Disease in High-School Students." *Lancet* i: 1209–11, 1971.

22. N. J. Vianna and A. K. Polan. "Epidemiological Evidence for Transmission of Hodgkin's Disease." *New Engl. J. Med.* 289: 499–502, 1973.

23. M.C.P. Pike and P. G. Smith. "Clustering of Cases of Hodgkin's Disease and Leukemia." *Cancer* 34: 1390–94, 1974.

24. Ibid.

25. L. J. Kinlen. "Evidence for an Infective Cause of Childhood Leukemia: Comparison of a Scottish New Town with Nuclear Reprocessing Sites in Britain." *Lancet* ii: 1323–1327, 1988.

26. L. J. Kinlen and S. M. John. "Wartime Evacuation and Mortality from Childhood Leukaemia in England and Wales in 1945–9." *Brit. Med. J.* 309: 1197–1202, 1994.

27. A. G. Knudson. "Mutation and Cancer. Statistical Study of Retinoblastoma." *Proc. Natl. Acad. Sci. Washington* 68: 820–23, 1971.

28. Y. Nakamura. "The Role of the Adenomatous Polyposis Coli (APC) Gene in Human Cancers." *Adv. Cancer Res.* 62: 65–87, 1993.

29. B. S. Bloom, R. S. Knorr, and A. E. Evans. "The Epidemiology of Disease Expenses. The Costs of Caring for Children with Cancer." *J. Amer. Med. Assoc.* 253: 2393–97, 1985.

30. R. R. West. "Valuation of Life in Long Run Health Care Programmes." *Brit. Med. J.* 291: 1139–1141, 1985.

31. R. Doll and R. Peto. *The Causes of Cancer.* (Oxford: Oxford University Press, 1981).

32. D. Albanes. "Total Calories, Body Weight, and Tumor Incidence in Mice." *Cancer Res.* 47: 1987–92, 1987.

33. D. Albanes, D. Y. Jones, A. Schatzkin, M. S. Micozzi, and P. R. Taylor. "Adult Stature and Risk of Cancer." *Cancer Res.* 48: 1658–62, 1988.

34. E. A. Lew and L. Garfinkel. "Variations in Mortality by Weight Among 750,000 Men and Women." *J. Chronic. Dis.* 32: 563–76, 1979.

35. S. Preston-Martin, M.C.P. Pike, R. K. Ross, P. A. Jones, and B. E. Henderson. "Increased Cell Division as a Cause of Human Cancer." *Cancer Res.* 50: 7415–20, 1990.

36. J. Cairns. "Mutation, Selection and the Natural History of Cancer." *Nature* 255: 197–200, 1975.

CHAPTER 6
POPULATION

1. World Resources Institute. *World Resources 1986.* (New York: Basic Books, 1986).

2. Thomas Robert Malthus. *An Essay on the Principle of Population, as It Affects the Future Improvement of Society, with Remarks on the Speculations of Mr. Godwin, M. Condorcet, and other writers* (1798). (London: Penguin Books, 1970).

3. William Godwin. *An Enquiry Concerning Political Justice and Its Influence on Morals and Happiness,* vol. 2, p. 332 (Dublin: 1793).

4. Ibid., p. 350.

5. P. H. Marshall. *William Godwin.* (New Haven, Conn.: Yale University Press, 1984).

6. William Godwin. *The Enquirer. Reflections on education, manner and literature, in a series of essays,* p. 177. (London: 1797).

7. Ibid., p. 169.

8. Godwin; see note 3, p. 392.

9. Ibid., p. 402.

10. Virginia Woolf. "Essay on Mary Wollstonecraft." In *The Second Common Reader.* (San Diego: Harcourt Brace Jovanovich, 1932).

11. A-N. de Condorcet. *Sketch for a Historical Picture of the Progress of the Human Mind* (1795). Translated by J. Barraclough. (London: Weidenfeld and Nicolson, 1955).

12. Patricia James. *Population Malthus. His Life and Times.* (London: Routledge and Kegan Paul, 1979).

13. Malthus; see note 2, pp. 93–94.

14. Adam Smith. *An Inquiry into the Nature and Causes of the Wealth of Nations* (1776). (London: Penguin Books, 1979), p. 182.

15. Ibid., p. 488–89.

16. Malthus; see note 2, pp. 172–73.

17. Ibid., p. 154.

18. Thomas Robert Malthus. *An Essay on the Principle of Population; or a View of Its Past and Present Effects on Human Happiness. With an Enquiry into our Prospects Respecting the Future Removal or Mitigation of the Evils which It Occasions* (1803),

vol. 1 and 2. Edited by Patricia James. (Cambridge: Cambridge University Press, 1989).

19. William Derham. *Physico-Theology or a Demonstration of the Being and Attributes of God from His Works of Creation,* chapter 10, p. 238. (London, 1711).

20. Johann Süssmilch. "Die Göttliche Ordnung in den Veränderungen des menschlichen Geschlechts, aus der Geburt, dem Tode, und der Fortplanzung desselben erwissen" (1741).

21. Robert Wallace. "A Dissertation on the Numbers of Mankind in Antient and Modern Times: in which the Superior Populousness of Antiquity Is Maintained." (Edinburgh: 1753).

22. Robert Wallace. "Various Prospects of Mankind, Nature and Providence." (London: 1761).

23. Ibid., pp. 116, 119.

24. Benjamin Franklin. "Observations Concerning the Increase of Mankind, Peopling of Countries, &c." In *The Papers of Benjamin Franklin* vol. 4, pp. 225–34. (New Haven, Conn. Yale University Press, 1961).

25. Malthus; see note 2, pp. 71–72.

26. Malthus; see note 19, p. 16.

27. Charles Darwin. *Natural Selection* 1858, but unpublished at the time. Edited by R. C. Stauffer. (Cambridge: Cambridge University Press, 1975), p. 176.

28. Charles Darwin. *Autobiography.* Edited by Francis Darwin, 1892. (New York: Dover Publications, 1958), p. 42.

29. Ibid., p. 200.

30. Malthus; see note 2, p. 213.

31. Malthus; see note 18, vol. 1, p. 226.

32. Malthus; see note 18, vol. 1, p. 3.

33. Malthus; see note 18, vol. 2, p. 209.

34. Ibid., p. 235.

35. Karl Marx. *Capital.* The English edition translated by Friedrich Engels, 1887. (London: Lawrence and Wishart, 1954), vol. 1, p. 578.

36. Ibid., p. 495.

37. Ibid., p. 606.

38. Ibid., p. 578.

39. Karl Marx. "Theories of Surplus Value." Quoted in R. L. Meek, *Marx and Engels on Malthus* (London: Lawrence and Wishart, 1953).

40. Malthus; see note 18, vol. 2, p. 161.

41. Engels, 1844. Quoted in R. L. Meek, *Marx and Engels on Malthus.* (London: Lawrence and Wishart, 1953), p. 109.

42. Anthony Flew. *Introduction to Malthus's First Essay.* (London: Penguin Classics, 1970).

43. E. A. Wrigley and R. S. Schofield. *The Population History of England, 1540–1871. A Reconstruction.* (Cambridge, Mass.: Harvard University Press, 1981).

44. Malthus; see note 2, p. 78.

45. J. Meuvret. "Demographic Crisis in France from the Sixteenth to the Eighteenth Century." In *Population History,* edited by D. V. Glass and D.E.C. Eversley, pp. 507–52. (London: Arnold, 1965).

46. World Population Monitoring 1991. United Nations Population Studies No. 126. (New York: UN, 1992).

47. W. C. Robinson. "Kenya Enters the Fertility Transition." *Population Studies* 46: 445–57, 1992.

48. L. F. Newman, ed. *Hunger in History: Food Shortage, Poverty, and Deprivation.* (Oxford: Blackwell, 1990).

49. L. R. Brown. *Building a Sustainable Society.* (New York: W. W. Norton, 1981).

50. T. Jacobsen and R. M. Adams. "Salt and Silt in Ancient Mesopotamian Agriculture." *Science* 128: 1251–58, 1958.

51. A. S. Issar. "Climate Change and the History of the Middle East." *Amer. Scientist* 83: 350–55, 1995.

52. E. S. Deevey, D. R. Rice, P. M. Rice, H. H. Vaughan, M. Brenner, and M. S. Flannery. "Mayan Urbanism: Impact on a Tropical Karst Environment." *Science* 206: 298–306, 1979.

53. "World Resources 1986." World Resources Institute. (New York: Basic Books, 1986).

54. "Climate Instability During the Last Interglacial Period Recorded in the GRIP Ice Core." Greenland Ice-core Project (GRIP) Members. *Nature* 364: 203–7, 1993.

55. J. Imbrie and J. Z. Imbrie. "Modeling the Climatic Response to Orbital Variations." *Science* 207: 943–53, 1980.

56. W. F. Lloyd. "Two Lectures on the Checks to Population." Oxford University, 1833.

57. J. C. Riley. "The Prevalence of Chronic Diseases during Mortality Increase: Hungary in the 1980s." *Population Studies* 45: 489–96, 1991.

58. H. C. Tuckwell and J. A. Koziol. "World Population." *Nature* 359: 200, 1992; Fifty-eight of the World's Scientific Academies. "Population Summit of the World's Scientific Academies." (Washington, D.C.: The National Academy Press, 1993).

59. "Technological Trends and National Policy Including the Social Implications of New Inventions." National Resources Committee. (Washington, D.C.: U.S. Government Printing Office, 1937).

60. Ibid., p. 26.

61. Ibid., p. 25.

62. Ibid., p. 14.

63. Ibid., p. 33.

64. Ibid., p. 8.

65. Ibid., p. 14.

66. *World Resources 1986: World Resources Institute.* (New York: Basic Books, 1986).

Index

Note: Page numbers listed here refer to the first page only of a continuous discussion that may or may not run over several consecutive pages. I have not documented every mention of each subject, but have chosen to list only truly informative sections.

John Cairns, M.D., is recently retired from the Harvard School of Public Health. Before that appointment, he held posts as Director of Cold Spring Harbor Laboratory and then as Director of one of the laboratories run by the Imperial Cancer Research Fund in London. He is the author of *Cancer, Science and Society*.